BRITISH COUNTRY LIFE
IN AUTUMN AND WINTER

THE WAGON.

From a water-colour by
Tatton Winter, R.B.A.

BRITISH COUNTRY LIFE

IN AUTUMN AND WINTER

THE BOOK OF THE OPEN AIR EDITED BY

EDWARD THOMAS

Author of 'Horæ Solitairæ,' 'Oxford,' 'Beautiful Wales,
'The Heart of England,' and Editor of 'The
Pocket Book of Poems and Songs
for the Open Air'

CONTENTS

CONTENTS

CONTENTS

CONTENTS

ILLUSTRATIONS

ILLUSTRATIONS

OPEN-AIR DIARY

OCTOBER

1   Juniper carpet moth.

2   Rich perfume of sage, dead grass and leaves, a mustard field and crumbling wild carrot seeds.

3   Harebells, dwarf red-rattle, sheep's scabious ragwort, hawkweed, field speedwell, yarrow, honeysuckle, tormentil, buttercup, bramble, dovesfoot, cranesbill, herb robert, wild thyme, eyebright, black knapweed, wild parsnip, flowering.

5   Redwings arrive.

7   Jack snipe arrive.

9   Winter moth.

10   Fieldfares arrive.

11   One swift, buffeted by a crowd of swallows gathering for migration.

12   Blackcap singing in leafless hazels.

13   Flowers of thrift, ivy-leafed toadflax.

16   Large flocks of wood-pigeons.

17   Wood-pigeons and rooks at the acorns.

18   Flowers of dwarf spurge.

20   Scattered sprays of hawthorn flower among purple leaves.   Fallow deer rutting.

21   Woodcocks arrive.   Flowers of least toadflax, common persicaria, sun spurge.

22   Flowers of corn feverfew, carline thistle, yellow toadflax, small nettle.

23   Flowers of lesser dodder, hoary plantain, fiddle dock.

25   Flowers of ribwort plantain, common pellitory of the wall.

26   Chaffinches in small bands.

27   Flowers of petty spurge.

28   Flowers of wall speedwell.

29   Flowers of cornflower.

30   Flowers of inelegant ragwort, sea beet.

31   Flowers of scarlet pimpernel.

OPEN-AIR DIARY

NOVEMBER

1 One swallow in London fog.

2 Harebell, field speedwell, black knapweed, bramble, fumitory, feverfew, small bugloss, creeping crowfoot, one flake of hawthorn, in flower. Solitary linnet sings.

3 November moth.

5 Fieldfares at the brier hips.

6 Flowers of corn woundwort, cut-leaved dead-nettle, red dead-nettle.

8 Bullfinches at the ash-keys which have a taste as of caraway. Linnets at the seeds of thistle and dock.

10 Last house-martins seen.

13 Mangolds carried in.

14 A bunch of hedgerow flowers : White dead-nettle, herb Robert, yarrow, white campion, red campion, dandelion, nipplewort, nettle-leaved bell-flower, knapweed, buttercup, germander speedwell, mouse-ear chickweed, camomile, barren strawberry, calamint, wood-sage, dog violet, ragwort, devil's bit scabious.

15 Flowers of annual knawel.

17 Blue-tits spend some days in suburban gardens, apparently in the course of a petty migration.

18 Colour in the woods to-day due not only to leaves and fungi, but to ivy blossom, the wool of traveller's joy and willow-herb, the berries of bryony, convolvulus, bramble, holly, juniper, privet, spindle, dog-wood, guelder-rose, brier, honeysuckle, ivy, yew, bittersweet.

19 Fresh shoots of goosegrass, garlic mustard and even cuckoo-pint are spring-like in the hedges ; vetchlings begin to climb again. Woods green underfoot with the bright leaves of wood sorrel, wood sanicle, dog's mercury, ground-ivy, woodruff. Heather sends up green sprays among the black.

20 Flowers of yellow oxeye.

21 Thatching mangold stacks.

23 Missel thrushes sing.

24 A thrush sings for an hour on a heavily misty gossamer morning, beginning before sunrise at 6.45 ; again at 11 ; last at 4.

26 Plants of bush vetch strong and flowering.

27 Birch catkins large. Willow beds cut.

28 December moth.

30 Hedge-sparrow, wren, blackbird, and above all, starling and robin, sing.

OPEN-AIR DIARY

DECEMBER

1 Flowers of corn-feverfew, cinquefoil, tormentil, field speedwell, fumitory, chickweed, dead nettles.

2 Very large flocks of wood-pigeons travelling in a south-westerly direction.

3 Willow buds, large, bright and golden-green in the rain. White lichen, shaped like stag-horns, white as a mushroom, conspicuous now on oak roots, etc.

5 Flowers of ivy-leaved toadflax.

7 New sprouts of nettle and wild parsnip; sticky young shoots on the yew.

8 More flocks of wood-pigeons travelling south-west.

9 New leaves of elder just visible but still closed —like moths with folded wings of gummy bronze.

11 Honeysuckle's twin leaves opening.

12 The last gossamer.

13 Flowers of white dead-nettle.

14 Long-tailed titmice in small flocks by themselves.

16 Pale brindled beauty moth.

17 Only these birds are still to be met singly— missel thrush (probably the native and not the immigrant), green wood-pecker, blackbird, robin, hedge-sparrow, wren, sparrow hawk ; even kestrels are chiefly in pairs.

18 Suddenly a spring-fed pool has all its dead leaves hidden by a deep green mossy vegetation so rounded and soft that it is like a thick liquid poured into the crystal water and slowly being absorbed by it.

19 Wood-pigeons coo.

20 Flocks of chaffinches, yellow-hammers and sparrows together in the hedges, broken up into twos and threes continually.

21 Fresh fronds of yarrow rising. Hazel catkins redden.

22 Missel thrushes sing.

25 Moles working, aided by a fall of snow that keeps the earth moist and soft.

29 Green foliage to-day of foxglove, brier, bramble, cinquefoil, crowfoots, violet, primrose, woodruff, parsleys, vetches, wood sanicle, goosegrass, bedstraw, ground ivy, polypody and hartstongue ferns, wild strawberry, dandelion, snow-thistle, yarrow, sorrel, dead-nettles, garlic mustard, great celandine, dovesfoot cranesbill, speedwells, thistles, brooklime, dock, hedge woundwort, ivy-leaved toadflax, " ground-ash."

30 To-day the last of the dog's mercury foliage crumpled in the frost.

31 Flowers of daisy, chickweed, groundsel, dandelion, dog-violet.

OPEN-AIR DIARY

JANUARY

1 Barren strawberry.

3 Trout spawn.

4 Moss at its best, embossing the fir-needle carpets and the tiles, making fur on the ash stoles and the beeches in misty woods, and fledging the dead stalks of summer flowers and the uppers of a tramp's discarded boot.

7 Many thrushes and blackbirds sing.

8 All the hips cleared from the briers.

10 Flowers of spurge laurel.

11 Dog-foxes bark at night from time to time, pursuing one another in the woods—their barking, hoarse and very malicious-sounding, is the wildest sound to be heard in England.

12 Flowers of ivy-leaved toadflax.

13 Earthworms busy, sparrows building.

14 At 7 a.m. many robins and missel thrushes began to sing, and a few thrushes and wood-pigeons.

15 Starlings at nests.

16 Flowers of butter-bur.

17 Corn-bunting sings.

18 A dead broken stem of teazle is feathered with moss—as if Yorick's skull should learn to laugh.

19 Rabbits eating bark of willow, hazel, ash and thorn, during frost.

20 New flannelly leaves of mullein.

22 After four mild still days, an adder seen.

23 Strong new shoots of crowfoot, thistle, dandelion, sorrel, goosegrass. Skylarks sing, but for another month there are still flocks of them.

25 A pleasant winter sight is the continuous movement of birds in search of food, from tree to tree, from field to field, from valley to valley. All the fields are visited every day, not so much because they may offer a succession of foods, but because there is always something left over from the feast. What with quarrelling, hurrying, and the joy of moving about, birds never exhaust a tree or a field, and their combination of exercise and feeding is a nice economy.

26 Green woodpeckers silent during frost and snow.

27 To wild animals, man is above all the creature that can produce effects at a distance. No bird or animal can. But a man is gardening and moving about, so that he perhaps resembles a windy tree, and the birds creep up and feed at his heels; suddenly a clod or a stone is cast near them quite by accident and they fly off, once more reminded of this extraordinary power of producing effects at a distance. It is an inconvenient power, because its effects are past calculation, and it has alienated the wild creature as much by those which are not intended as by those which are.

29 Young dock leaves conspicuous.

30 Gorse blooms abundantly.

OPEN-AIR DIARY

FEBRUARY

OPEN-AIR DIARY

MARCH

1 Goldfinch sings. Wood-pigeons coo. Larks have paired, and fly and feed in couples. Rooks and missel-thrushes build. White violets. Yew tree and elm flower. Spurge laurel flowers. Digging round hop roots. Frogs croak. Small eggar moth, dotted border.

2 Periwinkle flowers. Fresh brier leaves. Greenfinches sing.

3 An adder and a brimstone butterfly in the sun. Kingfisher builds. Chaffinches sing. Green hellebore flowers.

4 Mezereon flowers. Wheatears arrive. Tortoiseshell butterfly. Bees at the purple crocuses. Toads appear.

5 Elm flowers. Peacock butterfly. Thrushes build.

6 Moschatel flowers. The first lambs—in the north.

7 Peeling ash for hop poles.

8 Kingfishers in pairs. Blackbirds build. Dung-hauling.

9 First tortoiseshell butterfly.

10 Larger celandine leaves big and conspicuous now. Flowers of barren strawberry. Crows build. Sowing oats. Black ants abroad.

11 Hawthorn and crab tree leaves. Frogs spawning.

12 Pewits and chaffinches still in flocks.

13 Gannets begin to nest. Sallow flowers.

14 Flowers of ground ivy.

15 Hedgehogs abroad. Hazel flowers.

16 Ground ivy flowers. Pied wagtails arrive.

17 Great titmouse sings. Purple new shoots from the hop plants. Flowers of ivy-leaved speedwell.

18 Wrens begin to build. Flowers of wood-sorrel, ivy-leaved toadflax, anemone. Rolling hayfields.

19 Thrush's egg laid. Chiffchaff arrives and sings on the wing. Other birds that sing in flight are wren, pipits, buntings, linnet, whitethroat, cuckoo, all the *hirundines*, and sometimes nightingale (when the males are fighting), robin, wagtails and others. Dipping new hop poles in tar.

20 A dormouse awake. Pipistrelle bats begin to fly.

21 Bees abound on willow catkins. The " skating " beetle appears. Coltsfoot leaves appear. White poplar flowers. 5 a.m., rooks begin to fly over. 5.15, songs of missel thrush, thrush, blackbird, robin, lark, corn-bunting and chaffinch. Green woodpeckers drumming, and repeating their laughs so often and with so little interval that they become a song.

22 Blackbirds, robins and hedge-sparrows laying. Ash and alder flowers. Hillside covered with dog violets. New leaves of privet, brier and bramble.

23 Hazel leaves coming. Hairy bitter cress and cowslip flowers. Flags a foot above the water. Willows are gold. Tadpoles begin to appear.

24 Red campion and cowslip flowers. Peacock butterflies abroad.

25 Marsh-marigold, blackthorn, periwinkle, mistletoe, ladysmock in flower. Elm and chestnut in leaf. Black poplar flowers. Herons lay. The first sand-martins arrive.

26 Stinking hellebore flowers. Vetchlings four feet high in the hedge. Yew flowers.

27 Wryneck arrives. Wild daffodil, hairy bitter cress flowers. Large tortoiseshell butterflies.

28 Wood anemones and saxifrage and bitter sweet flower. Large convolvulus begins to climb. Robin's eggs. Early gray moth appears. Long after the end of a hard winter there are some ivy bushes where thousands of large berries are untouched, and only now do the robins and blackbirds thin them slowly but with evident joy.

29 Long-tailed titmouse begins to build : some nests all but finished. Young foxes born. Flowers of yellow alpine whitlow grass, woodspurge, box.

30 Cutting willow beds. Hebrew character moth, clouded drab, common quaker, powdered quaker, blossom underwing. Yellow wagtails arrive. Meadow pipits sing. Snipe pairing.

31 Larch leaves. Comma butterfly appears. March moth. Stonechat builds. Long-eared owl's eggs.

FLOWERS OF THE SHORE

"There is a pleasure in the pathless woods;
There is a rapture on the lonely shore;
There is society where none intrudes
By the deep sea, and music in its roar."—BYRON.

OUR maritime flora continues much later in the season than that of the woods and hedgerows and other inland localities. In the month of September, when but few flowers will be found on the open downs, and when most of the bog plants are gone to seed, many interesting species are still in blossom by the seashore. The salt marshes which stretch for miles along the east coast are now aglow with the purple of the sea-lavender: on the rocky cliffs of Cornwall and South Wales the sea mallow is not yet past flowering; while on the short sandy turf—from early spring a favourite haunt of sea-loving species—numbers of wild flowers continue in bloom.

Among the most stately plants that grace our sea cliffs on certain parts of the coast must undoubtedly be reckoned the tree mallow (*Lavatera arborea*, L.). It is a tall and picturesque species, often six feet in height, with soft downy angular leaves, and abundance of glossy purple flowers. Parkinson, in the year 1640, notes it as growing "about the cottages neere Hurst Castle, over against the Ile of Wight."

A few years later Merrett states that "Mr. Morgan received it from the Isle of Wight"; and John Ray says, "I have observed it in many places by the seaside, as at Hurst Castle over against the Isle of Wight; in Portland Island; and on the rocks of Caldey Island." It has now disappeared on the Hampshire coast and in the Isle of Wight, except here and there as an escape from cottage gardens; but on the rocks of Caldey Island, over against Tenby in South Pembrokeshire, it is as abundant as when, in 1662, Ray and Willughby visited the enchanting spot. Indeed "our tree mallow," as the early writers called it, is a conspicuous feature in the flora of the district. Magnificent plants, many of them still in flower, were to be seen last September, not only on Caldey Island, but also on the rocks at Tenby, in company with the wild sea-cabbage (*Brassica oleracea*, L.), the origin of our cultivated varieties, and fennel, samphire, wild sea-radish, and a rare kind of sea-lavender (*Statice occidentalis*, Lloyd) which prefers the hard precipitous rocks to the muddy stretches of marshland which is the home of the commoner species.

At Giltar Head, some two miles from Tenby, over against St. Margaret's Island, the golden samphire (*Inula crithmoides*, L.) was also in full flower last September. This conspicuous member of the *Compositæ*, with narrow succulent leaves and large bright yellow flowers, must not be confused with the samphire immortalized by Shakespeare (*Crithmum maritimum*), the gathering of which, for purposes of pickling, was in his day regularly carried on by the hardy fishermen of the coast. The passage in *King Lear* is well known where above the white chalk cliffs of Dover, Edgar says to the Earl of Gloucester :

" Come on, sir, here's the place ; stand still.
                              How fearful
And dizzy 'tis to cast one's eyes so low !
The crows and choughs that wing the midway air
Show scarce so gross as beetles ; half-way
     down
Hangs one that gathers samphire ; dreadful
     trade !
Methinks he seems no bigger than his head."

Gerarde, a contemporary of Shakespeare, who calls this plant " Rocke Samfier," states that it grows upon " the rocky clifts at Dover, about Southampton, the Isle of Wight, and most rocks about the west and north parts of England." He speaks of " its spicie taste, with a certain salt-nesse," and as " beeing of smell delightfull and pleasant," and adds that it makes " the pleasantest sauce, most familiar, and best agreeing with man's body." The custom of gathering samphire for pickling has now almost entirely ceased, but a hundred years ago it was a lucrative business in the Isle of Wight. " Great quantities of it," wrote in 1799 the Rev. Thomas Garnier, a distinguished botanist, who afterwards became Dean of Winchester, " are annually gathered for a pickle of the most exquisite flavour ; it may be had by being ordered at the public-house, Freshwater Gate, from whence I have been constantly supplied ; and where I have often seen, as Shakespeare literally describes it, a man gathering it midway on the perpendicular cliffs, suspended by a rope fastened on the top, and sitting on a short piece of wood with a basket slung to his shoulders, somewhat as colliers descend a coalpit, and as in that case, accidents have been known to happen in this." In consequence of the risk involved it appears that " some little fraud was often practised " in palming off other plants as the true samphire. Among these the golden samphire was a common substitute, and indeed it resembles the genuine kind in " being compassed about with a multitude of long fat leaves," and to a certain extent in its aromatic qualities. Moreover, it could be gathered with little trouble and no danger in the marshes of this district, especially at Newtown, where now as then it is abundant. Its favourite haunt is mostly on the muddy banks of estuaries, although sometimes it is found on rocks. Ray noticed it not only in the Essex marshes, but also " on the rocks at Llandywn in Anglesea " ; and at Giltar Head it flourishes in inaccessible places on the magnificent cliffs.

The " dunes " or sandhills and the short springy turf which on many parts of the coast borders the sea are sometimes famous places for rare and interesting plants. In addition to such generally distributed species as the beautiful sea-convolvulus with its large rose-coloured flowers striped with red, the yellow horned poppy with its cylindrical curved pod sometimes a foot long, the prickly saltwort, the scurvy-grass, once a famous remedy for scorbutic diseases and not without its virtue, the sea purslane, and sundry kinds of trefoils, choicer plants may sometimes be met with. On the coast of Suffolk between Lowestoft and Yarmouth the tall and stately lyme-grass (*Elymus arenarius*, L.) lends distinction to the sandy " denes " ; and not

far from the ruined church of Dunwich the sand cat's-tail grass (*Phleum arenarium*, L.) is plentiful. Here and there on the Hampshire shore, but very sparingly, the delicate little pink, *Dianthus prolifer*, is found ; and once the philosopher John Stuart Mill met with a single specimen of the purple spurge (*Euphorbia peplis*, L.) in Sandown bay. This latter plant, at once distinguished by the purple hue of its stem and leaves, has now become very rare, and like the seaside cotton-weed (*Diotis maritima*) frequently recorded by early botanists, has doubtless become extinct in many of its former haunts. Another most interesting species, to be seen in a few localities on the shores of Cornwall and Wales, is the wild asparagus. It still exists near the Lizard Point, where Ray found it in the year 1667, and only last autumn I noticed it on the stretch of sandy burrow which curiously enough crowns the lofty headland of Giltar in South Pembrokeshire already alluded to. The lovely little burnet rose (*R. spinosissima*), then conspicuous with its black globular fruit, was trailing all over the ground, an uncommon form of felwort or autumn gentian (*Gentiana Germanica*) and the rare sea-spurge (*Euphorbia Portlandica*) were plentiful, and a few plants of *Thalic-*

trum minus were to be seen ; but the choicest plant was the asparagus, known in old days as sparagus or sperage, corrupted, says Ray, into sparrow-grass. It was, beyond question, truly wild on this lofty, wind-swept eleva-tion, which in spring-time is starred with the exquisite blue flowers of *Scilla verna.*

In the Isle of Wight, justly cele-brated for the richness of its flora, there are several sandy spits or necks of land which will amply repay a botanical visit. The most famous of these is St. Helen's Spit at the mouth of Brading harbour. It is a small piece of ground, not exceeding fifty acres, and yet it is said to support over two hundred and fifty species of flowering plants. In this respect it is perhaps unequalled by any area of like extent in the United Kingdom. Formerly the " Dover " at Ryde vied with it in the number and variety of its botanical treasures, but the " Dover " is no longer a haunt of wild flowers, and the only locality in the island now to be compared with it is Norton Spit near Freshwater. At Norton, it is true, the rare grass *Phleum arenarium* may also be found, and a few plants of asparagus which, although hardly indigenous, have been known to exist there for a long number of years. But

the sandy tract near the early English tower of the now ruined church of St. Helen's can show greater rarities than these. One plant calls for special mention. Unknown on the mainland of Hampshire, unknown in the neigh-bouring counties of Wilts, Dorset, Sus-sex, and Berkshire, unknown elsewhere in the Isle of Wight, at St. Helen's Spit the autumnal squill (*Scilla autum-nalis*) may be seen in extraordinary profusion. All over the sandy ground it puts forth its lovely little pale blue star-like flowers every August and Sep-tember. Gerarde calls the plant " the small Autumne Jacinth," and Ray " the lesser Autumnal Star-Hyacinth," and the names are well chosen. How long the beautiful little jacinth has flourished at St. Helen's there is no means of telling, for the island flora received but little attention from the early botanists. But there is no reason to doubt that it is truly in-digenous. It seems to have been first recorded about the year 1823, and then it was as abundant as it is to-day, lending additional charm to this favoured spot.

Another striking species, not indeed rare and delicate like the vernal and autumnal squills, but characteristic of the loose sandhills of the coast, is the handsome sea-holly (*Eryngium mar-*

itinum). This stout and prickly plant, not unlike a thistle in general appearance, but of a pale glaucous hue, and bearing dense heads or " knops " of " glistering blew " flowers " of the bignesse of a wallnut," is often a conspicuous object on the seashore. In former days the long creeping roots, " of the bignesse of a man's finger and so very long as that it cannot be plucked up but very seldome," were highly esteemed when candied as a sweetmeat which was supposed to possess great virtues. It was known as " Eringoes," and under this name Shakespeare refers to it in *The Merry Wives of Windsor*. In his list of rare Essex plants which Ray drew up for Gibson's edition of Camden's *Britannia*, published in 1695, the great botanist includes the sea-holly or eryngo, but adds : " This being a plant common enough on sandy shores I should not have mentioned, but that Colchester is noted for the first inventing or practising the candying or conditing of its roots, the manner whereof may be seen in Gerarde's *Herbal*." It is interesting to know that in the Chamberlain's accounts for the borough in the reign of James I there are several entries with reference to the purchase of eryngo roots. The trade was then in the hands of one Robert Buxton,

an apothecary and alderman of the town, who in the time of the Civil War, after the famous siege of Colchester, was expelled from the Corporation for his political opinions. It was afterwards carried on by his apprentice, Samuel Great, or de Groot, a member of one of the refugee houses, in whose family the secret of the " candying " remained till the close of the eighteenth century. For a long period " Great's Candied Eryngo " was held in high repute, and a box of it was regarded as a present not unworthy for a queen. Indeed, when Princess Charlotte, on her arrival in England to be married to George III, passed through the town, she was duly presented with a box of the precious sweetmeat. The trade appears to have continued till about the middle of the last century when, owing, it is said, to the difficulty of obtaining roots, it gradually declined. This doubtless is the explanation of the comparative scarceness of *Eryngium maritinum* on the Essex coast. It is clear from Ray's statement that it was formerly abundant : it cannot be called abundant now, but plants may be found at Clacton and Harwich, on the shores of Mersea Island, and where old Gerarde noticed it in the sixteenth century, " at Landamer lading."

II

A SURREY PLATEAU

"The tribes who then lived on her breast,
Her vigorous primitive sons."
—MATTHEW ARNOLD.

THE fastidious young man of Miss May Kendall's poem who "owned the scenery was grand," but objected to the cliffs because they were Laurentian and not Pleistocene might, it is possible to think, find scenery and deposits to his liking on a certain plateau near the escarpment of the North Downs. There he could inspect thick beds of gravel, the flints much rolled and often of considerable size, reputed to be of either pre-glacial or early Pleistocene age, while scattered over the surface in other parts may be traced the old Southern Drift containing, with the rolled and subangular flints, pieces of chert from the Lower Greensand beds which are now separated from the Chalk by a valley 300 feet deep, the gravels having been deposited before the vast intervening hollow was formed. It would not be necessary to conduct this imaginary youth to the edge of the Chalk escarpment and point out the physical features of the country, due chiefly to the action of rain and rivers acting on the Greensands and the Gault, or to explain that his favourite Pleistocene rocks are comparatively recent accumulations, often of great thickness, and, where fossiliferous, contain shells belonging to existing species and remains of mammals, many of which are extinct or now resident in colder and warmer countries.—One small section here displayed contains the characteristic molluscan fauna of late Pleistocene age—land and freshwater shells, some of which are now rare or extinct in the neighbourhood. But these somewhat recent beds are limited in area, and the newest are on the edges of a depression which in prehistoric times was probably a diminutive lake which existed when the rounded pebbles were deposited by some temporary torrential stream in their present position. The present-day ponds, though small and shallow, never run dry even during the occurrence of a season like the rainless summer of 1906.

"We have no waters to delight
Our broad and brookless vales—
Only the dewpond on the height
Unfed, that never fails."

In the spring they are white with the pretty little flowers of the Ranunculus or Water Crowfoot, and later their borders are bright with Forget-me-not and Persicaria and adorned with the bold lance-shaped leaves of the Water Plantain. Certain species of small molluscs, such as the Limnœa, with graceful sharp-pointed spire and wide mouth, and the flat and coiled Planorbis, flourish at the bottom; while the Water Boatman and " Skater " and other curious creatures disport themselves in coolness and security on the surface.

The chief deposits lying on the most interesting portion of this plateau— a pleasant undulating wind-swept heath of 3,000 acres in area—are a puzzling mixture of sands and clays from what are termed the Lower London Tertiaries, perhaps from the Thanet Sands and Blackheath Pebble beds, which, though originally in position seem to have been disturbed and rearranged unequally over the surface of the eroded chalk. In some small pits are beds of thick red clay capped with small pebbles, and in other sections the sands prevail. Near the chalk outcrop where the Tertiaries are thinner may be seen beds of clay-with-flints, the flints in their original fantastic shapes but with their beautiful combination of lustrous black and sober white altered and discoloured by the solution of the chalk and contact with clay into dirty brown and sooty shades.

In a few places white sands are exposed, and from a distance with their background of brown heather almost seem to suggest the familiar image of " Snow upon the dusty desert's face." At one corner of the heath is a small coombe widened and deepened by excavations for flints, which when obtained are sorted and stacked in large rectangular heaps and finally sold as road material. It is pleasant to sit on the edge of this valley and watch the rabbits scamper and tumble to and from their sandy subterranean lairs, in numbers rivalling those at the antipodes, while occasionally the stoat, their chief enemy next to man, with uplifted head peeps round suspiciously and then with leisured pace continues his relentless pursuit of fur and feather. It seems an ideal spot for snakes and adders, but they appear to be rarely seen, though the slow worm, vulgarly classed with them, is common, and its skin and skeleton may often be seen bleaching in the sun. The little lizards with convenient tails may be detected by a quick and accustomed eye as frequently as Grant Allen could find them on his favourite Hindhead. Below on the piled stones wagtails flit, and at their appointed season build soft nests between the crevices and thus secure an original and safe retreat. The old poet in pre-migration days thus sang of the swallow :

> "In thy undiscovered nest
> Thou dost all the winter rest,"

and most of these nests are as undiscoverable as the swallow's mythical winter residence or as those of the stonechats and wheatears on the common. In the gorse one can sometimes find the nest and blue eggs of the hedge sparrow, and, rarely, among dark nettles the whitethroat's thin hairy nest is found, but only the keen eye and untiring enthusiasm of youth could hope to be successful here. The nests of most of the heather-loving birds are hidden too carefully by art and nature amid the thick vegetation, and the eggs of the goatsucker or nightjar are equally well concealed although laid on the bare ground among the small rounded Blackheath pebbles.

Down in the hollow small pinnacles of chalk are visible between masses of brick earth and gravel, and at the deep end on the northern slope is a good exposure of this pure limestone belonging to a zone of the Upper Chalk named after the familiar Echinoderm, Micraster cor-anguinum.

> "What is it ? A learned man
> Could give it a clumsy name."

The characteristic fossils of this zone have been found here, many of course in a fragmentary condition, but others beautifully preserved. The fossil which gives its name to the zone is not rare, the useful guide Echinoconus conicus is scarce, but the most important fossil at this horizon (for it should be stated that the Micraster cor-anguinum is also found in higher zones), namely, the special form of Echinocorys is fairly common and the other associated fossils have yielded to patient search and vigorous hammering. It is obvious that many fine specimens still remain "sealed within the iron hills." Around this end of the valley, equidistant from the opposite clumps of sand-grown pines and limestone beeches are traces of the chalk flora such as the bright blue Viper's Bugloss and Deadly Nightshade which are abundant on the near escarpment. One refuse heap in an old excavation is the local habitat of the rarer and curious Henbane with its peculiar bell or funnel-shaped corolla of dingy yellow prettily pencilled with purple brown veins. It is a sinister-looking plant and plainly suggests its evil nature. The delicate yellow of the Rock Rose and the pink flowers of a few straggling plants of Centaury are reminiscent of the wealth and beauty of these rather neglected flowers in their favourite soils. Except the gorse, which is proverbially ever in bloom, the earliest spring flower here is the leafless Coltsfoot, and a little later the Wood Anemones, continuous as the stars that shine, whiten the spaces between the heather. The tiny Hair Moss (*Polytrichum*) is common, and still more abundant and beautiful is the Scarlet Cup moss or Cladonia with pale tube-like stems and bright scarlet fruit. Near the open road the Traveller's Joy scrambles over the hawthorn hedges, its small summer flowers of greenish white developing later on into those feathery sprays of lengthened " styles " so conspicuous on bare hedge-rows in the winter and likened by the rustics to " Old Man's Beard." But the real victor in the plant struggle for existence is the Heather-Ling (*Calluna vulgaris*), which keeps the bracken at bay, and confident in its strength and success allows the fine-leaved Heath (*Erica Cinerea*) to share at intervals a portion of the soil and sunlight.

If this wide and beautiful stretch of country consists of sands, gravels, and clays sufficient to provide the geologist with physiographical and other problems for winter evenings, and he, unlike a certain famous statesman, usually has a weakness for recreation combined with instruction, it also possesses in or near its surface numerous relics of a bygone age over which philosophers may be compelled to ponder for many a century. These relics are the flint implements which under the old classification are styled " Neolithic," left by the vanished peoples on the surface of the ground, with the result that in many cases " hungry generations tread them down " or crush them with the heavy agricultural tools of an iron and industrial age. Here they fell on stony but benevolent ground, to be at once covered by sand and loam and protected for many a thousand years by the slow accumulation of peaty soil. A few years ago we found on the small bare patches left by local turf cutters in the borders of the heath—a veritable " Celtic fringe" as subsequent proceedings showed— and on the excavated valley slopes, a number of flakes, a delicate saw of white flint, some well worked scrapers and a celt or axehead of unusual type. Every exposure was searched, but as is too frequently the case in likely situations, turf, heather and bracken enjoyed uninterrupted possession of the land. It was known that Roman remains had been previously discovered and the outline of several small camps could be dimly traced, but with regard to the possibility of making additional "finds" it seemed, in the words of Thomas Hardy, that "no sod had been turned since the days of the Cæsars." The narrow paths and trackways of soft short grass looked, at a distance, like green bands between acres of dark interrupted heather. At last, when further search was nearly abandoned, on one budding morrow in our midnight of failure a small body of rough-jacketed genial workmen, doomed to labour and the mattock-hardened hand, suddenly descended on the heath and with welcome energy razed wide strips of the small jungle, ploughed up the tangled mass of roots, and harrowed and cleared the soil. The phrase "ploughing the sands" is often employed by political humorists to describe unsuccessful attempts at legislation and unremunerative experiments in general of their opponents, but here the saying, like many another of similar origin or appropriation, had little meaning. The plough turned out from the fresh loam numerous implements, which had already lain for centuries just beneath the turf when the Roman legions first tramped along Ermyn Street or pushed over the Downs from Noviomagus. These strenuous semi-agricultural operations were due to the remarkable revival and development of an ancient and royal pastime now enthusiastically followed, even in the absence of anything to kill, by an ever-increasing number of persons who apparently belong to the prosperous classes. The archæologist in anticipation of a bountiful harvest was scarcely in the humour to join in any cry of "spoiling the common." Wild nature near London is still something more than a phrase, and many acres of undiscovered country still remain for the nature lover—but good implements in some districts are scarce. The work, conducted with care and skill, unavoidably destroyed the primitive appearance of several "hut circles," dug out by the Neolithic people. They have been restored after the manner of certain fine old churches and now possess, no doubt, a peculiar attraction for the golfer or his balls. With this exception very little damage has been done, and but for the making of the "links" the unwritten history of this area might never have been read. One cannot help being reminded, though, of the recent picturesque remarks by Sir Frederick Treves on the desecration of the ancient Dorset earthwork, Buzbury Rings. "The rampart that the Britons built up so laboriously with their horn picks had thus degenerated into a bunker, while into the fosse there drops in place of the stone headed arrow an American golf ball."

Here was an opportunity, which was not missed, of following the plough literally along the freshly turned mould to examine the released flints and rescue the numerous and precious prehistoric trifles for them to rest once more in the possession of men, perhaps of a degenerate race, capable of appreciating their good points. Many specimens were found of the usual types pictured on the pages of the classic " Stone Implements" or resting on the ill-lighted shelves of museums, and in the convenient cabinets of friends. Scrapers, as usual, were common and of most of the shapes and sizes and colours, rounded, " duckbill " and " horseshoe." Worked flakes or knives lay in company with the numerous untrimmed flakes and cores or nodules from the sides of which they had been probably detached. The instruments employed in this ancient industry, such as hammerstones, fabricators, and small pointed tools lay scattered around. Several interesting celts were found and a dozen good arrowheads. No polished celts—the implements of the late Neolithic and the Bronze periods—were discovered, but one or two of the chipped celts showed signs of careful work. The majority were extremely rough,

merely rude sharp-pointed picks, especially those near the recent valley excavations. The arrowheads were of the usual leaf-shaped, triangular, double barbed and " winger " varieties, the double-barbed specimen being a particularly fine weapon of light brown flint. Perhaps the rarest and most valuable was one of thin black flint with the ripple-marked working characteristic of the Scandinavian type of implement.

Of man in the earliest period, according to the old classification, no trace has been found on this plateau, i.e., neither ovoid nor pear-shaped implements with any resemblance to the relics of early Palæolithic man of river drift age. To which succeeding period the recorded discoveries belong, is, in our present state of knowledge, a problem not easy of solution. Many of the celts, as we have seen, are very rough ; but as the best authorities have so frequently maintained, mere roughness of form unsupported by any other evidence, is no guarantee of antiquity. When found in tumuli, in the vicinity of megalithic monuments, or in caves with associated contemporary fauna there is less difficulty in determining age ; but when found alone on or immediately beneath the surface, the only evidence would appear to be form and workmanship. As we are tempted to suggest that a certain proportion of the implements from this district differ from the usual Neolithic types and should be classed with the tools of the later Cave men, we must remember the cautious words of General Pitt-Rivers : " Flints found on the surface of the soil cannot be legitimately disconnected from flints of the surface period except by form; and form alone is not conclusive in determining date."

III

DAY-FLYING MOTHS

" But she, God love her ! feared to brush
The dust from off its wings."
—WORDSWORTH.

MENTION will first be made of a few kinds that are distinctly sun lovers—Burnets and Foresters, Clearwings, day-flying Hawk Moths, etc.

The most generally distributed kind of Burnet is that known as the Six-spotted, and this is perhaps most abundant near the coast, where it may be found in large colonies in favourable hollows on cliffs, downs, and sandhills. In its inland homes on sheltered hill-sides, meadows, and railway banks, it is not much less common. The moth, which has the forewings glossy, deep bluish-green and the six spots thereon of the same crimson colour as the hindwings, flies about somewhat in the manner of a bee. It is fond of settling on thistles and other composite flowers, and sometimes quite a number may be seen resting together.

When the sun is obscured they become inactive and may then be easily captured, but directly the sun appears again they are quickly on the alert. The caterpillar, which is a flabby and sluggish sort of creature, is greenish in colour and is marked with black and yellow ; it feeds upon clover and bird's-foot trefoil. The cocoon is most conspicuous, fixed as it usually is about half-way up a grass stem. It is a shuttle-shaped affair, more or less white as regards colour, and of a glistening, papery texture. If one of these cocoons is opened a shining black chrysalis will be found within, or it may happen that the maker of the domicile will then be exposed still in its caterpillar state.

The female moth lays eggs of a yellowish colour in batches, and in large numbers. The caterpillars hibernate and many doubtless perish or fall victims to some foe. Those that survive until the spring are then subject to the attacks of parasitical flies, and the numbers destroyed in this way is sometimes, in hot seasons especially, very large. Even when the chrysalis state is attained without mishap, all danger is not over, as the contents of these cocoons appear to be to the taste of sundry birds, and even mice seem to have cultivated a liking for them. It is perhaps surprising that they escape complete annihilation. They come near such a catastrophe in some years.

Two nearly allied, but rather local, kinds of Burnet Moth have only five crimson spots on the forewings. These are the Broad-bordered and the Narrow-bordered. The former is found in marshes and meadows, and the latter in and around woods.

Three other species are very local. One is the New Forest Burnet and is like a small specimen of the Broad-border. In England it is confined to certain limited areas, of a somewhat marshy character, in the district from which it receives its name. Another species is the Transparent Burnet which is found in localities near the coast in some parts of Scotland, Ireland, and Wales. It was first noticed in Ireland, and was therefore called the Irish Burnet. The third of these very local kinds is the Scotch Burnet, which seems to be peculiar to the Aberdeenshire mountains.

Of the Foresters only three species are known to occur in Britain. The English names of these are the Green Forester, the Scarce Forester, and the Small or Cistus Forester. All have golden or coppery-green bodies [and forewings, and greyish hindwings. The first mentioned is the most widely distributed and is usually found in moist meadows. It is, however, curiously restricted to some particular portion of the field in which it occurs. The pink flowers of the Ragged Robin seem to be a favourite resting-place, and when it is thus reposing it is less easily seen than one would imagine. Under the influence of sunshine it is very active on the wing, but rarely flies far from its breeding ground, which, as has been adverted to, is of very limited area. The caterpillar is dull yellowish with pink markings, and it feeds on the leaves of sorrel.

The Clearwings, which, from their superficial resemblance to some species of Hawk Moths with transparent wings, were up to quite recent times associated in classification with the Sphinges, are for the most part only obtained in the winged state on bright sunny days. Fourteen species are found in Britain, and the two largest of these bear a strong likeness to hornets and wasps. These Hornet Clearwings, as they are called, are rather sedentary in habit, and are most often seen sitting on the leaves and boles of poplars and osiers, in the stems, trunks and roots of which their caterpillars were nourished. The other ten members of the group are individually less in size, but they also resemble species of Hymenoptera, to which order hornets, wasps and bees belong. They delight in resting on leaves to bask in the sunshine, and at such times they seem to offer the collector an easy chance of annexing them ; but when the sun shines the listlessness is in seeming only and not in fact. The Clearwing Moth is very much awake, and exceedingly nimble withal. Perhaps the best known, certainly the most generally distributed, species is the Currant Clearwing. In spite of its fairy-like appearance it is capable of doing considerable damage when it once succeeds in establishing itself in a garden where currants are grown. It has a particular fancy for the black currant bush.

The female moth lays a number of eggs and each one is carefully deposited near a bud, so that the caterpillar when it hatches is in a position to bore into the stem right away. When it has reached the centre of the stem it feeds on the pith both above and below the point of entry. In due time it attains full growth, and it then gnaws through the woody walls of the stem, but stops short at the thin outer skin, which is left intact so as to protect the chamber whilst the insect is in the chrysalis state. The chrysalis, about the time when the moth is ready to emerge therefrom, is worked towards the outlet by means of the hooks with which the body is provided. Subsequently pressure is brought to bear on the outer skin of the stem, this gives way and the front half of the chrysalis is then protruded from the opening. After a while the moth escapes from the chrysalis shell, and the latter remains with the hind portions still in the hole.

The Broad and the Narrow Bee Hawk Moths are true Sphinges, and although the wings are clear these moths are not directly related in any way to the Clearwings alluded to above. The Broad-bordered is the commoner of the two, and in late May and early June when the rhododendrons are in full bloom it is an interesting sight, on a sunny morning, to watch these pretty insects engaged upon the open flowers. Humble Bees, to which the moth is very similar in many respects, always settle on the blossom they investigate with felonious intent. The Hawk Moth on the other hand remains in front of the flower, as though suspended by a thread, and probes the nectary with its long sucking tube without alighting. How suddenly it darts to the right, or to the left, just as the would-be captor is making ready to envelope it in the net. When seen on the wing these moths always have the wings, except the edges, quite transparent. When freshly emerged from the chrysalis the wings have a covering of dusky scales, but these are so loosely attached that the first flight of the insect removes them.

A rather near relative of the Bee Hawks is the Humming Bird Hawk Moth, which although not observed in Britain every year is sometimes quite common, and may be seen in gardens even in large towns, and occasionally in London itself. The wings of this moth are fully scaled; the fore pair are brownish in colour, crossed by two black lines, and the hind pair are orange marked with brown. Like the Bee Hawks, it also takes nourishment in a hurry and remains on the wing whilst obtaining it. As an adept in eluding the toils of the entomologist's net it is even more accomplished than either of those moths. Although it may perhaps have a preference for the sweets to be found in tubular flowers, such as honeysuckle, jasmine, or valerian, it may often be seen probing and testing the saccharine productions of various kinds of blossom.

It is essentially a sun-loving and day-flying moth, but it apparently takes a midday nap, as it is chiefly seen in the forenoon and again after about two o'clock. These periods of rest and activity may synchronise with similar stages in plant life.

Among the divisions of Lepidoptera known as Arctiidæ, Noctuidæ, and Geometridæ there are several species with the day-flying habit strongly developed, but space will only suffice for brief mention of a few of the more generally distributed of these.

Although many of the Arctiidæ, or Tiger Moths, are more or less active in the daytime, they do not get on the wing in quite the same voluntary manner as does the Cinnabar Moth. This insect, with its crimson splashed blue-grey forewings and crimson hindwings, imparts life and colour to the rough fields and waste places in which it disports itself, on sunny days, in the early summer time. The caterpillars, which are orange with black rings, are often exceedingly abundant on ragwort, but the moths are rarely very numerous. It is one of the moths designated common that the tyro is enraptured with on first making its acquaintance. He shows it to the expert in great glee, but immediately feels sad when he learns that it has no claim to rarity.

In sanfoin and lucerne fields, and in rough fields with plenty of bindweed among the herbage, especially in chalky districts, will be found a pretty, active, little Noctuid Moth. It is black in colour with a white blotch on each wing, and is known to the collector as the Four-spotted. It flies briskly in the sunshine, but it is also on the wing in the evening.

Then there are the Beautiful Yellow Underwing, not uncommon on most heather-clad commons and moorlands; and the Small Yellow Underwing, often to be seen in some numbers in meadows, etc., in May and early June. Both these insects are lovers of the sun, and are only active in the daytime under its influence. As may be gathered from the English names, each species has yellow hindwings, but in the first named the forewings are purplish or reddish-brown marbled with white and otherwise marked with yellow; in the other species the forewings are brownish marked through the mid area with blackish.

In meadows, and flying with butterflies of the Skipper persuasion on rough grassy hill-sides, will be seen in early summer, the Mother Shipton and the Burnet Companion. The former of these species has the forewings brownish mixed with grey, and upon them a design in ochreous or whitish which may be likened to a grotesque profile of a human face, and distinctly of the conventional witch-like pattern. The wings of the latter species are as regards the upper pair greyish brown varied with a purple sheen, and crossed by darker brown bars; the lower pair are orange yellow, marked with brown.

The species now to refer to in the present connexion, are one or two members of the Geometridæ, a family of moths that afford the collector plenty of day sport throughout the season. The majority of these species are induced to break cover very readily, by means of the beating stick, but a few are day-fliers because they feel that way inclined. The first on the list is a pretty little fellow with black marked yellow wings; this is the Speckled Yellow Moth of our woodlands. Then in the pine woods there are the males of the Bordered

White, and on moors and heathery ground the same sex of the Common Heath. The females of these two species last mentioned do not fly freely until early evening, and then their chief business is egg-laying.

IV

THE SPHINX MOTH

"The beam-like ephemeris,
Whose path is the lightning's."

I HAVE just seen the sphinx moth bravely on the wing and feeding in the squalls of wind and rain! Though my charming little friend will sometimes fly on summer evenings about sundown, I have always imagined that he was a worshipper of bright hours and warmth. I thought him a sound sleeper, like a butterfly, during rude weather. Yet here he came on the wing, brisk as could be, on a dark, rough autumn day. He zigzagged from blossom to blossom—red and pink geraniums —and, buffeted by the wind and beaten on by the rain, he still held himself aloft, and plunged his trunk into the nectaries, seeking their sweet-meats.

Sometimes the wind would toss him from the blossom ere he could poise himself close enough to plunge trunk down nectary; but defeated once or twice, he would return and in the end succeed.

Whilst this humming-bird hawk moth hovers, its wings appear to whir not at right angles to its body —I should say they may be at an angle of 45 deg. or so, and away from the head. Often whilst drawing the sweets from a blossom, the insect is hung in the air, touching nothing with its legs, which are laid back close to the body, like those of a sea-gull in flight. But, look very closely, and you will see that now and then when the hawk moth appears to be hanging in the air it is really resting—so lightly, though, as not to crumple a petal!— on the flower, with its thin little grey legs.

Yet, resting so, it keeps whirring its wings as if it were hanging without support.

One thing I notice in my sphinx which shows it not so infallible of eye as it might be. It will sometimes visit dead blossoms of plants round which it is hovering. True, it discovers instantly that they are dead, and is gone in a flash to a fresh blossom. Still, were its sight extremely powerful, would it waste one beat of the lightning wing on a visit of inquiry to a flower that was spent and almost colourless ? I think not. The sphinx is not the only sweet-seeker that makes a momentary mistake of the kind. The cumbrous, droning humble bee has an eye for colour, but has it one for form ? It came to the handle of my garden roller when this was new and painted with gaudy colours. It took these rings of coarse colour for blossoms—to which they bore no likeness. The bee or butterfly appears to be only infallible of eye when it is close to the object, almost touching. At a little distance, perhaps it sees just a blob of colour ; it must come very near to make out the exact form and texture of the thing observed.

To read the flowers aright, it must have its face pressed close to the petals, as a short-sighted man must have his face pressed to the book. Once at close quarters, however, the insect sight is very powerful—it has every detail under microscope.

Another thing about the little sphinx moth is the quickness with which it discovers whether a blossom has honey or not—once it is up to the flower and poised. That fine feeler, the trunk, is out of the nectary in the flash of a second if there is no honey.

By the way, how does the sphinx carry its trunk when it is honey-seeking and roving from blossom to blossom ? Well, when the flowers are very close together, when they belong to one bed or patch, the sphinx does not neatly roll up the trunk and pack it away ; nor is the trunk carried about quite unrolled. A sort of compromise is more convenient. The trunk is kept out, quite loosely rolled up. Thus it does not impede the movements of the moth, and at the same time is ready to straighten out and plunge into the nectary of the flower.

V

HUMOURS OF INSECT LIFE IN OCTOBER

"Shake not his hour-glass, when his hasty sand
Is ebbing to the last;
A little longer, yet a little longer ——."
—DRYDEN.

IN the early morning a tattered blue butterfly comes from a hiding-place in the dewy grass, flits aimlessly across the field, and drops into the shelter of the hedgerow. Unseen he had rested, clinging to an upright stem, till disturbed as I walked through the meadow. Inquisitive, I stoop to examine the stalk from which he rose. It still sways lightly from the shock caused by the insect's hurried departure. All its dewdrops have been sprinkled on the soil, and near its root a brown beetle clings asleep. Among the grasses I find many other butterflies, one here, another there, sometimes two on a single stem. So closely folded are the insects' wings, so fittingly decorated in neutral hues of grey with yellow spots, that each butterfly seems to be part of the stalk on which it reposes. Saved from harm by the loving care with which Nature has made every minute scale on the fragile fans match some surrounding tint in the undergrowth, the motionless insects await patiently the disappearance of the dew. The warmth of the previous day called some of them to life, but others resemble their weather-worn companion that flew before me a moment ago: their summer is past; they will probably die when day closes over the fields.

Towards the south, a long bank of rose-tinged cloud, overhung with a thin curtain of pale primrose, hides the risen sun. A partridge calls from the silence of a distant stubble; the gossiping rooks caw harshly as they sail overhead on their way from the elms on the slope of the hill to the ploughlands near the river. Among the oaks near the outskirts of the wood the ringdoves are already astir, seeking among the branches a meal of ripe acorns; and the eager cooing of these most amorous of forest lovers is heard in every part of the valley.

Close by, the webs of the geometrical spiders glimmer among the bushes; and long silken strands, marking the wanderings of these weavers of the night, are stretched from twig to twig across my path. Now that the sun's power is waning, and insect life is rarer day by day, the spider becomes unusually diligent. She needs to be well fed before the wasting sleep of winter and so must not fail to secure a plentiful supply of flies. Though at other times careful of her store of silk, she does not hesitate now to weave a new net whenever she may require it, if but the day hold out a promise of fair weather. To prepare for her long sleep seems to be the spider's chief purpose when autumn comes. The law that determines her existence is the survival of the fittest : so, if through accident or extravagance her silken supply is exhausted, she quickly visits the web of a near neighbour, and contends with the owner for possession. Such a battle frequently results in the death of one of the combatants, and then the victor leisurely proceeds to feast on the body of the slain. Should the aggressor be also the conqueror, she makes a careful survey of her new abode, and soon settles down to the enjoyment of her ill-gotten gains. In time her store of silk is so renewed that when she lays her eggs she is able to enclose them in a watertight cocoon. This task completed, she at last retires to some sheltered cranny in the hedge, and there constructs a silken chamber in which, secure from rain and cold, she sleeps the winter away.

As the sun rises above the pink clouds at the horizon, the yellow curtain in mid-sky fades into an almost transparent veil, and gradually vanishes. The mist rises in steam from the grass, and collects in dense cloud-masses which, following one another, roll slowly across the meadow, and spread out over the rank herbage by the hedgerow, like smoke-puffs from the sportsman's gun on a November afternoon. Half an hour since, I noticed that all the webs in the furze brakes around had evidently been completed before the dawn ; for no spider continued at work among the strands. The reason for this early toil is apparent. Had the spiders delayed their tasks till the moisture rose from the grass in the growing heat, their threads would have been softened and rendered useless even as they were spun. But since the webs have been hardened by the cool night air, the passing mist only decks them with a thousand pearls, that trickle along the threads and fall to the grass, or are in turn absorbed by the heat.

When, later, I come again into the fields, the mist has gone, but in the shadows beneath the leaves the dew still lingers. The pearls of dew, that were flushed by the rose-tinge of the eastern sky, have, in the clearer light, become diamonds, that glow and sparkle with a dazzling radiance almost unbearable to the eye. A few late spiders, less learned, perhaps, in weather-lore than their companions which spun during the night, but finding that the mist has disappeared, are busy placing their snares among the brambles for the unwary flies. Passing some large trees in the hedge-row, I notice on the trunk a number of Vanessa butterflies. Just as with the little Blues, the colours on the underside of the larger insects are similar to those of their surroundings. A Painted-Lady, resting on a broken branch, seems like a patch of lichen ; while, near by, a Peacock, with closed wings, looks like a charred stick, and is scarcely distinct from the shadow in the crevice on the edge of which it rests.

Presently, enticed by the gentle warmth, the butterflies leave their hiding-places, for the flowers are full of honey and await their coming. They flit idly about the blossoms, but their favourite resort is a clump of valerian, on the crimson crowns of which three or four of them bask, with spread wings, and probe between the clustered petals. Not only the big Vanessas love the sweet juices of the valerian. A little Copper flits down from the oaks and drives away a Peacock from the flowers ; then, while her studded fans reflect on their burnished scales the brightness of the morning, she enjoys a sumptuous feast. Soon the Copper butterfly is pursued by an eager mate. Coyly, with trembling wings, she resists his advances, but the ardent admirer pursues her to the edge of the valerian ; then they flit into the air, and gambol round each other till, rising higher and yet higher, they disappear over the tops of the oaks.

The chirrup, chirrup, of the grasshoppers in the light is to-day almost as incessant as when the hot sun scorched the dry fields in July. In one spot, where a long, shaft-like shadow is thrown from a ruined wall, the insects are strangely silent, and seem to be endeavouring to escape from the darkness. Repeatedly they leap far above the shadow, as though wishful to feel for one brief moment the pleasurable glow of autumn sunshine beyond the gloom of their little world.

A spider, when viewed closely beneath a powerful glass, wears a sinister and forbidding aspect, befitting the cruel life she leads. But the grasshopper, a harmless vegetarian, possesses an almost owlish countenance suggestive of sober wisdom and grave responsibilities, as if she had heard every secret of Nature whispered by the passing wind in the grass. As I watch intently a female grasshopper nibbling quietly and carefully a single blade of grass I cannot fail to smile. Her antennæ project before her face almost like quill pens stuck forward in the ears of some village schoolmistress. Her big, bulging eyes ; her long-drawn visage fringed with the palpi, or lips, that continually move as she feeds ; and the blunt, beak-like mouth, all combine to render her appearance curious and antiquated. I can hardly imagine a suitor for the affections of this queer little dame. Nevertheless, he presently appears, peeping from behind a twig, and approaches cautiously—in trepidation, it would seem. His eyes are set further in front than hers, and his aspect is not so particularly venerable. He gently lifts his legs, and utters a faint chirrup, calculated, perhaps, to assure her of his admiration ; but she makes no response. Now he crawls still nearer, takes the grass-blade which she is daintily nibbling in his front claws, and holds it obligingly for her in a better position. But she gnaws away, and he, preoccupied with her charms, fails to notice that the grass-blade is gradually disappearing close to his claws, till with a sharp nip she reminds him that her business is eating, and causes him to relinquish hastily his hold. His next attitude is absurdly funny. While he grasps the surrounding stalks with his four hind-feet, his front-claws seem to have nothing to do. He clasps them in an unintentional attitude of supplication so comical that I laugh aloud ; and alas ! the grasshopper's wooing is indefinitely postponed. A grasshopper, while nibbling a green blade, holds it in such a position that her jaws cut through it edgewise, and in a curve of which the lower extremity is nearer to her body than the point at which she commences to gnaw.

All this I have seen as I crouched in the grass. As I walk by the fence I notice a dragon-fly, belonging to the largest of our British species, resting on a leaf. The body is rich olive-brown in colour, with a delicate bloom, like that of the sloes in the hedgerow, at the lower end of each overlapping spiracle, and is crossed with bands of white. The dark eyes glisten like polished greenstone ; and in the transparent gauze of the rainbow-wings lurks every colour of foliage and sky. A robin flits past, with a quick jerk of his wings, and alights on

DRAGON-FLY.

From a photograph by
F. Martin Duncan, F.R.P.S.

the grass. Disturbed, the dragon-fly flashes off into the sunlight, and, as if pretending to ignore the false alarm, commences in a business-like fashion to hawk for flies near the ditch. Now is witnessed a marvellous display of its powers of flight. Like a miniature airship balanced perfectly between swiftly revolving propellers, the dragon-fly goes straight as an arrow, skimming the heads of the valerian, and nearly touching the top of the furze under the oaks. Suddenly it halts, and its wings rattle and scintillate in the amber light of the morning. Then, reversing the action of its fans, the insect moves backward for an instant, and hangs above the crown of a blue field-scabious in the ditch. Finding that the small flies, which chiefly form its food, have gone from the neighbourhood of the flower, the dragon-fly, with a sharp alteration in the movements of the wings, turns head and thorax towards the sky, and, like a clubbed arrow shot from an invisible bow, ascends to the level of the midmost branches of the oaks. Thence, with another equally rapid change of flight, it passes along the outer leaves. Again it stops, and again the sunshine touches the trembling wings. Almost immediately afterwards it vanishes—

it has dropped so quickly that my eye is baffled in seeking to ascertain its whereabouts—till yet once more the shining film of lace-like wings may be observed among the brambles close at hand. Creeping stealthily towards the tangle, I notice that the head of the dragon-fly is turned restlessly, now on one side and again on another, as the insect keeps a sharp watch for its prey. The light green lips are opened and closed, as this marauder of the woods devours some savoury morsel just secured, but I am unable to discover the identity of the stricken insect. Having finished its meal, the dragon-fly dashes off in pursuit of one of its species which has come to trespass on its hunting preserve, and drives the intruder away. Returning from the chase, the ravenous creature spies a drone-fly quitting a broad leaf of plantain, and drops instantly, hoping for a richer repast, but rises again, reluctant to attack an opponent of such formidable appearance. It may be that the drone-fly owes its escape to the accuracy with which Nature has counterfeited the colour and shape of the hive-bee in this less intelligent wildling of the fields, which, however—as the dragon-fly is probably unaware—cannot sting. Gliding, pausing, rising, falling, the dragon-fly inspects the upper surface of every leaf and flower in its neighbourhood, and consequently a rather heavy rate of mortality takes place among the gnats. But the gnats are not the only sufferers. Down from an oak bough flits a long-tailed titmouse, evidently in pursuit of a fly; but it fails to catch its quarry, and returns to the fence-rail beneath the branch. Almost directly afterwards, the dragon-fly skims across between the trees, swoops down, and appears to pick off something from a thistle close to the spot where the tit turned back baffled in its chase. Whether the bird has attracted the attention of the dragon-fly to the thistle, or whether the sight of the insect is far more acute than that of the tit, I cannot tell; I recognize, however, that in the dragon-fly the power of wing is much more wonderful than in the titmouse, making the insect a perfect acrobat of the air, compared with which the bird is like a member of some untrained troupe. Having struck its prey, the dragon-fly carries it to a neighbouring plant, there feeding leisurely on what I afterwards find, from a fragment of chitine left on the spray, to have been a bright green insect, slightly similar, but for its colour, to the familiar house-fly.

While hawking, generally along the margins of the woods, the dragon-fly, if passing to and fro in a favourite line of flight, inclines its head towards the ground, and tilts its abdomen slightly above the thorax. Its large and almost spherical eyes cover a considerable field of vision, if not the entire surroundings. From the shape and size of the thorax, it is at once apparent to me that the muscles controlling the action of the wings are numerous and extremely powerful. This conclusion is fully warranted by an examination of the wings themselves, which in every part are tough and firm, but where joining the thorax are especially strengthened and stiffened by thick, tapering nervures forming the framework of a shining, elastic gauze stretched tightly between the dark brown veins.

From the moment of its transformation into the larval condition to the time of its death, the dragon-fly is a pitiless destroyer of weaker insects. During the larval and pupal stages of development it dwells in a pond or in a stream. There the creature's appetite is ravenous, and sometimes it becomes a cannibal, devouring even its own kin. Yet, in its perfect state, this swift-winged tyrant arouses admiration by the grace of every movement. The very audacity with which it approaches and dares to hover before me, as if inquisitive concerning my trespass among its haunts, causes me to regard it as an object of more than ordinary interest.

But there is a certain family of insects, similarly cruel, for which I can cherish no kind of regard—the robber-flies. The members of this tribe most commonly seen in the fields are comparatively sluggish in their habits, and are of a dull grey colour, or banded with black and yellow. On a wooden rail, not far from the dragon-fly's preserve, I find one of the grey robbers engaged in sucking the juices from the body of a small, wasp-like insect. Though effectual in screening the drone-fly from harm, the mimicry of Nature has evidently been insufficient to preserve the robber's victim. As is usually the case, the robber-fly may have struck its prey while both were on the wing, and when the protective colouring of the wasp-fly—which fulfils its purpose chiefly as the creature rests on a yellow flower—was of little avail.

The diligent wasps are still abroad in the fields, and are engaged, like the bees, in providing for their winter wants. As I pass a fallen tree trunk, an angry buzz warns me that I have started one of these insects while at some important task. The wasp circles several times about my head; then, reassured, flies to the prostrate tree, seeks a place where the bark has been stripped off by the wind, and begins to collect wood-pulp, with which, undoubtedly, to repair her nest. A leaf-cutter bee can be heard as she shears through the harder portions of the leaves; and, similarly, the sound produced by the jaws of the wasp, while she patiently tears away minute fragments of pulp, is at once noticeable as I stoop to watch this skilled mechanic of the hedgerow. The wood is hard; her labour difficult; and a considerable time elapses before she has gathered sufficient for one journey to her nest. Having apparently masticated the pulp and reduced it to a condition fit for her purpose, she flies to the hedge-row bank, where, behind a frond of brake fern, she disappears within the shadowed entrance of her underground abode.

The afternoon declines as I return homeward from the fields. Among the brake-fern on the outskirts of the woodlands the midges are numerous and troublesome, for the dragon-flies are at rest among the leaves. When the sun sinks in the west, dusky moths commence to flutter around the pale evening-primrose in the rough pastures on my way over the slope of the hill, while a noisy beetle booms up from the grassy lane leading to the village, and passes into the gloom, with a loud murmur that gradually becomes fainter and fainter, and at last dies away across the swollen river.

VI

THE MAKERS OF GOSSAMER

"Autumn grows old: he, like some simple one
In Summer's castaways is strangely clad;
Such withered things the winds in frolic mad
Shake from his feeble hand and forehead wan."—WILLIAM H. DAVIES.

AS a season for the out-door study of Nature, the month of November hardly strikes one as altogether congenial. To the enthusiastic ornithologist it may furnish an opportunity for the observation of many of our rarer birds; the energetic lepidopterist, too, may brave its dreariness in search of pupae: but to the man in the street—and, still more so, the man indoors—Nature appears to have put up her shutters and bidden her manifold creations rest—or perish.

Put on a pair of thick boots and come with me, my friend, and I will prove to you that Nature has not quite fallen asleep and that some, at least, of her children are as wide-awake as ever. No, do not bring your gun—the woods and fields are dreary enough already without any assistance on your part. We will walk through the park, although our ramble will be restricted by yonder serried row of iron railings which the owner has erected for the preservation of his hundreds of acres.

Why, what is the matter now? Another cobweb across your face? I am glad, for it foretells much sport in store for us. Where do you think these flying threads come from? You have read all about it? I am glad of that: perhaps you will tell me. No, my dear fellow, you are quite wrong. The book was right as far as it went, but it did not go far enough. There is no doubt that the orb-spinning spiders employ flying threads as a means of forming foundation lines in the construction of their snares. But these interesting creatures have, by now, in the majority of cases, laid their eggs, snugly enveloped in a thick silken covering and, having completed this all-important task, have come to the conclusion that life has no further attraction for them. A comparatively small number of half-grown individuals lie in hiding awaiting the return of spring, but they would hardly dare to venture abroad on such a cheerless day as this.

Look carefully at the tiny black spider perched upon the pinnacle of this railing. It is not a youngster as you might suppose, but an adult spider in the full glory of his manhood. How do I know ? Simply enough. Do you see those prominent organs in front of his head, somewhat resembling arms with very large, complicated hands ? They are known as palpi ; and the presence of the complex organs at the extremity of each of them is a sure criterion that the creature has arrived at the adult state. Had it been a female, your microscope would have been necessary in order to satisfactorily decide as to its condition of maturity.

Watch the antics of the little creature carefully, and you will be amused. See, it is dissatisfied with the pinnacle which at present supports it, and is taking advantage of a bridge of delicate silk, obligingly formed by one of its predecessors, to explore the next railing, which, to our eyes, appears exactly like the other. Still it is not satisfied. First it tries one point,

then another, striking curious attitudes, and, at intervals, pirouetting wildly upon its dainty feet, its whole demeanour obviously suggestive of extreme excitement. It is only natural, for the little creature is making its final preparations for a voyage of discovery and adventure to a land of which it knows nothing and from which there is little chance of its ever returning.

At last it seems satisfied with the particular railing upon which it stands, and is raising its body to the utmost extent by straightening its legs in an almost ludicrous manner. Do you notice that from the spinners at the extremity of its abdomen there has issued a line of web of such tenuity that it is only visible when the light strikes it in certain directions ? Incredible as it may seem, this thread is not simple, but consists, in reality, of quite a large number of filaments, being, in fact, somewhat of the nature of a ribbon, and intended to offer as considerable a resistance to the breeze as is possible. Although you cannot actually confirm it in the present instance, you may take my word for it that this ribbon is being paid out with wonderful rapidity.

It was formerly believed, chiefly by reason of the fact that these lines are often cast on days when there is no perceptible motion in the air, that the spider could project them where and when it chose : but experiments made with air rendered perfectly stationary by scientific means have demonstrated the fallacy of this supposition, and have shown that an air current is absolutely necessary. It is, however, manifest that a breeze quite inappreciable to the human senses would be sufficient to carry a ribbon whose delicacy is such that spun silk, by comparison, is coarse and heavy.

The thread is formed from a viscous liquid, secreted by special glands in the body of the spider, which liquid, when brought into contact with the air in the finely divided state exhibited in these filaments, hardens immediately, and forms one of the strongest cables, in proportion to its size, that Nature or man can produce. Notice how tenaciously the little creature clutches the railing. It is necessary, for he has probably, by this time, several yards of ribbon to contend with, and the pulling force must be considerable. There he goes ! He has estimated to a nicety the pull of the thread and away he sails over the meadow. His direction is controlled by the prevailing breeze, and by the rising air-currents ; but he is not altogether at the mercy of these fickle agencies for he is able, by lengthening or drawing in his thread, to rise or to descend. But whether he shall travel north, south, east or west he has no choice whatever.

We may premise that his voyage will end safely, for in all probability he will be brought to a standstill by yonder row of stately elms. But it is not always so. If you are fortunate enough to be on the cliffs in the late autumn, with a very gentle land-breeze blowing, you will be able to observe large numbers of minute spiders sailing out to sea. We are often told that man has been forestalled in many of his mechanical contrivances by spiders ; but few may be aware that, long before man essayed in one curious way or another to cross the channel, these tiny creatures had perished in millions, unconsciously attempting the same feat.

You thought spiders were more intelligent ? I remember, a few years ago, in the early autumn, noticing an orb-spinning spider perched upon a knapweed head on the very brink of the cliff at Dover. Closer inspection revealed the fact that it was paying out a thread as the foundation line for a snare, expecting, as is usually the case, that it would ultimately become entangled in some neighbouring object. Unfortunately, from the direction of the wind, the line was drifting directly towards the French coast, and the nearest available object was at a distance considerably more than twenty miles. After a prodigious amount of thread had been thus expended, the spider seemed to come to the conclusion that it must have caught somewhere, and, acting upon this supposition, walked boldly out to sea. I watched for some considerable time but never saw her again.

But let us return to our railings. Look at this little creature just preparing to vacate its perch. I will postpone its journey by breaking its thread, because I wish you to examine it closely. Take this lens : its magnifying capability is only about three diameters, but it will help you considerably in making out the structural peculiarities of your victim. Take particular notice of the shape of its head. Do you see that instead of being bluffly rounded as in the majority of spiders it is drawn out into a kind of conical elongation with a tuft of hairs at the top ? Extraordinary, is it not ?

You ask me what is the reason for this curious formation : I am afraid I cannot tell you. It has been suggested that its object is to increase the creature's range of vision, but this is hardly likely to be the true explanation because, in the first place, the eminences often exist quite apart from the eyes, and, even when any of the eyes are actually placed upon the raised portion, those which are thus elevated are, as a rule, of imperfect structure. The variety in the form of these prominences is remarkable, and the appearance presented by the spiders is often really ludicrous. They are, indeed, the gnomes of spiderland, and the designer of goblin masks for the Christmas pantomimes might well obtain original ideas from the quaint forms of these little creatures. Curiously enough, the strangely formed heads are almost peculiar to the males. Nearly a thousand species have been described, and we have considerably more than a hundred in this country : but practically nothing is known of them except by a few experts. Let us tear up a few tufts of grass by the roots from the bottom of these railings and beat them upon this sheet of newspaper. Do you see those small brown objects scampering towards the edge of the paper ? They, also, are Erigones, as the " big-heads " are scientifically termed. The grass in this place absolutely swarms with them, and yet in a similar situation a few yards away you might have difficulty in finding more than a few stray specimens. They seem to be quite fastidious in their selection of a dwelling-place ; and although the expert collector knows from experience exactly where he is likely to find any species which he may require, he is, in the majority of cases, quite unable to account for the creature's predilection for that particular locality.

What is that you say ? You understand now why these creatures indulge in aeronautical excursions. You think that they leave because the district is not in accordance with their tastes. Without being in any way pedantic, and without forgetting the caution which a long acquaintance with Nature's curious methods has engendered, I am afraid I must again disagree with you. You must remember that the mother spider makes strenuous efforts to place her eggs in such a position that the young spiders, when born, shall be under those conditions most conducive to their well-being. Why, then, should her offspring reject her choice of a home for them and wander far and wide in search of something better ? Let me hazard an explanation. The patch of herbage at our feet, as you can see for yourself, seems in every way to fulfil the Erigone's idea of a suitable abode, judging from the fact that in practically

every tuft of grass there is to be found one of these small beings resting beneath its frail horizontal saucer-like snare. Think, now, what will be the history of this small patch during the coming season. Within a couple of months the female spiders will have deposited their eggs, and leaving them to the mercy of the world, will have shrivelled up to unrecognizable specks. The eggs will hatch, even though the weather be still inclement, and several dozen tiny spiderlings will be ushered into the world to take their part in the struggle for existence.

The first problem, naturally, is that of food. Now in this respect spiders are fastidious. True, most creatures are somewhat particular in their selection of viands, and a caterpillar, for example, will often starve rather than partake of green-meat not exactly in accordance with its taste. But the eggs from which caterpillars are produced are usually laid near to an ample supply of the particular kind of food which the moth-mother instinctively knows her offspring will relish, and the difficulty vanishes. With spiders, however, the case is altogether different. Living creatures form their sole nourishment, and, failing this, they must inevitably perish. Now, if you will bring a lens to bear upon the surface of the ground at the roots of our grass-tuft, you will probably be surprised at the hordes of creatures of one sort and another which people the spot, and you may be tempted to suggest that the supply must be amply sufficient for the needs of a dozen or so of tiny spiders. But, without experience in the matter, you can form little idea of the two most potent factors in this little drama—a spider's appetite and a spider's prodigality. As long as suitable food presents itself, or is within a reasonable distance, a spider will kill with the utmost ferocity and eat with as much gusto as if it had not seen food for days.

As long as mites and springtails are to be procured with ease the spider's existence is one of killing and eating. There comes a time, however, when these minute comestibles become so scarce that he finds difficulties even in obtaining the bare necessities of life. He cannot borrow from his brother, for the whole family are probably in the same straits. So he makes the best of a bad business, and, borrowing his brother in person, transfers the liquid portions of his anatomy to his own little maw. The bad habit, once cultivated, soon grows stronger, and the spider, also growing stronger, becomes more and more capable of indulging in his unholy practices. As a consequence, before many weeks have passed, the original family of several dozen has dwindled to three or four well-favoured, robust spiders. Surely, it is not a matter for surprise that one or more of them should wander up a railing and sail quietly away.

And so, in the autumn mornings, when the grass is alive with tiny spiders, young and old, all attempting, with more or less success to change their quarters, the air becomes charged with quantities of their silken emanations ; and these threads, wafted hither and thither by fickle breezes, gradually become entangled, form visible flocculent masses, and descend to earth. And the rustic calls it gossamer, and blames the fairies for its appearance.

VII

FLOWERS IN LATE AUTUMN

"Departing summer hath assumed
An aspect tenderly illumed."
—Wordsworth.

SOME half a dozen plants only in the British Flora bear the specific name of *autumnalis*. Of these a late-flowering yellow Hawkbit, and a water Star-wort are of no particular interest. The lovely little Pheasant's Eye, a rare cornfield weed with bright scarlet flowers, though known to science as *Adonis autumnalis*, is usually in blossom in the month of May. The other three species, *Scilla*, *Colchicum*, and *Spiranthes*, are, however, choice and beautiful plants. The Scilla or Autumnal Squill, "the autumne Jacinth" of the early botanists, we noticed in a previous paper as flourishing in vast profusion on the sandy turf of St. Helen's Spit in the Isle of Wight. The *Spiranthes* or Lady's-tresses belongs to the distinguished family of the orchids, and is first-cousin to the rare New Forest species mentioned in a former chapter. Its name, both in Latin and English, has reference to the nature of the efflorescence, which consists of a slender spike of fragrant white flowers arranged in a spiral row. It is a striking little plant some six or eight inches in height, to be found in dry pastures and on open downs in late summer and autumn. It cannot be called a rare plant, at any rate on the chalk hills of Hampshire, where, around Winchester and in the Isle of Wight, it is frequently met with. Last autumn I also noticed it in great abundance on the sandy burrows near Tenby in South Pembrokeshire. The *Colchicum autumnale*, which "maye be called in Englishe wylde saffron," is a far more local plant, though often plentiful in "fat and fertile medowes" where it occurs. A member of the Lily tribe, it may at once be distinguished from the purple saffron Crocus which in colour and general appearance it resembles, by bearing six stamens instead of three. "Cholchicum," says Dr. William Turner in 1548, "hath leaves and seedes in sommer, and flowers lyke saffron flowres aboute Michelmesse. It is muche

AUTUMN.

From a photograph by
Mary Cottam.

in Germany about Bon in moyst middowes and in woddes." Old Gerarde mentions the plant growing in " great abundance " in several localities, " as about Vilford and Bathe, also in the medowes neere to a small village called Shepton Mallet and in the medowes about Bristoll." In the West of England I have met with it in fine profusion both near Charmouth and in the neighbourhood of Crewkerne. I have also found it " in the meadows under Malverne Hills in Worcestershire " as " plentifully " as when that " really curious and diligent botanist, Mr. Manningham " recorded it nearly two hundred years ago. In former days the plant was held in high repute for its medicinal virtues, especially in " curing of the gout," but it may be that Nicholas Culpeper was leaning to the side of wisdom when he said, " The roots are held to be hurtful to the stomach, therefore I let them alone."

But if the distinguishing title of *autumnalis* be restricted to a few species, yet a considerable number of plants may be seen in blossom late in the season. This is especially the case by the seaside, where, as already noticed, the flora continues to flourish for a longer period than inland. Many members of the somewhat sombre tribe of *Chenopodiaceae* are late-flowering species, and such plants as Seabeet, and Marsh Samphire, and the Sea-blites (both *Suaeda maritima* and *S. fruticosa*) may be seen in blossom as late as October and even November. The silvery-white Orache is also in flower, and the Prickly Saltwort. The handsome yellow Horned Poppy goes on flowering well into October, and so does the beautiful Sea Pink, while the marshes on the east coast have hardly lost the glow of purple which crept over them late in July when the Sea-lavender began to come into bloom. It is not, however, only in the neighbourhood of the sea that plants remain in flower till late in the autumn. After the harvest has been gathered in Yellow-weed or Ragwort is often plentiful, some purple Knapweeds will be seen in out-of-the-way places, with here and there a Bellflower or a few plants of St. John's Wort. Out on the downs the "everlasting" flowers of the Carline Thistle are very conspicuous where they occur, while the heaths and commons are still ablaze with the golden blossoms of the dwarf Furze (*Ulex nanus*), which must not be confused with the larger and commoner kind (*Ulex europaeus*), called, says the old botanist, Robert Turner, " in Norfolk *Whins*, in some countys *Goss*, and in Hampshire *Furres*." The normal time of flowering of this latter plant is the spring and early summer, although sometimes it blooms again in the autumn; while the dwarf Furze begins to come out in July and continues in flower as late as November.

One other late-flowering species must be mentioned. Among the "herbes which," as Gerarde says, "have need to be propped up, for they stand not of themselves," none is better known than the Ivy, though perhaps it is not generally realized that its time of flowering is October and November. The "floures are very small and mossie," of a pale green colour, arranged in spherical masses, and contain a large supply of honey in their nectaries. An ivy-bush on a still sunny afternoon in late autumn is sure to form a centre of attraction to myriads of insects. The splendid Red Admiral butterfly is almost certain to be there, and perhaps the Painted Lady or the small Tortoise-shell; while wasps and bees and flies of many descriptions flock to the banquet.

As the season advances, the flowers, as they say in Devonshire, "go underground," or in the more poetical language of Thomas Hood, in his ode to Autumn:

"The flowers are in their grassy tombs,
And tears of dew are on them all."

Yet, though comparatively few flowers are to be seen, the hedgerows are not devoid of beauty. If blossoms are rare, berries are plentiful. And, except when the dog-roses are in bloom, the hedgerows are perhaps never more attractive than when the berries are ripe. The foliage has now assumed great richness and variety of colour. Scarlet hips and haws are, in most seasons, plentiful, and the well-known fruit of the blackberry; while here and there glossy black clusters of privet berries will be seen, and the coral-like fruit of the spindle tree. The wild bryony with its profusion of brilliant scarlet berries festoons the hedges, together with the long twining stems of the fragrant honeysuckle, the fruit of which has been described by an old herbalist as "like to little bunches of grapes, red when they be ripe." "Old-man's Beard," the *Clematis vitalba* of botanists, is very conspicuous in the hedgerows, "each seed having a fine white plume like a feather fastened to it, which maketh in the autumn and winter a goodly show, covering the hedges white all over with its feather-like tops." So writes old Gerarde, who named the plant "Traveller's Joy," because "of its decking and adorning waies and hedges where people travel."

The autumn, too, is the season of the *Fungi*—a branch of the British Flora in which George Crabbe, one of the few English poets who was also distinguished as a botanist, took special interest and delight—and wonderful is the number of species to be found in certain favoured localities. The New Forest, which has not yet been exhaustively explored, has already produced some five hundred and seventy species ; while Epping Forest, which is far smaller in extent, has yielded upwards of six hundred species. Never shall I forget a few days' foray in the Surrey woods in the neighbourhood of Leith Hill a few autumns ago. The vast variety of species, their strange forms and delicate colours, were indeed marvellous. They were of " every size, shade and hue, from the slender filament of scarlet or yellow upon some decaying stump, to the bold broad agaric of a foot in height and diameter, standing in the forest as a fitting table for King Oberon." The following graphic passage from William Howitt's *Book of the Seasons* is worth quoting in this connexion : " In roaming the ancient wilds of Sherwood Forest in the autumn of 1827, I was particularly struck," he says, " with the varying character of the fungi ; some broad, tabular, and flecked with brown ; some in the shade of the trees, of a pearly whiteness ; others of a brilliant rose-colour ; some whose delicate surfaces were studded with dark embossments, some fashioned like a Chinese parasol, others gibbous and grotesque ; the massy puff-ball, which before it becomes dry has been known to weigh several pounds ; the pestilent, scented, and ginger mushrooms, for all the world the exact resemblance of a simnel cake." Gilbert White mentions that " Brother Ben " gathered a puff-ball in a meadow at Alton, not far from Selborne, which weighed seven pounds and a half, and " measured in girth, the longest way, three feet two inches and a half." In the autumn, the great naturalist tells us, a truffle-hunter with his little dogs would now and again come round. Truffles, we learn, were plentiful beneath the beech-trees on the famous Hanger and in High Wood, and half a crown a pound was the price asked for this commodity.

The delights of a fungi-foray are sometimes enhanced by one of those sublime and perfect days when we

"catch the last smile
Of autumn beaming o'er the yellow woods."

It is difficult to exaggerate the gorgeous splendour of woodland scenery at this season of the year. " If," says Gilbert White, in his *Naturalist's Journal*, " a masterly landscape painter was to take our hanging woods in their autumnal colours, persons unacquainted with the county would object to the strength and deepness of the tints, and would pronounce, at an exhibition, that they were heightened and shaded beyond nature. So wonderful and lovely are the colourings of our woodland scapes." William Gilpin, in his classical work on *Forest Scenery*, maintains that the autumn is " the most replete with *incidental beauty* of any season in the year." And even when the beauty of the landscape is gone, the charms of autumn may remain. There are often, as he says, days of such heavenly temperature that every mind must feel their effect.

VIII

THE BRITISH FUNGI

". . . I give my advice unto those that love such strange and new-fangled meates, to beware of licking honey among thornes, lest the sweetnesse of the one do not counteracte the sharpnesse and pricking of the other."—GERARDE.

WHAT are fungi ? While generally they have been defined as a large class of cryptogams distinguished from algae more by habit than by any general character, which growing above or under the ground, on decomposing vegetable or animal matter, on plants, and even on other fungi, are rapid alike in growth and in decay, so many and varied are their forms that to give a comprehensive yet terse definition in plain language seems hardly possible.

They are met with in all climates, and in situations where other forms of plant life cannot exist. As although the number of described species has increased from the 4,000 estimated to exist sixty years ago to a total of over 50,000 known to-day, nothing approaching a complete knowledge of the world's fungus-flora is as yet possessed ; this still presents a rich field for the investigator.

When we say that as rusts, mildews, slime fungi, and moulds are all true fungi, there are at a conservative estimate 4,000 species in Britain alone about which many volumes have been written, for the main part strictly and severely scientific in tone, it will be evident that in writing of the British fungi in a small compass severe limitations have to be enforced. Thus while

CLEARING TIMBER.

From a photograph by
Charles Reid, Wishaw.

in the view of the great public the range of the fungi is confined to the mushroom and a few others which are lumped together under the general heading of toadstools, in the forms of dry rot, moulds upon cheese and jam, and in the fungi of certain of the human diseases, there are in truth fungi present in every home. Therefore, so far from being comprehensive, our remarks can be but introductory to the study of mycology, and that to the few this forms an attractive hobby there is the plain evidence that gatherings of the brethren to engage in fungus forays are from time to time numerously attended and enthusiastically engaged in.

While the professional mycologist is more commonly employed in investigation of the many problems connected with the very important subject of fungoid plant diseases, the interested amateur is more likely to concern himself with the study, and perhaps collection, of the larger native fungi. And apart from their scientific interest and edible value—this last so very little understood in this country—it cannot be denied that there is also the attraction of there being a marked decorative value attaching to many of these. There are, however, only a very few species which at all

commonly attract praise by reason of their good looks. Most conspicuous among these are the Fly-blown Mushroom (*Agaricus muscarius*) a poisonous species, possessed of a remarkable intoxicating property and having a large cap, sometimes six inches in diameter, of a brilliant pink or crimson colour dotted over with white warts, and growing on a tall well-proportioned stalk, and the Carmine Peziza (*P. coccinea*), a splendid large cup-shaped fungus found growing upon decaying trees.

As the collecting spirit is both so very strong and widespread, and particularly as in contradistinction to birds' eggs, rare plants, and much more of the collector's prey their displacement is not at all a matter for deep regret, it will be well to afford a few hints concerning the collecting of fungi. This at home offers a considerably wider field than does that of any other class of natural history objects; while, no doubt owing to the supposed extreme difficulty of preserving good specimens, their collection in distant lands has hitherto been so much neglected that certainly a rich harvest of new forms still awaits those who have the opportunity combined with the requisite enthusiasm to collect.

While no close season can be said

to exist for fungi, the larger kinds are most abundant from the end of August onwards until the advent of winter. Microscopic forms are, however, to be found in abundance from early spring onwards. It is to be hoped that the beginner may be so fortunate as to have the friendly aid of an experienced enthusiast in mycology. Without this the most essential portion of his collecting outfit will be a handbook with which to identify his captures. Above all one should be chosen which contains illustrations and is not too severely technical in character. An open shallow basket is most suitable for the collection of large fleshy specimens, and when obtained it is advisable to wrap these up separately in soft paper. A clasp knife and a small saw must also be carried. The minute fungi are best conveyed between the leaves of a pocket book.

Once collected and identified, perhaps only a minority of the collectors of the larger fungi will essay their further preservation. By adopting the method of submitting a thin sectional slice of the fungus to slight pressure when placed upon blotting paper, a portrait of the growing fungus can, however, readily be obtained. Some small species may be dried whole in the usual manner that plants are dried. The poisoning of dried specimens by the application of carbolic acid with a brush is particularly important in the case of fungi.

In addition to the great variety of the conspicuous ground fungi, the agarics, morels, puff balls, and others, some beautiful, some repulsive in appearance, in autumn particularly it is a common sight to see fungi protruding from the trunks of trees, and this is lamentable inasmuch as it is a sure sign of the tree being in an unhealthy condition. While many of these fungi are so small as to be likely to escape notice by the ordinary observer, others attain to quite an astonishing size. All trees may be said to be subject to these growths, and not forgetting that every kind of plant is subject to fungoid attack, this particular liability extends also to shrubs, the gooseberry, and furze bushes, for example, being peculiarly subject to the attacks of certain fungi.

Most noticeable of the conspicuous fungi which grow upon living trees are various species of *Polyporus* and other allied genera belonging to the *Polyporae*. Prominent examples of these are *P. igniarius*, Tinder Fungus, which is particularly fond of the plum tree : *P. squamosus*, Scaly-tree Polyporus, a large showy fungus with a spotted skin somewhat suggestive of a giraffe, common upon many trees, and in particular the elm : *P. sulphureus*, a large yellow fungus with an unpleasant smell, common alike to conifers and broad-leaved forest trees : *P. dryadeus*, a destructive enemy of the oak : *P. cuticularis*, a species which attacks beech trees : *Trametes pini*, a fungus with brown flesh, appearing and growing to a large size upon conifers : and *Fistulina hepatica*, the handsome and attractively named Beefsteak Fungus.

Many tree fungi occur impartially upon a variety of trees, but others are only found upon one particular host.

One of the most interesting things about fungi is their food-value. Everybody is aware that this is greatly neglected in this country, but, nevertheless, in this matter we do not seem to progress. In other countries, and particularly in Northern Europe, several species are consumed in large quantities which here meet with no appreciation whatsoever. Although, of course, many undoubtedly highly poisonous species do exist, in the popular view the poisonous properties of fungi generally are very greatly exaggerated.

In this matter there exist an abundance of recipes for infallibly distinguishing the wholesome from the poisonous, but believing a little fancied knowledge to be truly a dangerous thing, we shall not present any one of them. A large number of species of British fungi certainly are edible, and, moreover, trials in this direction form an attractive bye-path in mycology, but it must be confessed that many of them are likely to be accounted palatable by the enthusiast only. The following have, however, some substantial claim to culinary consideration : Common Mushroom, St. George's Mushroom, Orange Milk Mushroom, Parasol Mushroom, Giant Fairy-ring Champignon, Morel, Vegetable Beefsteak, and Truffle.

The mushroom constitutes such an agreeable feature of country life as to be certainly deservous of particular mention. There is all the pleasure of the finding—the very prospect of mushrooms being discovered gives a zest to a walk which is otherwise lacking—and the mushroom gathered in the fields or on the downs, then taken home to be speedily cooked and eaten, is to the stale and journeyed mushroom of the shops almost as is wine to water. While some seasons are remarkably productive of mushrooms, in others these are sadly scarce. Localities also differ very greatly in their productivity. By far the best mushroom district with which we are acquainted is the Romney Marsh, where it is customary to go out to gather them with carts; but given a sufficiency of warm rains in August and September mushrooms will appear in surprising numbers where in a season of drought not one is to be seen.

Although it varies somewhat according to locality and soil the common mushroom (*Agaricus campestris*) is really so distinct in appearance from every other fungus as to render it remarkable that, save perhaps by small children or by slum-dwellers, mistakes in its identification should ever occur. Yet, so far from feasting on the abundance thus freely provided, a very large number of country dwellers are actually uncertain as to the identity of the common mushroom. The Horse Mushroom (*A. arvensis*) is an altogether larger and coarser form. It is perfectly wholesome and palatable, but is for culinary purposes decidedly inferior to the common mushroom. While we consider the product of cultivation decidedly inferior to that of the fields, mushroom growing is now a considerable industry in this country. Given abundant crops it is remarkably profitable, but it is certainly not a business to embark upon without practical experience.

The Truffles (*Tuber aestivum* is the English species) are a most interesting group of subterranean fungi which are greatly prized by gourmands. They are usually found under woods at about 1 foot depth, are abundant on the chalky downs of Hampshire, Wiltshire, and Kent, and probably grow in many districts where their presence is quite unsuspected. The common truffle varies in size from that of a plum to that of a large potato. Some success is said to have been attained at cultivating truffles on the Continent, but all attempts to do so in England have hitherto failed.

The origin of the familiar circles in pastures differing in colour from the rest of the grass, being either brown and withered or exceptionally green, remained a mystery until about a hundred years ago, when by accurately ascribing them to the growth of fungi a scientist bearing the well-fitting name of Withering effectively disposed of their supposed supernatural origin. While we cannot precisely account for the discolorations being usually so perfectly circular, we know that when the fungi are in progress, the consequent taking away of nourishment from the grass causes it to wither; while their decay, by nourishing the grass, causes it to become particularly green and vigorous.

WOOD-PIGEONS IN FLIGHT.

From a water-colour by
Frank Southgate, R.B.A.

IX

AN OCTOBER EAST-COAST RAMBLE

"Come, tell me now, sweet little bird,
Thou fly'st away! who bade thee soar?
Who bade thee seek the sky,
And wander through yon silver cloud,
A speck to mortal eye?"—JOHN PRINGLE.

VOLUMES have been written upon the subject of bird migration since an ancient naturalist referred to the coming of the "turtle and the crane," and to "the stork in the heavens knowing her appointed times": and the theme does not stale or grow wearisome, for there are always fresh phases and new facts yet remaining to arouse speculation and reward research.

My reader will kindly put on his top-coat, slip his binoculars across his shoulders, and join me on a lengthy October ramble in my favourite bird-haunts. I am always interested in the spring movements of our feathered visitors, and haunt the sands and mudflats to watch their ways and doings, but seldom expect to see them actually arriving. One wakes up some fine spring morning and finds the wheatear dodging about on many a little sand-knoll, the redshank clicking on the marsh-wall, and the grey plover reflecting his black breast in the opalescent water on the margin of the mudflat. One is content to find them there, and he is the much more pleased if perchance a flock is observed dropping in from a long voyage over seas. But the autumnal migratory movement is by far the more interesting one because, on occasion, one may actually observe the arrival of the migrants; and having regard to time and weather, as we have done to-day, can almost hope for, and expect, their incoming.

October is pre-eminently the flitting month of the birds inhabiting the more northerly parts of Europe, although, for some weeks previously, small parties of the early hatched youngsters have already taken it into their heads to wander southwards ahead of their parents and friends. Young dunlins are to be seen in family parties, simple and confiding almost to stupidity, on Breydon mud-flats before the end of July, and little stints (*Tringa minuta*) by the end of August, and with them noisy whimbrel, dingily attired turnstones, while young knots and grey plovers drop in either just before or on a south-easterly wind. More than once have I "noted" the plover's arrival and remarked in my log:

"Grey plovers—several on Breydon. Wind (perhaps) westerly: it will be coming from the S.E. directly," and seldom has my prophecy proved incorrect.

Our route beachwards will be by the North River (Bure) walls, the denes, and sandhills. We miss many of our summer favourites, which have left us for those warmer climates always abounding in insect life. You may think it odd that they should ever trouble to come hither, seeing that when it is summer with us, sunny days and abundant food are still their portion. Well, it would be just as difficult for me, when not taking into consideration the promptings of instinct, to give you a reason why many sea-fowl should leave their summer haunts among their native rocks, while the sea is still teeming with fish-life, and go south. I will admit that, in part, the pursuit of food may actuate them, as when the Northern-bred divers and auks pursue the inshoring herring shoals. Nearly all the swallows—the last of the *Hirundines* to clear out—are gone; here and there a belated individual, anxious still about its back-ward progeny in the old marsh-mill, flits silently by, gleaning a scanty livelihood by snapping up the flies drowsily sunning themselves on our house fronts, or furtively dashing up and down under the broken herbage at the ditch-sides, where a few tardy *diptera* are yet skulking. The swift led the way, the whitethroat followed suit, then the blackcap, and then the remnant of the juvenile wheatears. No summer migrants wilfully stay with us through October.

Scarcity of food, changes of temperature, and occasionally cyclonic disturbances—all have their influences on the movements as well as on the distribution of birds. There can be no doubt that the Northern-bred birds are "set going" definitely by approaching winter from the lakes and morasses of the polar circle; and they come to us for the sake of the food our marshes, estuaries, lakes and hedgerows promise them.

* * *

I am sorry I cannot show you the berry-laden hawthorns, and smiling market gardens, that made a veritable bird-land here in the days of my boyhood: the hawthorns remaining are scraggy and dying; and the gardens are being relentlessly overswept with an avalanche of houses. The redwings, blackbirds, fieldfares, and thrushes that used to swarm here are now seldom seen, and then but scantily when the countryside is white with snow. The nearer outskirts of a growing town are always depressing to the naturalist.

That merry party of crested wrens dodging and acrobating among the branches of that old apple tree, can only have just landed here. It seems odd to me that this smallest of British birds, and an *insectivore*, too, should not only skilfully navigate itself to our shores, but pick up a living when it comes; one would imagine there could be but little left in bark or chink, after our summer warblers had spent their summer and autumn among these trees, for the wren to discover; we suspect, though, its eyesight is microscopic, and it trusts not altogether to an insectivorous *menu*. Arriving simultaneously with the herring shoals, the fishermen nickname it the herring-spink; it sometimes wearily alights on board, when the weather is foggy, and stowing its tiny person into any and every crevice, puffs itself into a ball and sleeps until refreshed.

A solitary hooded crow rises heavily from the mud on our approach: he has been breakfasting on a dead tame rabbit that some fool threw into the river. This bird seldom hunts alone, but haunts Breydon in search of dead birds lost by the gunners, and hunts by the tide-mark for stranded dog-fish, broken herrings, and the carcasses of luckless guillemots. A stranded porpoise is a godsend, and may be the occasion of a gathering of the clans. A flock of mixed " hoodies " and rooks, fresh in from sea, passes leisurely overhead : on ordinary quiet days these *Corvines* come straggling in at more than gunshot distance from each other ; they fly erratically, but it is astonishing the distance they can cover in a very short time. In windy weather they fly much more compactly, and in more business-like fashion. This breaking or scattering applies to most species. Starlings, I think, fly in the densest flocks ; their mode of flight and superlatively gregarious ways conducing to this. Flock succeeding flock of corvines— now all rooks, now crows, and anon a medley of both, fly in at intervals. On some days you no sooner lose sight of the hindmost bird, flown over you, than you turn and " spot " the advance members of another contingent. The leader of one flock lustily called *Kræ! Kræ!* to the solitary fellow, who, although replying, preferred to remain. A flight of larks comes tripping in : there are twenty of them ; one and another trills a short joyous bar, which might be interpreted " *Hooray! we've arrived.*" It is similarly syllabled ; and in the bird's vocabulary means the same. Not one only, but half a dozen succeeding bunches fly over, with seldom less than a dozen in a flock : they, like the rooks and crows, fly in from direct east.

We arrive at a deneside gateway : there are two or three of these gates breaking the long fringe of firs and alders that skirt the road from Yarmouth to Caister. Between this " plant'ain," as it is called, in short for plantation, and the sea, stretch the sand-dunes, no longer smothered with sheltering furze, as in my boyhood's time, that harboured many a species of finch and warbler, rabbit and partridge, but bared of gorse and yellow bedstraw, hawkweed and restharrow, and turfed like a lawn by the unsentimental golfer. Even the migrant linnets and redpoles will have none of it, but pass on southward following the line of trees, and crossing marshwards at its ending. These finches, with many others, struck the coast up there at Cley and Blakeney, at the north of the county, and in

rapidly succeeding flocks came southwards, pushing on like the tiny waves that follow each other to the shore. The bird-catcher knows their " line of flight," and sets his nets therein. Yet oddly enough when the sterner days of early winter drive many more of the finches southwards that have halted on the way, they will skim along by the marrams that flourish nearer the sea, and there the trapper follows them.

This morning the wind is southerly but not forceful : it is dull and " clammy," and quite a " rush " of birds is observable. Sometimes there are days when there is a lull in the movement, and again it is fanned into quite an invasion by some strange premonitory impelling impulse. Such a morning was October 9, 1906. Let me give you my note for that date.

" Oct. 9. The influx of small birds this morning made the North Denes quite interesting. At six o'clock I went for a stroll as far as the third gateway, and hung around this deneside corner. The incoming birds struck the coast probably miles to the north'ard, and led along the nearest eastward fringe of scrub [the " plan'-tain "]. I noticed every four or five minutes, sometimes oftener, flocks of from six to thirty passing birds :

these included greenfinches, linnets, redpoles, twites, and in one instance, a bunch of a score was half composed of common sparrows! The sparrow is always chatty on migration. A few bunches of larks came in from the N.E. It was a typical migration morning. Wind S.W. by S. at 6; at 7 it was S.S.E."

Similar entries dot my note-books for many years previously. The following are picked haphazard:

"Oct. 19, 1903. Enormous numbers of rooks, crows, jackdaws, and small birds coming over."

"Oct. 20, 1903. *Corvidæ* pouring in to-day in thousands."

"Oct. 13, 1896. Migration fairly set in: larks, starlings, twites, crows, rooks flying in in numbers. Wind N.E."

"Oct. 19, 1890. Many lapwings arriving. Wind W. I never before saw so many starlings arriving: several woodcocks (arrived the previous night) were shot during the day. Kentish crows coming over in a continuous stream. Flocks of jackdaws coming in." A Buffon's and a Pomatorhine skua shot on the 20th.

Yon bird-catcher will take several dozen linnets this morning, and may-be, a mealy redpole or two, and the twites will annoy him by the per-tinacity with which they will join the devoted linnets. Find we ourselves now by the sea.

A flock of snow buntings are to be seen busily quartering the shingly patch, just below the marrams. They are worth watching: they feed in little parties, on the seeds of the dune plants laid bare by the blowing of the sands, closing up when taking to wing, and scattering the moment they alight. It is astonishing what they find to eat at times, but they are always plump. The earlier flocks are darker plumaged than those arriving later: they will whiten rapidly as the sharper weather comes on. Many go inland beyond the marshes, where too, at times, you will see parties of them gleaning the seeds of the Michaelmas daisy and the *Chenopodiums*.

Sometimes the bird-catcher sneaks down to the marrams, and sets his nets for "snowmen," and by the aid of decoy birds, often entraps with them the shorelark, the Lapland bunting and other interesting species. These species are exceedingly sociable, and are usually found together. Something like eighty shorelarks were shot near Yarmouth in October 1881, the greater portion of them males. They were at one time hawked about at sixpence each! What detestable and senseless slaughter.

Striding along through the marrams we nearly set foot on a skulking woodcock! He came over last night, with others of his fellows : you seldom hear of one being seen or shot but you hear of others also. Small parties drop in intermittently, but we usually look for a couple of " flights "—the " first flight " on the October moon ; the " second flight " in November ; but this is not always observable. I have in October seen the barn owl come over in broad daylight, but he comes singly, and looks very much out of place, and seems to know it! The short horned or " woodcock " owl arrives at night, but will cheekily hunt at all times of the day, not troubling himself about the sunlight. I have known the merlin and the kestrel freshly arrived, hungry as the proverbial hunter, to dash at the decoy birds in the first bird-nets they note in their line of flight. This audacity usually ends in disaster to themselves.

More rooks and crows, and some jackdaws.

Yet more skylarks,—now some starlings, and again rooks : this is the order of to-day. You may come to-morrow, and fail to see but the merest stragglers winnowing in, or you may come day after day and find migration still abundantly apparent.

* * *

It is high water, and the waves have pushed the sea's débris to the highest limit. It will be interesting to keep an eye on these sweepings of old ocean. We may find some drowned little warbler among the drift and seaweed. The chaffinch, the starling, and many another, even a woodcock, a harrier, or a buzzard may be found cast up, victims to sudden storm and wing-fag. Mayhap, some have struck the lantern on a light-vessel and fallen wounded in the sea, as birds often do in foggy weather.

Our lightship-men, since the fixed lights have been replaced by those that revolve, do not now find so many bewildered birds striking against their lanterns as in times gone by. They still flit around in hazy weather—the poor birds' greatest enemy, but do not so often strike. Occasionally some will alight on deck and bulwarks, and others, still more exhausted, drop around in the sea and miserably perish. You might ramble along here at night-time and still hear the " *syou!* " of the redwing, the shrill squeal of the dunlin, and the " *klee-a-ee* " of the plover ; and you may hear many a strange cry above the lighted town.

For hours they will fly bewildered and perplexed, around and about, until the dawn dispels their confusion, and on they go.

Notice yonder black and white sea-fowl dancing on the billows—use your glasses. You make them out to be guillemots and razorbills, and possibly you may discern a diver—a red-throated diver among them. These birds, as I told you, are pursuing the inshoring herrings; they began their southward trip in August—I steamed through hundreds of them last August in a tug.

They will remain here while the sprats inshore on the Suffolk coast in November; and so they will still work southward, dreading no lack of prey, but only in fear of the gale that springs up suddenly from the east. The gannet is common just a few miles off our coast; he, too, is an ardent admirer of *Clupea harengus*. The terns have passed—some weeks ago they went gaily and leisurely south, feasting on the abundant herring-syle as they playfully journeyed.

You notice the hosts of gulls working up and down the coast : they, too, have come to harass the herrings—content to scavenge the dead that the under-currents throw ashore, and ready on occasion to surround, in a screaming multitude, the fishermen's boats and take their toll ere the laden nets are hauled. Black-heads, black-backs, herring gulls, and rarer species gather to the fishing grounds; they too are unconsciously migrating and passing along south. They are in every stage of plumage. Observe that flock of ducks trailing along, just above the billows, half a mile out : they are common scoters (*Oedemia nigra*); they have worked southwards from the Polar regions—a few have been bred on the shores of the Baltic—and will remain, a little army scattered along the East coast, from the Faroe Islands to Essex; and will dive for mollusca all the winter through. They may be later on joined by scaups, and brents, if the weather be severe.

A flock of at least two hundred dunlins pass us : they may not halt, perhaps, until they reach the Essex saltings, although it is possible they may go a mile or so south, and re-membering Breydon, suddenly rise to a height, and make direct for the mudflats.

We were talking of light ships just now : I remember reading in a *Report on Migration* that in October of 1881, a Suffolk light vessel was visited by many little travellers. The excerpt is interesting :

" Oct. 6. Larks, starlings, mountain sparrows, common wrens, redbreasts, chaffinches and plover were picked up on the deck, and that it is calculated five to six hundred struck the rigging and fell overboard ; a large proportion of these were larks. Thousands of birds were flying round the lantern from 11.30 p.m. to 4.45 a.m., their white breasts, as they dashed to and fro in the circle of light, having the appearance of a heavy fall of snow."

*   *   *

We reach the village of Scratby whose lowly tenements look down on the wild North Sea. The five mile stroll on the yielding sand and grinding shingle had wearied us, but for the excitement of our pursuit, and the interest of our subject. It is but the matter of a few minutes' scramble, and we have clambered up the yielding cliff into the heart of the hamlet ; and a half-hour's walk brings us to the Ormesby Station, through which directly a convenient train will be coming on its way to Yarmouth.

We continue our gossip on the birds, and discuss the bearings of winds, and the vicissitudes of weather. How that the northerly gale drives southwards the various skuas, the petrels, rarer gulls and allied species. Birds do not like a wind behind them, but if left to their own devices prefer a shouldering breeze. The voyage across the North Sea, under favourable conditions, may be performed in a day, but contrary and baffling winds may be flown into, and sudden squalls and fogs may hamper them. On such occasions many birds arrive dead beat ; and no doubt many perish miserably on the way. We see their bodies cast up at times. I have found the Manx shearwater, kittiwakes, hawks and buzzards, wet and bedraggled, among the seaweeds. Lapwings invariably seem muddled out on arrival. Then, too, the manners and methods of individuals trooping in with their fellows afford diversion. Jackdaws always prate on their journey : they are the bird termagants of the northern climes. The rook is usually silent—whilst the Kentish crow has much to say *en route*, making comment no doubt to his fellows. Starlings come silently ; finches chirp a little ; and sparrows cannot hold their peace. Twites " cheep," and larks chortle ; missel thrushes crake, and redwings squeal, but blackbirds are as silent as the starlings. Flocks are more numerously noted in the early morning ; sometimes the " rush " is going on all day, whilst now and again the movement ceases long before noon.

One might wonder why the impulse does not seize the birds *en masse ;* but it does not, and contingents, save in exceptional cases, troop in day after day, a wise procedure enough, for it prevents over-crowding and the possibility of greater mishaps that might await a simultaneous exit. By the first week in November most of the land-birds will have left the early northern winter behind them ; but right away until January there may be large flights of the hardier water-fowl passing.

" The inspector is coming round for our tickets ! "

X

CONCERNING THE CHOUGH

"The Crows and Choughs that wing the midway air
Show scarce so gross as beetles."
KING LEAR.

THE chough is now only to be obtained in Ireland, and, in smaller numbers and more scattered, on the cliffs of Wales and Scotland and the western counties, and inland in certain mountainous Welsh retreats.

To assign a satisfactory reason for the banishment of the chough from so many an ancient fastness—for at one epoch it inhabited most of our littoral cliffs—would be mere guess-work. But it is perfectly clear that in some instances the ruffianly daw has been responsible for the exile of its aristocratic cousin, and, in others, that the princely peregrine has des-troyed not a few. Nevertheless these two factors alone are not commensurate with the wholesale thinning of its ranks, and, wonderful to relate, man is not to blame, so that it would seem that there must be some baneful agency at work which carries off the greater percentage of the young. To cite one special case. I know a dis-trict in Ireland where, of fully sixty nests annually, only some half-dozen are takeable, even to an expert crags-man ; jackdaws there are non-existent ; and from an examination of the pere-grine's gallows, few are captured by these marauders. Consequently most of the broods should reach maturity. But apparently it is otherwise, for the choughs do not increase at all. The subject offers a wide and interesting field for investigation.

The haunt of the chough is invariably a rocky one, and a decided preference is evinced for maritime rather than inland cliffs ; the chough must now be followed to the most desolate of regions, where the mighty breakers of the Atlantic rage unceasingly with baffled fury against the storm-rent, tunnelled faces of the beetling cliffs, just such a spot as the erne and peregrine, rock dove and seal revel in.

In appearance the chough is one of our most attractive species. Its elegant poise, dainty manners, purple-green glossed ebon plumes, rather long, red, decurved bill and vermilion legs all help it to an air of special distinction. It shuns trees altogether and obtains its food, which amongst other things comprises beetles, spiders, grubs and certain kinds of worms, in the open. But contrary to the example of most creatures which love exposed places, it is often extremely confiding, and when thus engaged may sometimes be cautiously approached to within the simplest of shots. Sometimes a flock or small party feed together ; at others only a pair or even a single bird. It delights in loose and sandy or friable soil in which to delve for prey, where its curved and sensitive bill is specially adapted for the work and particularly for worming into crevices and holes. A pair feeding in company is a fas-

cinating spectacle. At first both birds are close together : then one runs nimbly for several yards, stops, preens its glossy coat and now beckons to its mate with a clear " *kwāār*," flicking its wings up at the same moment. At this, the other starts by walking sedately towards it, halting at intervals ; then it gives a few big leaps and now both, with bills slightly opened, pluck greedily at the loose turf, either by a rapid, downward pickaxe motion or by sweeping sidelong scoops. At each stroke the soil flies up in miniature showers. If a slit or cranny in a detached lump has to be explored, the upper mandible is inserted into it to act as a prize, and, to steady it, the lump is often tenaciously grasped by the left foot, as is the way of parrots. Food is variously procured amongst scrubby heather, in rocks, and from the grassy strand, as well as from the plots of dubious cultivation within reasonable touch of its haunt.

At all seasons choughs are frolicsome. It is nothing uncommon—where the bird is still plentiful—to see from thirty to fifty playing sportively above the cliffs. Their antics are then replete with interest. As they all wheel—but each pair keeping rather apart—in devious flight, one will suddenly tumble over on its back like a raven, another spins over from side to side, whilst a third, rising obliquely for thirty or forty yards, dives rapidly down again.

The chough possesses two distinct modes of flight. The first is where it progresses by a succession of leisurely flaps and glides; the second, which is often a continuation of the first, by a series of big, spasmodic dives or inverted arcs, the wings being most tightly shut at the bottom of each dip. On the ascent of the curve the bird nearly always "*kwaārs*," and from time to time, especially during a 'long, slanting dive of several hundred feet to the cliff below, a leg is dropped hurriedly as if balance had momentarily been lost. They are most noisy and active towards evening.

In the breeding season some of their antics are peculiarly diverting. At one time a pair—close to their nest—dashing about low down over the slopes of or along the face of the cliff with far quicker flight than usual, will madly and erratically twist, first this way then that, with lightning turns as if for the nonce bereaved of their senses; at other times a couple will climb high into the heavens, sailing round each other in slow spirals or soaring head to wind just as is the habit of so many of the raptors.

Although when viewed at a distance the chough's flight is somewhat reminiscent of the jackdaw's, it is ever more buoyant and soaring than that species', the wings are longer and more curved, whilst the primaries all stand out more distinctly; and of course once the characteristic diving flight is witnessed confusion is impossible; and besides, the two birds rarely inhabit even the same district, they certainly never breed on the same cliffs. In fact, on the wing the chough suggests a miniature raven rather than anything else, a likeness which is further intensified when the two birds are seen in the air together. It may be of interest to add that in Ireland the chough is almost universally called jackdaw.

Whilst it is true that choughs are very socially inclined, inasmuch as they often feed in companies and otherwise consort together, yet I have found (and I know districts where the bird merits the prenomen common) that nowadays seldom indeed do they breed even in scattered colonies. For example, on some ranges of cliffs large enough to accommodate a hundred pairs there will be but one nest, whilst on longer ranges nests will be dotted about here and there. Yet in the latter case the birds frequently return from the feeding grounds in parties, each pair dropping out and diving straight to its home with a farewell "*kwāār*" as the troop pass merrily over the spot. But even during building operations the birds are frequently absent from their nests for a long period, and when one is sitting the other may be away for an hour or more.

Choughs are affectionate and amorous; long after the eggs are laid they pay court to one another. A pair will settle on a boulder or bare patch of soil on the cliff : then one— the hen presumably—will pirouette, fluttering her well-extended wings and giving vent to a curious "chackle," whilst the male rubs his beak against hers or even seizes her lower mandible and waltzes round her in a crouching attitude. Sometimes they caress after this fashion in mid-air.

The nest is always in a covered site and that generally in a cliff, but occasionally it is found in a disused shaft or a ruined tower. In a cliff, the site is either a hole, a crack, a small oven-shaped recess or even a protected ledge inside a gloomy cave ; but in a shaft or tower some hole where the woodwork or masonry has been dislodged. Unlike many of our maritime-land birds, the chough does not appear to give any preference either to the top or bottom half of a cliff ; many

nests are found in both situations : but it revels in a spot which is fearsomely overhung. This, combined with the fact that the nest is sometimes as much as six feet in, renders the majority of them absolutely impregnable. A partiality may possibly be evinced for a precipice composed of big boulders and more or less turf covered or plant grown in places. Some pairs breed on little, detached stack rocks close inshore ; a few on larger islets as much as six miles from land, but the majority nestle on the main land or on islands of considerable size.

The nest itself, always built at the extreme end of the selected cavity, and only in rare cases quite visible by merely lifting a flap of sheltering turf, is composed of sticks or heather sprigs according to locality, withered rushy grass and occasionally a *flake* or two of moss, lined with rather fine rootlets, masses of wool and now and then a tuft of hair or any fur that is procurable ; I have seen fox's fur in one nest. I have, however, never found odds and ends, such as paper and rags, adorning the nest, as is the general custom of the jackdaw. The whole structure, if rough, untidy and rather flat, is compact and firmly wedged into its site and considering that, as a rule, remarkably small cavities in comparison with the birds' size are chosen, a marvellous amount of material is used. Both sexes assist in building it.

Paired for life, they frequently resort to the same nest year after year, and although there is at least one alternative the birds usually only patronize it when their favourite site has been tampered with.

The eggs are from three to six or even seven in number, but clutches of four and five are most frequent. In ground colour they range from pale creamy or yellowish white to dirty white with a tinge of green, whilst the blotches, spots and streaks are browns of different shades, fawn and grey. On some specimens a few nearly black marks or lines occur. One type is zoned at either end, another is evenly marked over the entire surface, a third is scantily but boldly blotched, whilst a fourth is curiously streaked and lined ; and on some eggs the grey underlying markings predominate. As a rule eggs in a clutch are not all of one type. Incubation, chiefly the duty of the female, lasts, for one egg, eighteen days, for the chough frequently sits on its first egg.

The chough's breeding season commences in April, and very exceptionally eggs are found during the first half of the month, but full sets are prevalent from between the 25th and 30th, whilst some pairs have not laid till the third week in May.

The chough's cries are rather daw-like but are more metallic, more melodious and shriller. The ordinary note is a single " *kwāār* " or " *kwear*," sometimes " *kwā—ār* " the corresponding cry with the nestlings—a call for food—being more modulated and rather " *jaār*," quickly reiterated and resembling the whinings of a set of very young kittens. Its other notes are " *chow*," " *kwow-wow-wow-wow*," " *kwuk-uk-uk*," a sharp " *quek* " and a short, subdued, tremulous and guttural " *quarr*."

Choughs are plucky and will fearlessly mob eagles, ravens, gulls and, in short, any bird but the peregrine. I have seen this well exemplified when watching a party of choughs circling and cackling above the cliffs : a peregrine has " winnowed " through, when without a sound they have dispersed instantly.

XI

A PLAGUE OF FIELD-RATS

"Acorns ripe down pattering
While the autumn breezes sing."
KEATS.

AS, gun in hand, I linger by the hedge, a rat comes suddenly from his burrow in the bank, and moves quietly through the brambles into the ditch. There, sitting on his haunches, he gnaws at the exposed root of a hazel. But not finding the fibres quite as succulent as he had expected, he creeps away through the thicket to drink at a little hollow, scarcely more than a hoof-print, filled by the autumn rains. Having slaked his thirst, he resumes his foraging, and, not noticing my presence, pauses quite close to my feet, where a number of acorns, some parted from their cups, others still attached to them, lie scattered on the grass. Having selected one of the acorns which has lost its cup, the rat takes it in his fore paws, and, sitting again on his haunches, nibbles the light green husk at the base of the fruit, then, tearing off the covering, begins to feed on the white flesh within. Evidently, however, this acorn is not quite to his taste, so he throws it aside and chooses a second, which, also, is without its cup. Of this he eats a considerable portion, but at last abandons it, and seeks another that might prove more palatable. Following every movement of the animal, I am impressed with the significance of the common incident before my eyes. The rat evidently chooses the acorns that are severed from their green cups, because they are more easily stripped of their husks than are the others. Possibly he is attracted by the pale, ripe-looking rind at the base of the fruit, just in the spot he knows to be thin and soft. Anyhow it is clear that, when the first falling acorns are welcomed as a change of diet and sought with avidity by many of the woodland folk, those protected at the base have a greater chance of escape than those deprived of such a covering. It may follow, then, that most of our oaks spring from acorns thrown down by the wind while yet they are not ripe enough to shrink and to become detached from the cups. And it may be presumed that the fixed habit of simultaneously dropping both cups and fruit is gradually being acquired by the trees for the purpose of self-defence. This conclusion is borne out, when in the spring the first dark red leaves are observed unfolding on the fragile stem of the tiny saplings by the wayside. Then, in nearly every instance, a cup, its purpose fulfilled, is found lying beside the split halves of the sprouting acorn.

Still unsatisfied, the rat returns to the ditch, and wanders hither and thither, searching for green shoots of herbage. Somehow he becomes entangled in a matted growth of goosegrass and bramble. Attracted by his struggles, I approach the spot. But just then he escapes, and, making straight for his burrow, is about to disappear, when a charge of shot arrests his progress. As I walk down the field to pick up my victim, another rat leaps from the brambles, and, running along the ditch, receives the contents of my second barrel. I soon find that the first rat has a varied assortment of the dried seeds of goosegrass, meadow fescue, and foxtail fastened to his fur. Carefully examining the entrance to the burrow, I discover, in the bare brown soil, many more such seeds—all evidently rubbed or shaken off by these hedgerow pests as they have passed to and fro after feeding in the undergrowth. Seeking further evidence of the devices of plant life

for the distribution of seed, I now observe that the second rat has also unwittingly collected on his coat, especially about his shoulders, the seed spikes of several plants.

More than ever inquisitive, I cross the field into the woods. Almost from beneath my feet a rabbit bolts, and, rushing quickly down the glade, is shot as he crosses the path. Like the rat, the rabbit acts as an agent for the dissemination of seed. The prickly ball of a burdock has become matted in his fur close to the ear, but is already half torn away, apparently by the hind foot of the unwilling carrier in his attempts to get rid of his encumbrance. Clover-seeds are afterwards found in the whiter fur between his fore legs. Still eagerly curious, I resort to the lane below the woods, where the mounds are honeycombed by the dwellings of the brown bank-voles. Four of these little animals are soon destroyed. In the coats of two I find no trace of anything like a seed, but in the fur of the third I notice several husks from which seeds have fallen, and, on the fourth a dozen dark grains, probably from the capsule of the pink campion. These are the only seeds I can discover ; but it is likely that the presence of many others, too minute for the unaided eye, might be detected by means of a lens.

When the weather grows warm at the beginning of summer, the common brown rat often forsakes his winter quarters at the farm, and takes up his abode in some adjacent hedge. He may even prefer a haystack, or the loosely built walls of a cowshed in the meadow; but wherever may be his home his career of destruction is the same. The burying-beetles, alert to undertake the funeral arrangements of any dead bird or vole, find in the rat a keen competitor in such work. Perhaps just as they are about to complete the interment of some little creature recently slain in that struggle for life which is hourly taking place in the fields, and the female beetles have crept beneath the corpse to lay their eggs in such a position that the future grubs may find a rich and savoury repast immediately they are hatched, the ubiquitous rat comes and effectually puts an end to their plans. He digs out the body, feasts on it, and finds in the mother beetles themselves a dainty that lends variety to his repast. Fond of tunnelling in the bank close to a slowly trickling stream, he pollutes the water so that the mud becomes slimy and the pool in the corner of the field stagnant and evil-smelling. He is the villain in many a meadow tragedy. The fledgling that happens to fall from the nest in the hawthorn, or ventures too early from beneath the hen-bird's sheltering breast, has a poor chance of life if the rat is prowling in the grass. The doe-hare, indulging in some brief recreation, hears the piteous cry of a leveret, and returns in haste to her home among the withered bents near the gate opening into the cornfield, but finds that she is too late to save one of her young from death. The pheasant and the partridge lose many an olive-brown egg, and many a promising chick; moorhen, coot, water-rail, and corncrake, all dread a visit in nesting time from their enemy the rat. Even the skylark and the meadow pipit, among the furrows and the mounds, are never secure from harm.

In the corn and root-crops the rat, throughout the summer, is a plague. Here he is fastidious in the midst of plenty, and eats only a small portion of the countless sappy shoots which he spoils and destroys. In many districts where farming is carelessly carried on, and pasture land probably occupies the entire holding, the common brown rat abounds in such numbers that in comparison with his depredations those of the field vole are insignificant. Field voles and rats are especially destructive on poor and neglected farms near estates where game is vigilantly preserved. This is due to the wholesale slaughter of the weasel tribe, and of owls and hawks, which takes place in the neighbouring woodlands. Incidentally, however, carrion crows, jays, and magpies also suffer. It is undoubtedly essential to the successful rearing of game birds that some of the creatures known as " vermin " should be shot or trapped. But keepers, as a class, are so wedded to the traditions of their calling that their intelligence is undeveloped, and they lack originality. Speaking personally I confess that among the keepers I have known anything like an intimate and correct knowledge of the life of the fields has rarely been found. A keeper's marvellous tales concerning the habits of wild creatures must almost invariably be taken with the proverbial grain of salt. If the professional game-watcher only exercised that power of close Nature-observation which might reasonably be expected in a man who, ears and eyes alert, is always in the open air, it would be almost certain that such comparatively harmless and exceedingly useful creatures as the kestrel and owl would not be destroyed. I am perfectly well aware that at times the owl and the kestrel are guilty of the death of young partridges or pheasants ; but these occasions are exceptions to the rule.

Naturalists have for many years pleaded that the kestrel and the owl might be spared ; but all their pleadings have been wholly unheeded by the majority of our landowners, who leave such affairs in the hands of their keepers. The student of Nature has learned, from much patient observation, that in certain districts the kestrel and the owl are necessary to successful farming ; and almost everywhere the farmer finds in these birds inexpensive assistants which, by their labour night and day, prevent disaster to his crops. After nightfall I have seen the white owl appear like a ghost above the hazels, hover for a moment on slow-beating wings, then drop silently and suddenly into a ditch, and bear away through the gloom a squealing rat. Repeatedly I have watched the bird come to the same spot, that thus she might supply her nestlings with abundant food. In the early morning I have seen the kestrel fall like a stone from the sky, and snatch up a young rat feeding in the grass. I have also observed the bloodthirsty stoat, fit enemy of the scarcely less cruel rat, wander along the fence in company with his family, and enter the burrows to carry on a slaughter grim and great. But the stoat seldom ventures alone into a large rat-warren ; he prefers to lurk in the neighbourhood, waiting for his unsuspecting prey. The weasel is still more cautious, and rarely seizes a full-grown rat ; his quarry is usually the field vole, which he attacks with the same vigour as that with which a parent polecat, having young in her burrow, pursues either rat or rabbit. Three or four weasels simultaneously at work among a colony of field voles are wont to create such a commotion that their presence is not forgotten for many a day. Some of the marauders stay outside, while others raid the burrows ; the voles bolt like rabbits in every direction, and frequently, while rushing from danger within, blunder, panic-stricken, into the very jaws of an enemy crouching, vigilant, in the thicket without. Many of the timid animals, fleeing along their underground passages, find escape barred both before and behind ; and then, unquestionably, the law as to the survival of the fittest finds ample demonstration.

The barn-owl, the kestrel, and the different members of the weasel tribe are the chief foes of rats and voles, but they are assisted in their mission by the brown owl and the sparrow hawk. All these, except the owls and kestrel, feed also on the young or eggs of game birds, and on leverets and rabbits. They are persistently persecuted, not without reason, by keepers. But while game preservers circumvent in every conceivable way every creature that is likely to spoil their sport, they completely upset the balance of Nature, simply because the rat and the vole are not taken sufficiently into consideration. In woods and fields under the keeper's care, rats, and sometimes even voles, are killed whenever it is possible to do so. But on farms outside the " preserves " the pests flourish beyond the reach of the keeper. They are local in their habits : the keeper, therefore, does not suffer. But in shooting every stray bird or beast for which, perhaps, his grandfather ignorantly avowed a strong dislike, the keeper deprives his neighbour, the agriculturist, of the very assistance which he most needs in his conflict with a plague that does far more damage for him than many kestrels or owls can do for the game preserver. Only two hundred years have passed since the brown rat was brought oversea—unintentionally, it may well be imagined—into Britain, and in this comparatively short time he has spread throughout the country in alarmingly increasing numbers. Single-handed, man has been unable to exterminate the plague ; and it seems that, in years to come, the exceedingly favourable conditions under which voles and rats exist in this country will claim the attention of legislators. Then, probably, instead of being destroyed, the carnivorous birds and mammals that are the enemies of the rats, though also of game, will be imported and diligently protected. Unless, meanwhile, owls, kestrels, and, perhaps, weasels are allowed to multiply, some legislation on the point may become an absolute necessity.

Often during the morning or afternoon the rats, but not in great numbers, may be observed passing from burrow to burrow along the hedge. Like the field voles, they remain indoors while the evening shadows gather on the grass, for they know well when the owl goes on the first of his twilight journeys. In the day the rats are not nearly so wary as in the evening and at night. From this it may readily be inferred that they dread the kestrel far less than the owl and other nocturnal enemies. As the long sleep of winter begins to steal over the woodlands, the burrows become gradually forsaken, and the stables and haylofts at the farm are tenanted once more. The rats, having assisted in the dispersal of seed—almost the only useful purpose served by their existence—leave the tiny germs to root in the bare soil about the numerous entrances to their galleries in the fields ; so that when, next summer, the migration of these animals again takes place, the slimy ditch and the fetid mud of the hedgerow present, for a time, fresh verdure. But the spoilers of the fields soon desecrate the abode of summer.

In the bank-vole colony below the woods most of the young mice have grown to maturity, and the passages are being enlarged to provide for their accommodation. The vole, when burrowing, uses his fore feet to scratch away the soil, which he pulls towards him till it forms a small mound beneath his body. He then advances a little further, and with his more powerful hind feet kicks the heap towards the entrance to the chamber. The earth falls about him as he works, so, now and again, he shakes himself thoroughly, to prevent the loam from sticking to his fur. By these violent efforts to get rid of anything which might prove a burden, the vole also throws off the seeds he has unwittingly brought into his dwelling from the undergrowth outside ; the seeds are thus mingled with the débris of his excavations. When the vole finds behind him a neat little hillock of soil awaiting removal beyond the door of his house, he turns, and, placing his fore paws close together, makes a natural shovel, which he thrusts beneath the heap. He then pushes the loose loam right along the tunnel, and deposits it without. At the same time he inadvertently sows, in a mound of new earth, the seeds he has carried away from their parent plants. During the vole's semi-hibernation in the winter, these seeds are left protected and undisturbed, so that when, with the advent of spring, his labours are resumed, he finds new verdure beginning to form in the hedgerow bank a screen behind which, unseen for a time by kestrel and owl, he can work and play in safety.

XII

ENGLISH CHALK COUNTRY

"Downs that swerve and aspire in curve and change of height that the dawn holds dear."
A. C. SWINBURNE.

NO type of English scenery is so distinct from all others, and so deeply marked at the present day by the most ancient and storied features of rural life, as the vast curved hills and rolling downlands of the chalk. From the point where it rises from the sea in Dorset and the fringe of Devon, to the white, bird-haunted precipices where its most northern limb confronts the sea again in the crag of Flamborough Head, its smooth, huge folds and serene and airy skylines offer the same deeply satisfying landscapes, stamped with a beauty of which the inmost life and spirit is a Hellenic simplicity and restraint. Wherever the surface of the chalk is freely revealed, and not covered by subsequent deposits of gravel, as it is in some parts of the Eastern counties, it shows the same vast, unbroken curves and contours, folded into deep green combes, with farmsteads nested in trees under the rise of the hill, and at considerable intervals, in the larger valleys, the crystal trout-streams and emerald stretches of bubbling water-meadows. There is an utter absence of all turbulent confusion, all laboured and fretful detail, in the outlines of the great chalk hills; on the high, bare skyline one league-long heave sweeps downwards into the next with

THE CHALK COUNTRY.

From a photograph by
Frith & Co., Ltd.

an unbroken purity of curve; and all the lesser details of the combes and hill-slopes have the same underlying quality of restraint in their beauty of colour and form. To eyes that have once grown fully familiar with a country of such noble purity and calm, other and wilder landscapes of torn boulder, splintered pinnacle, and shouldering crags always convey an underlying impression of something tortured and overladen in their characteristic lines. However great is the pleasure in the scenery of mountain and moorland, or in the native features of other English shires, the eye comes back from them to the chalk again with a singular renewal of harmony and ordered peace. The beauty which is rooted in true sanity has moulded the great chalk hills for its eternal and visible kingdom; they form the humanest of all English landscapes, and the spirit's most kindly home.

Few British scenes have retained so much of their bygone character in other ages and centuries as the green folds and rolling hill-tops of the many ranges of the downs. That underlying sense of ancient human associations, which so deeply tinges every landscape of English soil, is never so potent and unfailing in its appeal as on the virgin turf of these wide and ancient sheep-walks, never enclosed until this day, and still scarred with a thousand traces and memorials of the peoples of an uncharted antiquity. Even as preserving for our eyes the aspect of the English countryside in the days before the chief centuries of hedge-planting, the rolling downlands of Berkshire and Wiltshire, still scored by the deep trails of the pack-horses, and traversable from market-town to market-town by rough and unmade roads, offer a remarkable picture of the country's bygone state. Stranger and infinitely more ancient still are the turf-clothed trenches and roadways, camps and funeral barrows, of the neolithic races who once clustered so thickly on these dry and open hill-tops, in an era when the lowlands were still impassable with quagmire and forest, and full of the wild beasts' lairs. Since the earliest dawn of time, in striking contradiction to the vast growth of the general population, the solitude of the great chalk downs has been steadily deepening and increasing up to the date of the latest census. The chalk supports no great manufacturing industries; the coal and iron which multiply thronged centres of population in the west and north are here plunged deeply beyond human reach, and the tide of humanity still ebbs steadily year by year from all the hamlets and villages of the downs. Season after season, old cottages are abandoned on the hill, old farmsteads dismantled at the head of the cultivated combe ; and the sense of loneliness upon these wide, thyme-scented slopes is increased to a singular degree as the mind's eye ranges backwards through so many centuries, finding in each, remoter than the last, a fuller story of the presence and business of man, till in the earliest ages, from the silent and turf-lapped memorials, there pour forth once more the skin-clothed peoples of the dawn.

It is very noticeable that while these primaeval relics are common on all the more open ranges of the chalk, from the camps on the Dorsetshire crests to the flint-workings of the Brandon heaths, they are far scarcer among the dense beech forests of the slopes of the Chiltern Hills. This difference in the distribution of these remains thus offers the strongest evidence that the present contrast between the wooded chalk hills and the open chalk downs is of very ancient standing. In very ancient ages, as now, it appears that the " Chiltern hundreds " of a later day were covered with dense woodland, while the other tracts of the chalk bore only those scattered

brakes and isolated, open thickets which sprinkle them to-day with a markedly distinct and interesting vegetation. A considerable proportion of the original thickets and brushwood of the downs has undoubtedly been cleared away in the course of ages for pasturage and occasional tillage ; but there is little real evidence that the high downs of Wiltshire and Berkshire were ever covered with dense tracts of forest, as Richard Jefferies was sometimes desirous of believing. Where the high chalk slopes are still studded with dark, innumerable junipers, or fledged with a mingled thicket of guelder-rose and whitebeam, elder and hoary thorn, we still have before us to-day some of the most ancient lineaments of the land. Many of the individual hawthorns and yews of the downs are of great antiquity, for all their cramped and wind-beaten growth. Their vigour has long expended itself, among the gales of the open hill, rather in gnarled, encrusted convolutions of trunk and bough than in green foliage and leaf-bearing twigs. Many an old yew upon the downs to-day must have seen for centuries the tall bustards trooping on the knolls, in spots where even the shy stone curlews are year by year more fitful in their visits to the flinty fields and wide turf summits where their strange call rises in the falling dark of May.

Towards the end of May the short, sweet haycrop of the wild downland pastures begins to rise and cover the slopes with an endless profusion of blossoms, of which the dominant and characteristic feature is jewel-like perfection in small stature. No tall and flaunting weeds, like cow-parsley and yellow ragwort or even the pink lychnis and ragged robin of the lowland hedgerows and hayfields, are native to the unbroken sward of the down ; there are no pools or mires to foster the long, rank blossoms of the waterside, nor tangled undergrowth upon the wide expanse to support lank, straggling creepers. Beneath the vast arch of the sky, and the titanic simplicity of the enfolding curves and summits, the precise, articulate beauty of each of the downland flowers displays itself with a heightened emphasis of contrast. There is none of them but the spare ox-eye daisy which outtops the slender, foot-high grass-stems of the downland hay-crop in June. Most of the blossoms cling closely to the elastic carpet of the sward, embroidering it for league on league with minute and brilliant profusion. Dwarf white and yellow bedstraws curl plumes of needle-sculptured foam ; the fiercer orange of the bird's-foot trefoil kindles a glow on the slanting turf, and here and there the pale sulphur of the ladies' fingers, like a larger and downy clover-bloom, pours a milder tinge of yellow among the softly interfusing hues. Everywhere the tiny milkworts gleam like sapphires, changing occasionally to bright pink, or purple, or pure white ; across the deep, fine sward the quaintly named squinancy-wort of the old herbalists lays its pink-tinged wreath of microscopic blossoms, almost the most delicate and subtly wrought of all which gem the downs. Here and there the creamy plumes of the dropwort, or down spiraea, are drifted like foam-flakes on the green, appearing in their delicate surroundings almost a giant growth. Many of the strangest and rarest of British orchises are found on the turf of the chalk ; on the slope of a long green hill the bee orchis often lifts in plenty the curious mockery of its blooms, and the turf is dotted with the lilac cones of the pyramidal, stiff and precise in shape as the farmyard trees in a box of German toys, or their originals endlessly ranked by a long undeviating highway on the North Sea shore. Even before the new grass comes to the midsummer downlands with the innumerable flowers of the hay, that beautiful wild anemone, the purple and silky-petalled pasque flower, uncurls under the lee of the dry brown tussocks in the April winds. Here and there, on the broken and chalky warrens, a different and much larger midsummer flora makes play of colour on the rabbit-tunnelled slope. The deadly nightshade droops its livid bells, and the large, buff, purple-veined blossoms of the henbane spread their throats above its hairy and viscid leaves ; tall mulleins light their yellow torches, up which the flame creeps slowly to the apex through July ; viper's bugloss clusters its sky-blue columns, and the dull purple eyes of the hound's-tongue fitfully open among its rank and dusty-looking leaves. But all this larger company of strange and sometimes sinister blossoms needs invariably some disturbance or mutilation of the soil ; by their occasional congregation on a pitted and upturned slope they emphasize by very contrast the calm and delicate serenity of all the wide-spread blossoms of the short, sweet haycrop of the open down. Long after the hay has been carried in the lowland meadows, and their stubble is bleached and bare, the blossoms of this wild, unharvested growth gleam on beneath August and September skies. The more ardent stains of yellow vanish as the high year wanes, and the prevailing tints become the tender blues and lilacs of the intermingling harebells and scabious bloom, that blend upon the crowns and edges of the down into the filmier blue of the early autumn heaven.

Though in many districts of the down country the racehorse in training has now become the dominant animal, the ancient lordship of the sheep is still deeply stamped on the landscape and features of the soil. It is for watering the sheep that the strange, isolated dewponds are still preserved on the crests of the absorbent chalk, through which the natural rainfall sinks to the remoter strata which are tapped by the enormously deep old wells of the downland cottages and farms. High on some great heave of the chalk, against a background of the sky, the shepherd, crook in hand, may still be seen leading his straggling flock among the black, dotted junipers to a pasturage over the ridge. On the steepest, concave hillsides the turf may sometimes be seen moulded by ages of grazing into innumerable parallel lines running horizontally round all the sweep of the hill, and as even as the tiers of seats in some great amphitheatre. These terraced sheep-paths are sometimes on so vast a scale, and so strikingly regular in design, as to suggest their being due to some such deep and ancient geological causes as have produced the well-known "raised beaches" on the slopes of certain other hills. Here, however, the terraces are far narrower, and are set more closely together, than either the raised beaches or the terraced "lynches" formed on steep hillsides by the plough ; nor do they correspond to any underlying stratification of the chalk, being merely worn for a depth of three or four inches into the turf and superficial soil. This strange arrangement of terraced paths is simply due to the sheep's two habits of following in the footsteps of its fellows, and of grazing neither up nor down a very steep slope, but straight along it, on one level. Each of the terraces is simply a narrow and trampled sheep-path, and the whole of the slope between each path and the next above it is just so wide as can be covered by the animal as it feeds. All kinds of path-systems worn by the feet of sheep can be studied in hill pastures of old standing, either in our own mountainous countries or in the Alps ; but it seems only possible for an arrangement of terraces of such complete regularity to be developed where the perfect evenness of the chalk's smooth contours puts no impeding hillocks in the way of the sheep's advance, and the whole of the slope of the hill offers pasturage of the same sweet quality. Amid that vast and heartening conjunction of freedom and order which so deeply inspires the beauty of the downs, even the feet of the sheep have struck out, in dim, mechanic obedience, a colossal rhythm of their own, and stamped it upon the eternal hills.

XIII

THE SAND-DUNES

"The western tide crept up along the sand,
And o'er and o'er the sand,
And round and round the sand,
As far as eye could see."

C. KINGSLEY.

THESE cordons of dunes, standing guard over the unruly breakers of the North Sea, have a history which modern students can outline with some precision. The Roman colonists, recognizing that a flat land is a fat land, and observing that the tides were wont to overflow the fertile strip of alluvial soil which here forms the seaboard, reared, at great labour, a protective earthen rampart along the wind-swept shore. Material gnawed from the cliffs further Northward was redeposited here as silt and sand. Muddy islets appeared, a new wall was raised outside the first, and the ever-drifting sand accumulated until it formed hills 30 or 40 feet high, and some quarter of a mile in width.

Far-seeing land-reclaimers then planted certain grasses on the dunes, to bind the material together and prevent further disasters. Mainly, these plants were the marram, or mat grass, and the sea lyme grass. Glaucous tinted, with channelled stems and glumes of parchment, harsh and disagreeable to the touch, each species has a rootstock provided with long stolons or runners. The innumerable fibrous rootlets and root-hairs grip the particles of sand and render them firm and compact. The grasses have now spread till they dominate the dunes. Dreary, desolate hills are the result, but hills throbbing with life.

The swirl of the wind forms little eddies between the coarse tussocks of herbage, and as the leaf-blades dip down they trace curious little curved patterns on the surface of the dune. The sand is squeezed and packed between the plant stems ; almost one would expect the grass to be choked.

Yet it thrives, as do the coarse sea barley, the manna grass, and other kindred species.

Furze with its velvet and gold has made itself a home here, and brambles cling and climb over bush and bank. Never surely were there such luscious blackberries as these, nurtured by heavy dews and ripened by the fierce sun. Those dewberries, usually deemed to represent a separate species, lack the choicest flavour, but their glossy fruits, covered with a delicate bloom, attain a size never equalled by the poor seedy fruit of the inland hedge-row. The leaves of the dewberry are deeply cleft, and the whole plant has a bolder look than the real bramble. Most striking of the plant denizens, however, is that somewhat low, spiny shrub, the sea sallow, or sea buck-thorn. Above, its long narrow leaves are of a dull olive or leaden hue, but as they are fanned by the breeze the undersides are seen to be silvered over with tiny scales. The globular orange fruit clustered around the stem is appetizing only to the schoolboy, to whose palate it is suggestive of a sour apple. The greys and greens and orange-reds of fruit and foliage present a harmonious combination as singular as it is satisfying.

Underneath this buckthorn where

we are sitting, a hungry thrush, keen of vision, has found a flat stone which has become lodged here in the sand. All around lie the remains of his breakfast, broken whorls of the wood-snail. We look about for more shells ; they are abundant, but the more fragile kinds have been crushed and comminuted by the sand blast. Tiny pupas and virgatas, which seem to have no folk-name, have escaped the general destruction. As we search, unwittingly we surprise a sheldrake, just about to emerge from a burrow, whose owner has perhaps been unlawfully displaced. With loud, tremulous, scolding cry it flies away over the new sea-bank to the mud-flats of the shore. We get a glimpse of its lustrous green head, black and white body, its red bill and its pink legs stretching out behind. Shortly the bird will return with a feast of molluscs for its young. The sheldrake's angry note has alarmed a redshank, or yelper, most wary and suspicious of birds. Wading about near the bounds of the ebbing tide in quest of food, this turbulent creature has caught the signal, and the clamour increases ten-fold. With slow wavering flight, fluttering betimes as if wounded, the yelper attempts to lure the watcher from its haunts. One last piercing pipe, and it

disappears below the margin of yonder creek. Follow this avine actor, and the manœuvre will be repeated.

What was that smoky cloud away to the right, that inexplicable mass of foam rising where it ought not to rise ? We watch, and the white cloud, evidently composed of living units, seems to turn a somersault. Flashes of silver, reddish reflections, a kaleidoscope of colour and form, a dash along the tide-line, and then the same brilliant pageant as before. It is a flock of dunlins, or ox-birds, little long-legged waders, which have been dibbling for worms amid the sticky clay. A " fling " of dunlins, never resting from moment to moment, yet not noticeably shy and distrustful, was one of the most characteristic sights of a boyhood spent near these dunes, a picture which can be recalled on the instant. Another common bird, closely allied, is the stint, a creature of spring and autumn. Its body is no larger than that of a sparrow, but this tiny gregarious bird in its dress of white and chestnut is ever welcome.

Turning the eyes to the hills once more, our gaze rests on the sea-holly, whose spiky lobed leaves seem whimsically to suggest the webs of a duck's foot. The sea holly, or sea holm, as old writers have it, is unique among the umbelliferous order in possessing blue flowers. How such a plant gets nourishment from the ungrateful sand is a mystery. Like the marram, it is anchored by spreading roots ; herein is security, if not nutriment. That large plant near the eryngium appears to have a stalk growing where the flower should be found. It is the yellow horned poppy. Examination shows that the " stalk " is a two-valved pod, most of the bright yellow petals having dropped off, and the fruit being by this time half ripe. An odd-looking animal now steps out of his hole at the root of the poppy. It is a toad, yet it does not move like a toad. Mouse-like in its actions, the natterjack neither crawls nor hops, but walks nimbly forward. One may distinguish it from its well-known congener by its more warty skin, and by the yellow stripe running down its back. Its throat pulsates as it gulps down draughts of the brine-laden air. Suddenly the creature snaps up an incautious spider, smartly retires, and is seen no more. Lizards dressed in buff and brown and grey glide swiftly through the wiry grasses. A month or two ago a friend thought to pick up a bronze fibula ; the warm fingers touched a half-torpid lizard and the Roman ornament vanished. But to-day all is life,

with its rhythmic accompaniment of concords and discords. The perpetual creaking of the stridulous grasshopper, the shriek of the sea-mew, now fearful and appealing, now triumphantly joyous as it wheels off from the ploughed field to the grassy saltings, the hum of the golden-tipped bee and the gentle twang of the hover-fly, each has its own voice and language. There is vigorous life among the crows and curlews, prospecting along the sinuous line of flotsam and jetsam left by the retreating tide ; among the oyster-catchers pushing their long wedge-shaped bills of orange under the brown algae in search of shrimp or mussel ; among the sand-loving beetles with glossy, iridescent shards ; among the hosts of butterflies zigzagging noiselessly from blossom to blossom.

The burnet moths which flit about with crimson - spotted fore - wings whose ground colour is so dark that the red appears almost black, have a steel-blue band on the margin of the hind wings. Larger and more handsome is the cinnabar, dusky red, with a knobbed stripe of crimson and two spots of the same hue. The larvae, ringed alternately black and orange, a little while back were devouring those clumps of yellow ragwort.

Tired of inaction, we clamber over

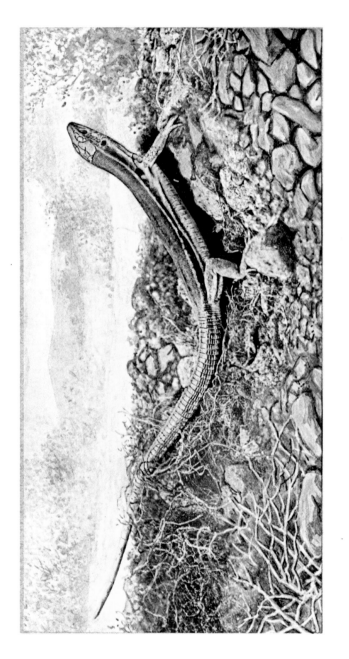

THE LIZARD.

From a photograph by
Reginald G. Lodge.

the seaward bank, parapeted with fascines composed of bundles of thorns. At once scores of rabbits rush in all directions to their burrows. The top of the bank, roughly turfed over, bears a cushion of yellow stone-crop. On the silted clay below, the pink sea-stock and the slender, fleshy-leaved milkwort abound. There are roods of the mauve thrift and the frosted sea-orache. The storksbill's fruit is a green dagger, tinging to red ; soldanella, the maritime convolvulus, carries a lilac trumpet ; and cochlearia, the scurvy grass, is furnished with brave shields. Patches of land where these plants occur will ere long be enclosed ; this have the sand-hills rendered possible. Yet the dunes are never the same ; change with them is cardinal. Never were the everlasting hills anything but a poet's vision.

XIV

A WESTERN BAY

"The tottering palaces of wind and sand,
Pride and vain pomp, tears, ashes, rapture, dust."
WALTER DE LA MARE.

NEAR the centre of the western bay is a small cove of pure white sand through which a brooklet wanders softly to the sea. It is fed by tiny sluggish tributaries, occasionally half-choked by bright green masses of tempting water cress, and the banks lined luxuriantly with flower and rush. The sand is composed of finely comminuted shells, minute particles of quartz and felspar, and minuter mica. Bleached landshells cover the slopes among the tough grass which slowly recedes before the advancing snow-like drift. The commonest shells are those of the flattened and coiled Zonites (recently renamed), two or three species of the usual snails, such as *Helix hortensis* and *Helix nemoralis* are plentiful, and at times *Helix pisana*, whose father snails grew fat on Lusitanian summers, a rare and local species, may be found. The spire-shaped Bulimus mingles with the other empty shells and in the soft grass above the cove, near the inland limit of the blown granitic and shelly sands, they seem to live in countless numbers, and when the air is damp, one can scarcely walk without hearing the noise of cracking shells. Several fishermen's cottages of rough hewn granite lie concealed in the cove with simple gardens containing tall thin fuchsias and tamarisks and the bright warmth-loving escallonia. Building and garden space is limited, but a little extension down the sides of the cove would provide, for each cottage, a lawn as white as driven snow. On the richer waste spots and where the sand is thin grows the horned poppy with its gay yellow flowers and long curious horns, while the peculiar and attractive sea holly with rigid spines and blue gray head keeps it company, and seems to flourish even nearer the shore and half buried in the sand. The sea convolvulus grows apace and with the tough grass helps to bind and hold together the ever-shifting material. On the low cliffs it is possible to gather samphire without the feeling that one is engaged in any perilous or "dreadful trade," and above the old raised beach rare and delicate ferns peep from beneath huge tumbled blocks of porphyritic granite. In this far western silver bay with grassy sloping cliffs, descending from rough weathered lichen-covered granite stacks and bluffs, and rich with pale pink thrift and yellow ragwort, the traveller fresh from the busy hum of cities and the long unlovely streets, is tempted to forget the Wordsworthian philosophy for awhile, and to endeavour, once again, to look at nature as in the hour of thoughtless youth.

But here the most thoughtless of youths would soon be attracted by the sight of other beauties and delights. He would notice the lovely seashells left in long irregular rows by the receding tide, lying bare on the drying sand or under tangled masses of seaweed. Small pectens (*Chlamys*) of many colours, white, light yellow, pink, orange and dark olive, though thin and delicate, lie unbroken among great numbers of topshells (*Trochus*) and the tough shells of Nassa and the single valves of a species of Venus with its graceful shape and curved beak. The little cowry (*Trivia europoea*) reminds one in name and shape of specimens from the far East and it is fairly conspicuous, but keen eyes are necessary to see the tiny ruddy pink Phasianella and the dark turreted Cerithiopsis, and the still smaller wonders of the deep, many of which live beyond the littoral zone " full fathom five," and more are washed up from the deeper sea. Minute echinoderms—prickly sea urchins— are among the trophies of the shore, and the spines of larger species, white, yellow and mauve, may be sifted from the sand.

But if the temptation to indolence is strong for the moment it is easily resisted. Besides the wealth of interest near the sea, the country inland, though bare and almost treeless and occasionally dull and disappointing, is generally wild and wonderful, and above all, among the purple heather or on the sun-scorched grass rest the mysterious stone monuments of the nameless dead—cromlechs, dolmens and menhirion, erected most probably by the peoples of the Later Stone Age, who resisted in cliff castles and on hill top forts of huge rough masonry the onslaughts of the conquering Celts. There is a strange fascination for many persons in the

" Grey recumbent tombs of the dead in
deserted places,
Standing stones on the vacant wine-red moor."

Curious clusters of bee-hive huts, homes of the silent vanished races, are hidden away in pleasant hollows, but whether they are as ancient as the dolmens and cromlechs, it is hard to determine. One thing is certain, most of the monuments are difficult to find even with the necessary help of maps. The footpaths lead now across waste lands of thick heather and now through well cultivated fields, the soil, thin and light, of decomposed granite, and surrounded by low massive stone walls. The narrow tracks run in bewildering fashion into broader sunken

paths between the granite hedgerows, moss and lichen covered, and the banks fragrant with wild thyme and bright with foxgloves and campions, but these wider ways seem only to connect distant farms and land the unfamiliar traveller through droves of straying pigs and tame villatic fowl into bare old-fashioned farm yards. Nearly every meadow has its small heap of refuse, not, as in counties nearer London, placed near the sides, but standing exactly in the centre. According to the local explanation, cattle are unable to use it in this central position in their desperate attempts to scale the low walls.

Less than a mile from the sunny corner of the cove there is a pleasant walk along the rugged cliffs, the actual path being among huge fragments of weather-beaten stone, on which the wheatears alight and flit away a few yards ahead of the disturbers of their peace, and magpies noisily take up fresh positions. It leads through a deserted hamlet of rough cottages, half decayed, on to a quiet heath and there, almost concealed by bramble and bracken, is a small and simple dolmen. By judicious handling of the thick and prickly growth we are able to obtain a sight of the capstone resting on the upright stones. Of the old warrior who rested undisturbed for centuries in this picturesque moorland tomb until prying antiquaries dug roughly for his old bones and rude weapons, not a trace now remains. On the neighbouring downs overlooking the sea, across a swampy vale on the borders of which the so-called flowering fern (*Osmunda regalis*) displays its cinnamon-coloured spores, and the tiny insectivorous sundew tinges the damp turf with rusty red, there are still traces of the old warrior and his tribe. In the deep-cut paths and on the bare patches left by peat-cutters, are numerous remains of neolithic work. The most noticeable are spalls or rough flakes of flint and chert, associated with broken crystals of quartz and felspar from the weathered granite, and there are a few neatly worked end-scrapers and small knives. A rude arrowhead and a well worked oval knife of grey translucent flint were recently discovered, but perhaps the most interesting trifles were several small scrapers made from rounded beach pebbles, split in half and neatly worked at one end. The material for the implements was probably obtained from the ancient raised beach below, though in two small areas in this district the flints worked and unworked were plentiful enough to suggest traces of

beds of flints, the remnants of ancient valley gravels carried westward by the agency of ice or water. A mile or so inland the remains of two stone circles lie beneath the shadow of huge irregular masses of rock, which, harder than the surrounding granite, and resisting better the sharp tooth of time, stand boldly pointing to the skies. Small worked flints lie amongst the blackened stems of gorse and heather left by recent fires. A little further eastward is a huge and famous dolmen, the capstone, of many tons in weight, resting on three large unequal stones. According to the pleasing exaggeration of some old guide books it was lofty enough to shelter a man on horseback ! Further south is a beautiful and perfect circle of nineteen stones all still standing with the menhir in the middle. This is one of the famous rings known locally as " Merry Maidens," for according to the popular legend certain girls were caught dancing on a Sunday and they and the piper who stood playing in the centre were turned into stone,

> " and so fitly earned
> Their stony transformation."

Probably the cromlech and the menhir, like the chambered dolmen, were in their origin connected with the ideas of death and burial and commemoration. Opinion now seems to favour Lord

A WESTERN BAY.

From a photograph by
Gibson & Sons, Penzance.

Avebury's theory that "The great majority were tombs. Some, no doubt, are memorial monuments; some were temples; but the idea and plan is still that of an interment." The old historians and later antiquaries generally attributed the erection of these stone monuments to the semi-mythical Druids who are popularly supposed to have been discovered, and their villanies exposed, by Caesar, but the modern theories of scholars and workers as to their connexion with the ages of Stone or Bronze are certainly more satisfactory. To the peasant mind the tumuli are still "giants' graves," and the capstone of the dolmen is a "quoit" which was once hurled by some powerful saint or mythical hero at the unfortunate head of the usually invisible enemy of mankind.

XV

OUR FUNGUS HARVEST

"And agarics, and fungi, with mildew and mould,
Started like mist from the wet ground cold;
Pale, fleshy, as if the decaying dead
With a spirit of growth had been animated."
SHELLEY.

IN one of the Home Counties there is a wide heathery waste, containing thick groves of pine. Nature seems to have purposely fashioned the spot for the mycologist, or lover of fungi. First there is the flat, swampy ground of the lower parts of the common; this is followed by a belt of ling and furze, anon comes a fringe of ancient oaks and graceful silver birches guarding the gloomy hilltop citadel of the heavy Scotch pines. Each of these soils yields its own crop of fungi, from the clay below to the Bagshot Sands above. As the autumn days grow short, and the withered leaves rustle underfoot, one may here find a feast of form and colour.

First to meet the eye, even of the unexperienced, is the fly agaric, with its deep crimson pileus, flecked with patches of yellow or dirty white, relics of a protective envelope now cast away. Poison to man, this agaric once destroyed a Czar, yet men, with strange perversity, have in Siberia prized it as an intoxicant. Russules of all hues, yellow, red, white and scarlet, nestle among the dead pine needles, and bolets, ochrey brown and russet, bear their heavy heads aloft on bulbous stems. The boleti merit a moment's

6

inspection. The spores from which the next generation is to emerge are borne, not on fleshy gills as in the mushroom, but on the lining of hundreds of narrow vertical tubes, and these make up the greater mass of the pileus. Here are the lactars, from whose flesh issues, at the slightest pressure, milky fluid, sweetish perhaps, or it may be as biting as pepper. The reds and yellows and blues of the fantastic parrakeet mushroom have given it its nickname. The virgin ivory-cap is of purest white ; the " golden-fleece," alas, is patched with dirty brown ; peziza has a scarlet cup. Here is a toadstool with violet head and another is washed with verdigris. Some are dry and brittle, some are uncannily glutinous ; the weeping dryad exudes nectar.

Many artists and designers visit our pinewood for impressions of form alone. Protean in the individual life-history and in the various species, fungi reveal the most diverse outlines. The fairy cap and the parasol, the goblet and the saucer, bunch of coral, piece of stag's horn, satiny leaf and velvet cushion, a sheaf of clubs, a handful of sea-weeds, a sphere of lattice-work, here are beauteous shapes in astonishing variety.

"Grey, purple, yellow, white or brown,
A Grecian shield, or prelate's crown,
Like Freedom's cap, or friar's cowl,
Or China's bright inverted bowl."

The most curious form is perhaps seen in the Jew's ear, a fungus which grows on old elders a little remote from the sandy plateau, moulded like a human ear with its ridges and veins ; this moist fungus, olive hued and velvety, frequently dries up, becoming shrivelled, leathery, and to all seeming dead. Placed in water it revives, swells out and regains its peachy bloom. The alternative name of Judas' ear was given because that disciple is traditionally believed to have hanged himself on an elder. On the paradoxical principle, the Jew's ear had of old supposed virtues for throat complaints.

Creeping along the dry needles, clustering round stumps of trees, or clinging to the boles, are tough, papery fungi which are often zoned and banded in colours. On the older trees are gnarled woody fungi, veterans of many summers ; such are the polypores and the rusty-hoofs. Once they were soft but always they were tough. The oaks on the clay border bear tiers of red-lobed, thick-fleshed edible fungi, the beef-steak or oak-tongue. Its pink juice colours the gravy of the breakfast rasher, and is much appreciated by the epicure. One kind of polypore often seen on a decaying ash or elm resembles a pommel in form, and grows to an enormous size; shelf above shelf of these fungi jut out from the trunk.

The writer will not readily forget finding the quaint " hen-of-the-woods " at the root of a tree on the heath. The specimen weighed several pounds, but though the odour was inviting, he did not test the statement that it is esculent —as soon would one try to eat a leather glove. The odours are frequently very distinctive, though the scent from the resinous pines masks that of the fungi, unless these are close at hand. The dainty chantarelle, of cinnamon hue, has a faint odour of ripe apricots, nor does it belie its apparent delicacy when cooked. There are fungi, says Dr. M. C. Cooke, which smell of tarragon, of anise, of violets. Commonly there is a reminder of good sweet meal or crushed nuts; occasionally the odour is not so pleasant, being of a fishy nature. The common stinkhorn has a sickening repulsive smell; you may detect it a hundred yards away from its haunt. When young, it is a gelatinous mass with a tough integument; in forty-eight hours it will shoot up half a foot, standing erect like a club. Two days more, or one day mayhap, it is a decomposing, putrescent hollow pillar, the lure of all flies.

Puff balls abound, the pepper-boxes of the schoolboy who loves to scatter abroad the million ripe spores. Several species may be counted in our area. Some are good for the table, if gathered young, when the interior is pure white. The giant puff-ball, or lycoperdon, occasionally grows to a huge size, but the Southern records cannot equal that of the specimen exhibited at Edinburgh in 1878; that monster was $4\frac{1}{2}$ feet in circumference and weighed 20 lbs. Peeping from the close turf covering the barren sand you will see the earth-ball, or scleroderma, rounder than the puff-ball, which is somewhat conical. The earth-ball is hard, of rank odour, and not safe for the table. Even the tyro will recognize its interior, which is intensely blue-black, speckled with white.

On the clay bottom at the foot of the hill lies a pond, dark and unruffled. Its margins are lined with reeds and sedges; the interspaces of swamp support such marsh-lovers as the bog-pimpernel, the water St. John's wort, and the sundews. Even here in the swamp fungi may be discovered, for the pretty little mitrula, two inches high, raises its brilliant orange mace from a slender, flexuous stem. Treasures everywhere for the searcher, on tree, grass, bark, and dead leaf. Minute fungi stud the very twigs and pine needles. Others envelop the green plants of the heath, or invest and injure the delicate root-hairs of the forest giants. There are also species of untold number, to examine which needs the aid of the microscope. Such are the smuts and bunts of yonder corn-fields, the moulds and mucor on that refuse thrown aside by the thoughtless rambler, the black fungus which spots the fallen leaves of the sycamore.

Chlorophyll, the green colouring matter of the flowering plant, fungi possess not. They can manufacture no starch; they must get food as parasites on some other organism, or they must play the part of scavengers in Nature. Degenerate they may be, but the creaking monarch of the forest must not complain; disease was probably at work ere the fungus began its work of disintegration.

As we wander along, a fungologist passes with a basket of spoils. The old gibe about distinguishing edible species is pointless: " Eat the fungus, you live if it is a mushroom, you die if it is a toadstool." All are mushrooms, all are toadstools. The principles of classification, intricate and confusing even to the expert, proceed

on other lines. Many of the toad-stools are delicious food, contrariwise the mushroom, if old and tough, is an indigestible morsel. Our pine-wood and its neighbourhood have yielded the present writer about a score of sound edible fungi, ranging in flavour from poor to excellent.

Dr. Badham once lamented the waste of hundredweights of rich, wholesome food. Amid blights, bad harvests, poverty and privation, the woods teem with esculent fungi, but the store is allowed to rot away. The champignon, the fragrant morel, the French truffle, who knows not these? Yet the heath and the coppice bear also their despised harvest. The scaly-capped hydnum gives a feast of oysters, a white gilled amanita, with its elegantly frilled stem, blushing red when cut, makes a vegetarian feast, whilst the true chantarelle might tempt the dying anchorite.

Setting our noble selves aside, let us notice how the humbler creation view the fungi. At once we see that the russules and their allies are furrowed by scars and gullies where the slugs have been feeding. The bolets, appetizing in odour, have been nibbled by field-mice. Here are amanitas bored by larvae. Under the sooty grey cap of maned coprinus dwells an empire of tiny beetles and flies, with kings and leaders perchance. When all these creatures have worked their will, the despised fungus sinks to the earth, and provides nourishment for unborn generations of woodland plants.

XVI

WINTER VISITORS

"The stork in the heaven knoweth her appointed times."
JEREMIAH.

IF we ever arrive at a full understanding of the causes that determine and control the migration of birds, it will probably be by means of the winter visitors, and not through study of the species that arrive here in early summer to breed, and depart when the nesting season is over. Research in this direction is more promising because there are fewer species in the class, because they spend that portion of the year during which they are absent from Great Britain in parts of Europe which are civilized, where their nesting and coming and going may easily be observed, and where many naturalists, wholly as skilful as our own, are already watching them in a careful and scientific way : and because the passage is shorter, the choice of landing more varied, and the number of resting-places on the journey more numerous and more accessible to observers. In this inquiry, many winter visitors will be of the least possible help, because they vary extensively in their migrations, because they never come inland, and so their comings and goings are hard to prove, or because they are scarce. In this category are included all the wading birds, swans, geese and " wild fowl," and a few others, like the grey plover, which is shy and uncommon. The inquiry must be confined to those three species which are inland birds, which betray no bewildering irregularity in their habits (such irregularity in other birds being probably a myth due to insufficient knowledge), and which are passably common : namely, the brambling, field-fare and redwing. A detailed, scientific, systematic inquiry into the habits of these three winter visitants, assisted by as many scattered observers as are obtainable, should within ten years produce an extremely valuable contribution to our knowledge of the system of bird migration, if not of its causes and laws. The main *rationale* of migration in the case of both our summer and our winter visitors is the same. Each class of bird seems to know that a certain country at a certain period of the year provides the most suitable temperature and weather for nesting, together with the food supply best suited to rearing its young ; each class of bird realizes that a milder winter than its nesting country affords is advisable both for itself and its young progeny, if they are to survive ; and each class of bird, as some would say, contains in its composition a sense of time far more accurate than mere calendar knowledge, since their coming and going is alleged to be independent of either wind, weather or the clemency of the seasons. This last is certainly claimed with every appearance of truth for the summer visitants by the Research Committee of the British Ornithologists Club—but my first attempt is to disprove it of both summer and winter visitors. If this could be done conclusively, that superstitious mystery which has long been attached by ornithologists to the " migratory instincts " would disappear to the exact extent of a half ; for the question usually asked and left unanswered is, " How do birds fix on the time of their migration ? " If we were convinced they left their wintering country at the instant of a definite and perceptible change in the weather, the only question would relate to the nature of that instinct which tells them where suitable weather is to be found, and which never fails, as has been proved by ringing visitant birds with miniature rubber fetters, such as pigeon fanciers use on a larger scale, to bring them yearly to the same country, and to the same district within that country. Much would still remain to be explained, but at present a large section of students are assured a migratory bird has a sort of calendar in its bones, as it were, that causes it to emigrate and re-immigrate at fixed dates independent of the weather. This has been deduced from the arrival of our summer migrants, and naturally they arrive here independent of the weather. For the weather here is not the same as exists simultaneously in Africa and India and Asia Minor and China, whence they come, and we might well remain hopelessly puzzled if a chiff-chaff in Algiers, for instance, was proved to have foretold the time of its arrival at Brighton would coincide invariably with a sunny afternoon. The main immediate question is, does not a change in the temperature at Algiers remind the chiff-chaff's experience (or inherited instinct, according as the bird is contemplating its first or a repeated migration) that if it flies over into Kent at once, the weather will be tolerably clement, and the spring advancing.

So far no one has succeeded, or so far as I know even tried, to prove that this is or is not the motive of the spring immigrations. But there is excellent evidence for supposing that it is true of the brambling, redwing, and fieldfare; and we owe this evidence to the fact that these birds live the summer, and nest, in an accessible, civilized and neighbouring part of Europe (the sub-Arctic pine and birch forests from Norway to Kamchatka). Every ornithological textbook, and every naturalist, be he author or not, possessing Scandinavian experience, asserts that these three birds migrate to England and Europe at a date and in numbers depending on the date and the severity of the winter in the countries where they nest. More than that, the severity of the winter is definitely asserted, and practically proved, to affect the extent of their wanderings in a southerly direction. In exceptionally severe winters they cross from Kamchatka to Japan, from Russia into Italy and Spain, and thence on into Northern Africa and Egypt. What is now needed is the systematic accumulation, by an ornithologist of wide experience and scientific method, of all the data from which this premise is obtained. The data need no finding—they exist, and demand rearrangement only. To support them, an even easier, but totally unattempted, task is essential, viz., the proof that the departure of our summer visitors is in the main timed by the failure of their main food supply (increasing cold is only another name for the same fact), and not by the termination of the rearing of the young, as is commonly supposed. Then we have a foundation premise for building a syllogistic theory of migration, namely, that migratory birds quit their nesting countries solely owing to the approach of winter and the growing scarcity of food. If this were established, the idea of a mysterious parallel to the homing pigeons' instinct would be considerably weakened, and factors of time and weather would assume greater prominence in the problem than they have now, although it is foolish to assert that the problem is single, and confined only to one tangible influence. The next question is, then, the reason fixing the date of re-migration to the nesting place from the winter quarters, and in this young and old birds may be temporarily classed together, as the winter visitors, for which I claim this special attention and promise of reward, certainly begin their migration already in flocks, and so the young reap the benefit of their elders' ripe experience. It is by no means proved, though in another paper I give adverse inferences on partial evidence, that all the summer visitors do not likewise start for this country in large flights. Now since the departure from the nesting country may well be proved to depend on external indications of the season, it is at least possible that the eager migration to the nesting quarters also depends on external indications of the season. This we shall not be able to prove or disprove from the summer migrants, because their haunts are alike distant, vast and inaccessible. But if the three commonest birds that winter here, brambling, fieldfare and redwing, were given the undivided attention of the naturalists of the country for ten consecutive springs with a view to ascertaining outward flights from the coast itself, diminish-

ing numbers inland, flights travelling from inland to seaboard, and dates of last seeing flocks or individuals of each species, it is at least probable a theory of the sort described might soon be well grounded. The migration of birds would then be understood in principle, and a very little application of the general principle to particular species by naturalists having good local facilities would perhaps reduce what is an outstanding puzzle of natural science to a series of comprehended laws.

The practical difficulties are greater than any which beset the observation of arrivals. Diminution in numbers, and vigilant notification of every remaining specimen require great accuracy and diligence and a thorough acquaintance with the bird, even down to the most *pianissimo* renderings of his call note, and a great help is to observe specimens of each in captivity, which aids to the recognition of contour, posture, or little unrecognizable sounds uttered in feeding or alighting at a perch. But a full and accurate knowledge of the periods of the emigration of these three species might actually settle the ground-work of the migration puzzle once and for all.

PLOUGHING.

From a water-colour by
Tatton Winter, R.B.A.

XVII

SOME BIRDS OF THE MARSH

"One question answer in the fewest words,
What sort of life is it among the birds?"
—ARISTOPHANES.

NEXT to the sea, the marshes are the oldest things in the world. Before the mountains burst from the tormented bosom of the earth, millions of square miles of slobbery land brooded over the surface of the globe. Born of, and but dimly distinguishable from, the waste of waters, they shuddered in their dreams at the huge explosions which tossed the crags on high, and rent the valleys for the habitation of the races of men. Truly, as awe-struck Ruskin whispered, a cloud which none may pierce cloaked the womb of Nature when it gaped for her great sons, the mountain ranges, to come forth. That mist had hung for aeons already over the firstborn sea and over the marshland, for the mother was young when she bore them.

The marshes, then, are old, incalculably old, and therefore very dear. Though memory faints in pursuing their origin, let the man who treads them never forget that he rests upon the bosom of the earliest friend of the human race, the everlasting victor over his first and last enemy, the sea, whose voice he may perhaps hear booming near, the desolate voice of a thing insatiable, but never again to be filled.

Never think that old Ocean has made peace or even a truce with you. Smile he never so sunnily, kissing the crinkled sands, or crooning over the rocks, as he gently stirs their amber manes of seaweed, he is still at war with man, and his murmuring is but the echo of the loud trumpets. *Timeo Danaos.* The vessel out at sea moves, like an army surrounded by a horde of savages, tense with precautions. On the decks the pickets lie always awake, apprehension in their eyes, their means of flight as ready for instant use as their weapons; for there is no quarter in case of surprise, and flight itself is too hazardous a matter to be dishonourable. Then, when the voyage is nearly over (take care! the ambushes lie thickest about the end of the march)— "Land ho!" A friend, *the* friend in sight; nay the mother, and she dearest of all when she looks forth from her

"Charm'd magic casement opening on the foam,
  Of perilous seas,"

7

not frontletted with white cliffs, which are of the sea, and as dangerous, but gravely kerchiefed with the vapour of the fenny flats.

The dwellers on the marshes are few in number, sparing of speech, and sober of dress, as becomes the children of so venerable a parent. Of all men the fenman is most taciturn and unostentatious. Yet not dour, like the hillman, or depressed like the overdone town-man, but reserved, with a little dignified melancholy, having the air of one who listens for faint and far-off sounds. His very cottage, built low, sometimes even below the level of canal or mere, is often difficult to discern behind the dyke, or under the belt of mist, from which its chimney top emerges like the stump of a dead tree. There he dwells, in such solitude, making so little noise, that I have often flushed the fearful snipe at his very door, where his child played dreamily under the old stone lintel with the rune scratch upon it. The snipe are often his only neighbours. The marshes, though at times they have many avine visitors, hold but few other regular inhabitants, and those are of a secret and silent nature, who move about but little, and when they do, steal so warily that even the slender reeds and grasses are scarcely stirred at their passage. Of these the bittern, less rare than is supposed, is the largest both of body and voice, a strange spear-visaged creature, with fierce topaz eyes, which glare like those of a cat from the shadow between the reed stems. And his song! Well is he named *Botaurus*, the bull-voiced. What dreariness of " old, unhappy, far-off things " falls upon the heart of the wayfarer when, hearing

" The bittern booming in the weeds, he shrinks
    From the dismaying solitude."

No other sound in Nature will strike upon his ear more mournfully, no other but one, that is the sobbing of the sea on a calm night in some cave deep cut beneath the cliffs, surely the secret weeping of a huge, elemental grief. Other cries, scarcely less melancholy, which resound over the swamps are the tenor drum, keyed in a minor, of the breeding snipe, the lost soul wail of the curlew, the howl like that of " the wolf on Oonalaska's shore," of the gray Heath Owl, an apparition prone to flap up in the twilight before the startled traveller as noiselessly as his own pale shadow. An old Irishman I knew used to declare that having once winged one of these ground owls as it flitted away before him, the bird, alighting, gave him one dreadful look over its shoulder, then turned and walked *towards* him! Whereupon he fled, and arrived home shuddering, with the vengeance of the spirit of the marshes so strongly upon him, that to this day his wife avers that even his breath *smelled of peat*. (N.B.—In lone recesses of the hills of Ireland once dwelt, and for all I know may illicitly still dwell, wizards who by black art could confine this spirit, smell and all, into bottles! It must have been one of these "bottle-imps,"[1] probably him known as *Uisge-'beatha*, that had laid his spell upon my friend.) Compared to these dismal noises the clear whistle of the widgeon, who by night haunt in thousands marshes near the sea, is a cheerful pipe, nor is there anything sepulchral in the green plover's nasal dissyllable, the hoarse ejaculation of the "lone fisher of the solitude," the heron, the argumentative quacking of the mallard, or the pochard's file-like rasp. Of the ducks, few are true sons of the marshes, the majority visiting them only for food after dark, and taking wing for their sleeping-places on sea or mere at the first breath of morning. Teal, however, may be looked for at any time and anywhere, especially on little reed-

fringed pools, from which, when alarmed, they spring with the perpendicular leap of a Spring-heeled Jock, sending the sportsman's heart into his mouth, and his shot into the innocent horizon whose pencilling at dawn is scarcely less lovely than the bird's. Now that the dusky gadwall has become so scarce, the shoveller is the only other surface-feeding duck who may be said to dwell habitually on the marshes, a brilliantly-hued oddity, with a bill splayed and coloured like a large Britannia-metal spoon. These, with two of the divers, viz., the tufted duck, with eyes of pure gold set in his purple-shot head, and the portly black-waistcoated pochard, almost complete the list of true marsh ducks. A pair or two of mallard, however (widgeon never, in my experience), so constantly remain behind after their regiment has departed to its sea-girt bivouac, that were an avine census for the electorate of sea and land to be taken, Mr. Bottle-green would be found to have established (and Mrs. no doubt to claim) a vote for each constituency.

The visits of the great grey geese are like those of angels, "few and far between." Yet, on wild nights their "trumpet-tongues" may now and then be heard clanging in the sky, and it behoves the sportsman next day to

---

[1] The word, and the necromancy, is as old as the early Hebrews, who, like the Scotch, calling the inhabitant by the name of his abode, termed their familiar spirits *oboth*, or leathern bottles.

search the marshes with his glass. I once shot a pink-footed goose with No. 8 shot when after snipe, missing another at close range from sheer astonishment ; and a Dissenting Minister of my acquaintance bagged no less than three of the same noble fowl with two barrels of the like paltry pellets. Can the Established Church, with all its canons and other great guns, loaded with the heaviest of Bishops' " Charges," say the like ?

Should all else fail, the green plover, or peewits, will nearly always give sport to the marsh gunner. When the gale is high, they may be seen in vast herds blowing up and down over the flats like clouds of torn-up newspaper, and about as easy to hit with a gun. Their favourite haunts, however, are not the swamps themselves, but the rough pastures and grainlands which border on them. There they love to stand, covering the broad acres, alert and motionless, each individual ten yards from his neighbour, like an army composed entirely of sentries. How differently the sea fowl, the brent geese, the widgeon, and the curlew herd upon the mud-banks of the estuary ; close-locked shoulder to shoulder, a phalanx of feathers, watchful, it is true, as a Zulu *impi*, yet not seldom paying that murderous toll to the artillery of the punt-gunner which modern arms exact from old-fashioned close formations in the field. Peewits, although amongst the most difficult of birds to stalk, are peculiarly easy to lure within range by a good imitation of their call. This the sportsman may do even when standing visibly in the open, so long as he remains motionless.

The poor plover have never heard of Ulysses with his masts and his wax-deadened ears, and at the voice of the Siren some of the flock rarely fail to lay their bones at the feet of the deceiver on the flowery mead. The device is most deadly, however, when the birds are scattered over a field, and the call can be sounded from the concealment of the nearest hedgerow. In this connexion a dreadful event came to the knowledge of the writer. An old marshman had been wont to add to his board and income by the shooting of green plover, his plan being as described, to crouch behind a bank and thither, with plaintive *pee-wits* to draw, as with a magnet the feeding flock within range of his muzzle-loading 8-bore. So wary by his constant persecution grew the birds that he finally adopted a practice much employed by the Boers in the late war at what time shrapnel and other typhoons were bursting over their lair to clear a path for the attacking infantry, viz., to lay their rifles in approximate alignment on top of the bank, and keeping unseen and unseeing below it, to pull trigger when the quarry was judged to be within the zone of the charge. One day a series of pee-wits, issuing apparently from the surface of an adjoining pasture, brought him to his knees behind the " party " bank near by, and his gun to its level upon it. Nearer and nearer drew the whistles ; a dozen plover at least as good as in the bag ! and fourpence apiece waiting in the market ; better earning than peat-cutting, with little David sorely needing winter clothes ; nearer and nearer— bang ! The 8-bore vomited its three ounces of lead, and the old man scrambled over the bank to gather his victims. Alas ! no ring of dead to be seen, nor even any living fanning away in the air ; but little David lay stretched like a fallen scarecrow across the furrows, the first and last prize for proficiency in bird-calling won from his proud instructor.

Golden plover, though far more local than their green relation, are always to be expected on the marshes, and on occasions will be encountered in vast congregations. Colossal " family

shots," from 160 downwards, are on record against them when thus collected. Such feats, however, are the exception, for whether as single spies, or as battalions, they have tricks of flight which puzzle the oldest gunner. In the former case they are commonly travelling at tremendous speed, skimming close to the rushes or herbage, with the colour of which their plumage so exactly harmonizes that it is no easy matter, sometimes, even to see them. When on the wing in flocks, they have a habit of darting, or rather hurling themselves towards the ground *en masse* at the exact instant of your pulling trigger, so that the sportsman, expectant of " browning," is too often *like* Browning's

"This high man, aiming at a million, Misses an unit."

Last, and least in all but interest, must come the little water rail, a mere wedge of delicately-toned feathers, relieved by ruby eyes. He is the truest bog-trotter of them all, revelling in the rottenest ooze, over which he runs unhampered, often appearing even to trip on the water itself, like his cousin the Jacana of Brazil, so slightly are the water-leaves immersed under his infinitesimal weight and filamental toes. Considering how numerous these birds are, they are but little known. Men who have shot the marshes for years have never seen them, or if they have, have mistaken them for rats as they wriggled rapidly in and out of the stems of the rushes and undergrowth. Whilst they are thus of little value to the sportsman, they might well be more familiar to the *gourmet,* for the snipe himself doth not furnish a more aromatic ounce or two.

XVIII

GILBERT WHITE

"Our simple life wants little, and true taste
Hires not the pale drudge luxury, to waste
The scene it would adorn, and therefore still
Nature with all her children haunts the hill."
—SHELLEY.

GILBERT WHITE belonged to an old family that grew abundantly in Hampshire and Oxfordshire. Charles II knighted a Sampson White, who was Mayor of Oxford, a mercer and a fool. This Sampson's son, Gilbert, became a Fellow of Magdalen College, Oxford, and, in 1681, vicar of Selborne, and he left money for the purchase of land of which the rents were partly to supply the Selborne children with instruction in reading, writing, saying prayers, knitting and sewing, partly to provide for the improvement of Honey Lane, the rocky, hollow lane from Oakhanger to the village. John White, son of this Gilbert, a barrister-at-law and justice of the peace, married a Sussex woman, Anne Holt, and their eldest son, our Gilbert White, was born in his grandfather's house, the vicarage at Selborne, in 1720. As a child he lived at Compton, near Guildford, and at East Harting in Sussex, and was at Basingstoke Grammar School and probably also at Farnham Grammar School; but he was only ten when his father settled finally in Selborne at "The Wakes." Before he was twelve, he planted an oak and an ash in his father's garden. When he was sixteen he noticed the northward flying of wild geese on March 31 and the coming of the cuckoo on April 6. As a schoolboy he took to Basingstoke, together with *The Whole Duty of Man, Cicero's Letters, Virgil, Homer, Isocrates, Tacitus, Sallust,* and other books, a copy of James Thomson's *Seasons.* We who know what he became have only these things upon which to feed our fancy about his childhood in remote Selborne, cut off from the world by

SELBORNE VILLAGE.

From a photograph by
W. T. Green.

obscurity and difficult and ill-kept roads.

In 1740 he entered Oriel College. At Oxford he shot, he rode, he listened to music, how much is not known, and he made a friendship with one John Mulso, an Oriel contemporary, which lasted until 1791. In 1743 he took his bachelor's degree, but he went up to Oxford again with his dog and his gun, and in the next year was elected a Fellow of his college. Mulso writes to him and asks after " Jenny," and " the Stamfordian," advises him not to play so much with " the tangles of Neaera's hair," and wants confirmation of the report that he is to marry. He was frequently going to and fro between Selborne and Oxford. His love of the south country is clear in his correspondence. Mulso tells him of the partridges which he has seen when a-field and wishes that White had been there ; he speaks of White's love for " cool, brown days " ; and he thinks, from White's letters describing his travels, that his friend is " a great and masterly hand " at landscape-painting in words. " I never," wrote Mulso in one letter, " I never see a spot which lies much out of the level but I think of you and say, ' Now this would please White.' " From the letters of Mulso it is easy to see that White was a man of original character, with a humour and a turn of speaking all his own. He was much out of doors in many parts of England, on visits of business or friendship and sport in Devon, Northampton, Bedfordshire, Essex, Kent, Surrey, Sussex, Wiltshire and Oxfordshire. He travelled and noticed so much that his friend begged him to make a useful book out of his observations and so " enable young men to travel with taste and improve at home." White's character, as it appeared in his letters and in her brother's talk, seems to have delighted Hester Mulso, afterwards Mrs. Chapone, who was seven years younger than he ; and Mulso often mentions her in his letters, playfully and very likely with a feeling that she might one day marry his friend. The naturalist enjoyed her society, wrote to her, sent his " Invitation to Selborne," but from her playful signature of " Yes Papa," and the tone of Mulso's letter at the time of her marriage with Chapone, it is almost certain that White had not been deeply moved. His nature, genial, self-centred, slow, perhaps phlegmatic, was not disturbed. His one show of passion came when he said that Pennant did not behave " like a gentleman." While still in his youth he was methodical, calm, with a temperament already quite precipitated, it appears. He was minute and businesslike, for example, in looking over some family estates in Essex in 1764, just as many years later he was shrewd and hard in writing of a debateable will, by which it was uncertain whether he or a hospital would profit. There is, indeed, a hint of dissatisfaction in Mulso's letter to him saying: " I sincerely wish you had a living like Deane and the thorough good sort of *damoiselle* that you mention that your wishes might be completed ; " but certainly he was living within his income, saving and investing.

In 1747 he received deacon's orders and became curate to an uncle at Swanaton, but he was still often at Oriel, where he had smallpox in the same year, and perhaps gave only Sundays to his curacy. In 1751 he was curate to Dr. Bristow, vicar of Selborne, and the next year Proctor of Oxford University and Dean of Oriel. But a letter from Mulso in 1750 suggests that he was getting tired of Oxford ways, though he was still shooting and sociable.

It was in 1747 that he bought Philip Miller's *Gardening Dictionary*, his first purchase of the kind, and in 1751 that he began the " Garden Kalendar," a diary of seed-sowing, weather, plant-

ing, etc., which he kept going until his death in this style :

" 1759, May 1. Pulled away the hedge round the fir-quincunx, and hoed the ground clean.

" 2. The Hanger out in full leaf; but much banged about by the continual strong east wind that has blown for many days. The buds and blossoms of all trees much injured by the wind. The ground parched and bound very hard. The cold air keeps the nightingales very silent. No vegetation seems to stir at present. Disbudded some of the vines. The buds are about an inch long.

" 3. Made second annual bed with six barrows of grass and weeds only ; no dung. Planted out the five handglasses with the great white Dutch cucumbers four plants in a hill. The plants are pretty much drawn. This evening the vehement east wind seems to be abated ; and the air is soft and cloudy. Ground bound like a stone.

" 4. Sowed—first, four rows of small dwarf white kidney beans in the lower field garden. Earthed the Cantaleupes [melons sent him by Philip Miller] the third time : found all the plants in a very flourishing way, and the fibres extended to the very outsides of the hills. Cut away the plants to one in some of the hills ; and left two in some, stopping down the worst plant very short towards the bottom of the runners, for experiment's sake, to see what the small wood about the stems will do. Some of the plants offer for male bloom. Saw first Redstart and Cherrysucker [Spotted Fly Catcher]. Sowed about two dozen of the large white Dutch cucumber seeds for the latter hand-glasses : the first sowing got full tall and big. Delicate soft rain all afternoon and night, which soaked the ground well to the root of all the vegetables."

In 1753 he bought a new edition of Miller and the *Methodus Plantarum Nova* of John Ray, and he sub-scribed towards the making of a zig-zag path up Selborne Hanger and placed the rude stone or obelisk at the upper end. In that year, too, he be-came curate of Durley, near Bishop's Waltham, riding for the Sunday service from Selborne ; and for a time he was also curate at West Deane, near Salisbury, accepting it, writes Mulso, " because it was; your sentiment that a clergyman should not be idle and unemployed." He often rode from Deane to Selborne,—a fine ride to one with an eye for the Downs. At one time he combined the duty at Deane with that at Newton Valence. In 1757 he accepted the living of Moreton Binkey, Hampshire, where he never

lived, and after putting a curate in, derived £30 a year from it ; and he exchanged Durley for Faringdon at about the same time. He was still in Oxford now and then, and was in 1757 unsuccessful candidate for the provostship at Oriel.

On the death of his father at this time, he was thought a rich man, but his private income did not exceed the sum due from his fellowship, which he therefore retained : he kept a maid and a man, and now and then employed another hand for gardening. For six months in 1759–60 he was away at Lyndon in Rutland with his naturalist brother-in-law, Barker. That was his last long absence from Selborne, where he was now apparently well-content to be settled for ever, the only one of his family living there after 1761 ; and we have a right to assume that he was in a condition to smile cheerfully at Mulso's letter on Hester's marriage in 1761 :

" You will give your good wishes that, as they have long wished for this happy state (I don't know whether I speak to be understood by you who continue an old bachelor), they may continue happy in it."

He seems to have thought of marriage, but without any temptation : his faithful and admirable biographer, Mr.

Rashleigh Holt-White, says that the obstacle was the fact that he could not have supported a family without seeking preferment elsewhere and giving up " The Wakes." In this present year, 1906, at least, it is hard to find a flaw in the life he led, which we may be excused for looking back upon dotingly as upon some past inaccessible and imperturbable tract of our own life. What satisfaction we must suppose to have been his, in buying now and then small plots of land with which to round off his estate ; building a ha-ha, an arbour, a fruit wall, buying a sundial, post and slab and dial, to record the hours of serenity ; planting trees against the walls. The names of some of his wall trees survive, as, for example —Sweet-water vine, Mr. Snooke's black-cluster vine, Nobless peach, white Muscadine vine ; and of his pears, as, for example—Chaumontelle, Virgoleuse, Brown Bury, St. Germain, Swan's Egg. Year by year he went to Ringmer to stay with his aunt, Mrs. Snooke, always noticing her tortoise. In 1763 " The Wakes " became his own house. It was often full and seldom empty of guests whom he loved, and there is at least one record of a party there which cannot soon be forgotten. A Miss Catherine Battie, a beautiful girl of twenty, who was staying at Selborne in 1763, left a diary of some of her pleasures at " The Wakes " and in the neighbouring fields. Thus she writes of a dance at White's house :

" The morn was spent at the Harpsichord, a Ball at night, began minuets at half an hour after 7, then danced country dances till near 11, went to supper, after supper sat some time, sung, laught, talked, and then went to dancing again, danced till 3 in the morning, at half an hour after 4 the company all went away, we danced 30, never had I such a dance in my life, nor ever shall I have such a one again I believe " . . . [Next day] " got up at 10 in very good spirits (who can be otherwise in this dear place)." Mr. White, she records, read an acrostic " made upon Nanny," i.e., Miss Anna Battie. Again :

" In the evening walked to Noar Hill. Oh sweet evening, sure there never was anything equal to the romantickness of that dear dear hill, never never shall I forget Empshot and the gloomy woods, the distant hills, the South Down, the woody hills on the right hand, the forest, the valleys, oh all are heavenly, almost too much for me to bear, the sight of this beauteous prospect gives one a pleasing melancholy."

White suggested that the young women should dress as shepherdesses for a dance, and wrote :

"Gilbert a meddling luckless swain
    Must alter ladies' dresses
To dapper hats and tuck'd up train
    And flower-enwoven tresses.
But now the Lout with loss of heart
    Must for his rashness pay ;
He rues for tamp'ring with a dart
    Too prompt before to slay !"

Reading this diary of a hundred and fifty years ago and looking at Catherine's face it is hard to believe that she is dead.

In 1769, White bought Hudson's *Flora Anglica* and, says his biographer, began the serious study of botany.

In 1767 his " Garden Kalendar " developed into the elaborate " Naturalist's Journal," and he began his correspondence with Thomas Pennant, to whom he was perhaps introduced by his brother Benjamin White, Pennant's publisher. Two years later he met Daines Barrington and began the letters which, with those to Pennant, formed his " Natural History." He was writing also to his brother John White, a naturalist, at Gibraltar, giving him this excellent advice :

" Learn as much as possible *the manners of animals*, they are worth reams of descriptions. Frequent your markets and see what birds are exposed for sale." Birds, animals and drawings came frequently from Gibraltar to Selborne.

As early as 1770 his sight was decaying, but on November 13, 1771, he could yet count sixteen fork-tailed kites together on the Downs. Mulso, still writing to him, calls him " the richest man that I know, for you are the only man of my acquaintance that does not want money."

Now he is reading *Tristram Shandy* and now Johnson's *Hebrides*, and again *Boswell*. Dryden is for him " the greatest master of numbers of any of our English bards." He reads Thomson, who " falls into fustian sometimes . . . though he thinks like a poet is often faulty in his diction." His nephew, the young John White, stays with him and they read Horace together, finding the epistles " a fine body of ethics and very entertaining and sensible." They never fell out about anything except the quantity of a Latin syllable. Apparently Jack learned from him how to write, for his letters are absurdly like his uncle's in style. He understood the schoolmaster, if he could not have been one himself. " Unless," he writes, " a schoolmaster is somewhat of a pedant, and a little sufficient in his way, he must expect to be soon faded with his drudgery." With the two friendly families at the vicarages of Selborne and Newton Valence life went very well. As to the world, he says in 1775 that America " is at present the subject of conversation " and finds a quotation from Seneca " prophetic of the discovery of that vast continent," and he sees soldiers on their way to the war through the Hampshire lanes ; but as the Journal says in 1776 :

" Brother Harry's strong beer which was brewed last Easter Monday with the *hordeum nudum* is now tapped and incomparably good." And he knew his happiness. " When the children are buzzing at the spinet," he writes, " and we grave folks sit round the chimney, I am put in mind of the following couplet which you will remember :

"All the distant din that world can keep
Rolls o'er my grotto and improves my
sleep."

He notes the coming of the ring ousels in September and he praises the snuff-pincers for extinguishing his candles " in a very neat manner." He builds a new Hermitage on the hill. He adds a new parlour to his house and buys " long annuities." He rejoices, in 1777, that he can at last purchase " the fields behind his house, that *angulus iste* which the family have so long desired."

He weighs the tortoise at Ringmer and notices the increase of an ounce in its weight. Even in London he keeps up his journal, noticing, in 1785, two martins and a swift in Fleet Street, and hearing owls and a green woodpecker at Vauxhall. In 1780 his aunt, Mrs. Snooke, died, and he received from her a farm and the old tortoise, Timothy. That year he reached " with only one infirmity," deafness. His income was about £100 from inherited property and sometimes as much as £150 from his fellowship. He puts Timothy into a tub of water and finds him " quite out of his element and much dismayed ; " he addresses him through a speaking tube without effect. He makes a gentle sloping path up the Hanger, called the Bostal, instead of the steep zig-zag : but there is " a junto of Zigzaggians " among the neighbours. Though deaf, he can still enjoy hearing his nieces play jigs and minuets that run importunately in his head of a morning. He still goes to Oxford for an election now and then. He sends out verses about crocuses and about wasps in treacle. He plants mullein and foxgloves from the Hanger in his garden, and sows beech mast in the hedges and on the bare parts of the Down. He writes how his hepaticas do and his Persian iris, and what he adds to his borders, and when the first black-cap came, and how late the swifts have young. He is careful about the state of the roads ; and it is a legend that when children saw him coming they began to put stones in the ruts and got pennies for their diligence. As late as 1786 he is " in a sad fright, having no silk breeches and stockings to make a wedding visit in." In 1788 he is proud that his nephews and nieces number fifty-one.

In 1789 at last his book was published. As early as 1776 Mulso had written with remarkable foresight :

" Your work upon the whole will immortalize your place of abode as well as yourself. . . . No man communicates the pleasure of his excursions, or makes the world partake of them in a more useful manner, than you do." He had, in fact, made a book which had three extraordinary merits. It contained valuable and new observations ; it overflowed with evidence of a new spirit—a spirit of minute and even loving inquiry into the life and personality of animals in their native surroundings—that was coming into natural history ; and thirdly, it had style or whatever we like - to call the breath of life in written words, and it was delightfully and easily full of the man himself and of the delicate eighteenth century southern country side which he knew. But the observations are no longer new ; the new spirit has been renovated by the gun-less naturalists from Thoreau to Mr. W. H. Hudson of our own day. The man himself is still fresh to succeeding generations, and thousands who care not at all how many willow wrens there be, delight to read these letters from a man so happy and remote from our time that he thought the dying fall of the true willow wren " a joyous easy laughing note." We are always pleasantly conscious of the man in his style, which strikes us as the lines and motions of a person's face strike us for good or for bad, and, even so, in a manner that defies analysis. His quack who ate a toad, his boys twisting the nests out of rabbit holes with a forked stick, his love of the " shapely-figured aspect of the chalk hills " above that of the " abrupt and shapeless " mountains, his swallows feeding their young and treading on the wing, his friendly horse and fowl, his prodigious many-littered half-bred bantam sow that proved " when fat, good bacon, juicy and tender," his honey-loving idiot, his crickets (" a good Christmas fire is to them like the heats of the dog days ")

—these things have in his pages a value which can only be attributed to his literary genius, by which his book survives.

In 1790 he records how the trees which he planted have grown : the oak of 1731 is 4 feet 5 inches in circumference ; the ash of the same year is 4 feet 6½ inches ; the spruce of 1751 is 5 feet ; the beech 4 ; the elm of 1750 is 5 feet 3 inches ; the lime of 1756 is 5 feet 5 inches. In 1793 he " made rhubarb tarts and a rhubarb pudding, which was very good ; " but a bad nervous cough and a wandering gout made him languid and indolent ; he suffered much pain ; and on June 26, after his bed had been moved into the old family parlour at the back of his house, so that the Hanger was in sight, he died.

XIX

IN HARD WEATHER

"When icicles hang by the wall,
  And Dick the shepherd blows his nail ;
And Tom bears logs into the hall,
  And milk comes frozen home in pail."
—SHAKESPEARE.

BITTERLY cold days, overhung with a light mist that vanishes at noon, but in the dusk of morning and evening floats like a dim blue film above the red sun, and still colder nights, bathed in the white light of the moon and the stars, have succeeded the rainy weather that accompanied the advent of winter. Hardened by successive frosts, the snow lies thick on the fields. Since the fall of the flaky showers the heat of the day sufficed to melt from the boughs their jewelled incrustations ; but along the northern side of the hedges and the margins of the woods the drifts are now almost as deep as immediately after the storm. All the broad pools of the river are icebound. To the fast-flowing trout reach below the bathing-pool an otter comes every day at noon to fish the stretch by the cottage gardens. If only the watcher remain motionless and silent, the creature continues a systematic search from bank to bank, now and again showing itself at the surface when it rises to breathe. Forced by hunger to abandon many of its wild ways, the otter is sometimes seen at night in the lane at the end of the village, whence it is chased back to the river by any wandering terrier that may chance to cross its path. Its favourite resorts are the refuse heaps in the gardens and beyond the high wall built as a breakwater against the river floods. During long-continued hard weather every fish in the river vanishes. The trout are there, however, though not visible. They have forsaken the streams for the still pools, where the temperature beneath the ice is not so variable as in the open water among the rapids. The otter, unable, because of the ice, to drive the trout from their hiding-places at the bottom of the deep pits they frequent, is forced to feed on anything it may find in the streams— an occasional " kelt " salmon, or salmon " pink," or a stray morsel from the cottagers' kitchens—and finds but scanty fare. Yet fortune sometimes favours it. A half-pound fish, chased by a cannibal of its own tribe, will now and then drop down from the hollow of the pool to the shallows, where the ice becomes thin and at last disappears on the edge of the rapids. Here, if anywhere, a stray " blue dun " is to be found loitering at the surface in the brief sunlight of the winter noon. The trout know this, and lurk among the ripples for a half-hour in the warmest time of the day. The otter, learned in all the ways of its prey, and having forsaken its nocturnal habits, spends most of its time on the look-out for roving fish by the fringe of the ice.

Around the trunks of the willows growing by the river are cleared spaces where the water-voles have scratched away the snow in their quest for food. Under the trees the ground thaws more rapidly than elsewhere ; the latent heat in the trees themselves is, in part, the cause of this. Finding the earth comparatively soft close by the willows, the voles have here and there dug a shallow trench, that they may obtain a frugal meal of grass-roots and reeds. They are timid little creatures ; their burrows by the waterside are like miniature dwelling-places of the otter, one entrance opening on the top of the bank and the other below the surface of the stream. In summer, the voles are rarely seen by day, but when darkness falls they sit out with their families by the reeds near the river's brim. At the slightest disturbance they drop into the water and enter their burrows by the hidden passages. Like the otter, they are night-feeders. But hard frost causes a change in their habits ; they now take full advantage of the warmth of noon. During the least thaw the voles must work hard, if life is to be kept aflame. Perhaps only for a little while in the day can the hungry creatures have easy access to the succulent shoots of water plants and grasses, which form their simple diet, and then, in certain unfrequented places, they throng the river bank.

None but the student of Nature recognises how marked is the change in the life of the fields after a week of uninterrupted frost. An unforeseen catastrophe has befallen the weaklings of Nature's flock. No sufficient provision has been made to meet the sudden cruelty with which an erstwhile bountiful hand turns the key that locks the storehouse door. Disinherited and forlorn, the wild wanderers by wood and hedgerow eke out a bitter existence in mute appeal against the inexorable fate that has driven them forth upon the bleak face of a barren world. When the mildness of our climate is rudely disturbed by piercing east or north-east winds succeeding a fall of snow, the conditions of life in our temperate latitudes are similar to those existing in Arctic regions. But the habits of our wild creatures are different. Along lines of migration known for ages, Arctic birds and animals move south-wards in the dusk of the darkening winter night. Once arrived at their usual resting-place, they for some unaccountable reason seem disinclined to journey further south.

Overtaken by unexpected severity of weather, redwings and fieldfares die in thousands from privation and cold. One morning in a recent winter, thirty-three of these birds were picked up dead on a small farm of forty acres. Even our native birds suffer greatly from any unusual continuance of cold. Wood-pigeons, among the hardiest of forest dwellers, collect in large flocks and associate with rooks and jack-daws. The birds fly from field to field, and by unremitting labour among the furrows—labour directed by shrewd-ness and intelligence—manage in places to tear up the ground and obtain the necessaries of life. The wood-pigeons watch the resourceful rooks, and in the fresh-turned earth find here and there some welcome morsel rejected by their companions. But the cushat is no longer the plump, fleet-winged bird that filled the summer wood with soft continuous cooing. Wasted by privation to a mere bag of bones covered with feathers, it wearily wings its way to the home meadows, there alighting to pick a meal from the turnips provided by the farmer for his hungry sheep.

SNOWSTORM.

From a photograph by
Edith L. Willis.

By the river side, the water-vole, as well as the pigeon, discovers in the ubiquitous rook a friend. The rook is a keen entomologist. Books would not suffice to contain all the knowledge of insect life possessed by the tribe-father of the rookery on the hill. Every tree in summer sheltered amid its leaves a hundred little families of promising caterpillars, destined, if fate were propitious, to develop into delicate, soft-winged moths. When autumn came these caterpillars spun their robes of silk and passed into the third, the sleeping, stage of their existence. With the fall of the leaf they dropped to the ground. Some, however, when about to sleep, crawled down the trunk and burrowed in the warm soil at the roots, before putting on their garments of " chitine." All this is known to the observant rook. In the thaw of the winter noon the wise bird comes to the foot of the tree, digs beneath the snow among the rotting leaves, and, foraging for the hidden grubs, assists unconsciously the little vole to hollow out a shallow trench around the trunk.

The increasing cold of night drives every creature to cover. The rooks forsake the elms on the slope for the oaks in the valley below, where they cluster together almost as closely as leaves. Hares and partridges lurk in the furze-brakes near the haunts of man, and at dawn steal through the gaps into the home meadows, to join the pigeons among the turnips or to pick up stray grains near the feeding-troughs. Blackbirds, thrushes, and finches collect in the thickets for shelter from the bitter wind. When morning comes, they too join the wood-pigeons in the fields near the farm. The pheasant goes to roost in the middle of the larch plantation. Shyer than the partridge, the wild-bred pheasant trusts to the woodland sanctuaries, and there, during the day, searches the tangles on the outskirts of the trees for acorns and berries.

Many creatures now become torpid. Others fall into a state of lethargy from which the call of hunger every day arouses them. Except when thus awakened, the weasel, stoat, and polecat lie curled up in the furthest corner of their burrows, doubtless longing for winter to pass away. Like the otter, they abandon some of their wild ways at this season. Occasionally the stoat is seen to peep from a hole in the farmyard wall, when hunting the rats that have forsaken the fields to take up an abode in warmer quarters. The members of the weasel tribe, were it not for the rats and the mice at the farm, would find it difficult to live through a long period of frost. The keen air of night benumbs them. After dusk they seldom, if ever, venture forth from their burrows. By force of circumstance the habits of all three animals are changed. So sensitive seem these creatures to cold that they choose the warmest part of the day for a visit to the neighbouring warren or corn stack. But at that time the rabbits are generally abroad, enjoying the slight thaw; and the stoat and the polecat have no choice but to pursue them through the furze or along the hedges. Such a hunt is seldom successful, unless time be at the disposal of the hunters. Yet in the afternoon, should the rabbits be driven to their burrows, the raiders find their task an easy one, for, caught in blind alleys among the galleries below ground, the timid rodents choose rather to submit to death than by one bold effort to make their escape. No satisfactory reason can be given for the paralysing fear that possesses the rabbit directly it ascertains the presence of a stoat. Nor can it be explained why the rabbit should "bolt" before its cruel foe more readily in the morning than in the afternoon. For ages, from causes which naturalists have clearly described, those creatures most capable of taking care of themselves have outlived their weaker and less intelligent brethren; and, when this is borne in mind, it is difficult to understand how a senseless stupidity which often results in death can have become hereditary.

In hard weather the fox and the hawk approach the homestead. The kestrel descends suddenly, like a stone dropped from the sky, into the barnyard, and rises with a mouse in its claws. The sparrow-hawk, bolder and more cruel still, dashes along the hedgerow and "stoops" upon a thrush that is trying to obtain a worm in the "miskin" near the cowsheds. At night, when the unclouded moon shines from the indigo sky with a strange, weird brightness upon the white coverlet of the sleeping world, the fox steals through the shadows of the woods and enters the fowls' house at the farm. Presently, awakened by the cackling of the poultry and the barking of the dogs, the farmer appears at his window. A shot rings out into the silence. Stung by a stray pellet from the old muzzle-loader, Reynard drops his prey and, followed by the loud-tongued dogs, disappears within the wood.

XX

GAME SHOOTING

"Now mercy goes to kill,
And shooting well is then accounted ill,
Then will I save my credit in the shoot;
Not wounding, mercy would not let me do't."—*Love's Labour's Lost.*

ONE cannot but marvel at the change which has taken place in the methods of game shooting and game preservation during the last quarter of a century. Nor can one help being amazed at the greediness of the age, the general absence of that ideal sportsmanship—woodcraft, knowledge of the habits of birds and beasts, call it what you will—without which no man who shot could formerly hope for satisfaction or success.

Shooting nowadays is more often a pastime than a sport; game is brought to the gun, not the gun to the game. And as game has attained its full speed by the time it reaches the shooter, to hit it calls for greater quickness and accuracy of aim than did the old-fashioned method of shooting birds as they rise. In these modern days of crowded concentration, when a man may be hunting in the Midlands one day, the next shooting in Hampshire, and fishing on the third in Scotland, it is not necessary for the follower of either sport to possess those practical qualities which were once indispensable to him who hunted, shot, or fished.

But does your modern sportsman—how insulted he would be if you told him he was no real sportsman—reap anything like the measure of enjoyment he would were he to plan with his own wits the tactics by which his game is brought within gun-shot? No!—decidedly no! It is given to him to taste one tithe only of the pleasures of the ideal sportsman. To be a successful game shooter, all that is now required is to kill as often as possible. And were the fact of killing the sole reward which came to me from the sport of shooting, I would give it up to-morrow. There are to-day any number of successful sportsmen of the mechanical type; but, send out ten of them to bring home five brace of strong, wild grouse or partridges in mid-October, and nine would fail utterly; they could hit the birds but know not how to circumvent them.

The mandate of fashion says you must be of the herd rushing north for grouse shooting, which certainly has some advantages over the pursuit of partridges, not the least being that the season for grouse is at its best in the great month of holidays, August. To the hard-worked professional man there is no more enjoyable way of spending the inside of a week than in tramping the moorland on the chance of a few shots at red grouse. For all that, it seems to me that the charm of such shooting must lie chiefly in the exercise of woodcraft, in the fresh scenery, and exhilarating air—clearing the cobwebs from the tired brain— and the feeling that the day is one's very own—no telephone calls, no letters to write—rather than in the hitting of birds which calls for but moderate skill in aiming. If you feel inclined, you can stretch yourself on the springy heather and refresh yourself with great soul-satisfying draughts of Nature's abundance. The shooting of a few brace of grouse gives you just sufficient excuse to repel a charge of absolute idleness ; you must bag a few brace—or patronize a poulterer. Personally, I know nothing in the whole world of shooting which would sicken me sooner than to pile up a big bag of birds which have almost to be kicked up.

Fine grouse shooting, by driving, falls only to those of gilded pocket ; and there is no gainsaying to the man who handles his gun like an artist the pleasure—while it lasts, for ten minutes or so—of a drive when birds are stringing past his butt. If you can once gauge the deceptive pace of grouse, they are not so hard to hit as the bonny partridges ; for if you shoot at a grouse coming straight at your face and miss it, on it comes still straight. And, as a rule, you can see approaching grouse far in front of you, but when shooting driven partridges—to my mind the finest sport in the world—you know not where birds may top the fence. Just as you have marked the leading bird for your own, off it goes at a lightning tangent and—you miss.

If I could avoid it, I would never shoot a partridge otherwise than by driving. I never can understand all I hear about driving being butchery. The making of mammoth bags by parties of shooters who combine the most brilliant accuracy with marvellous quickness of hand and lightning judgment of brain, is a very poor reason for calling the performance butchery. To prove this, all you have to do is to take your stand for a drive and butcher partridges—if you can. True, by driving, many more shots are obtained in a day ; but picture to yourself a team of really good shots walking up birds which lie well—this would mean veritable carnage, for close-lying part-ridges are, as a rule, only missed by *moderate* shooters through carelessness. Besides, just think of the birds which would be wounded by indifferent shooters, who are generally the worst sinners at firing at all sorts of dis-tances—I should call this worse than butchery.

There can be few things more annoy-ing to the man who is a genuine sports-man than to lose game he has shot. For the mere accurate marksman who measures his enjoyment and sport solely by the amount of game he hits, there was never a finer invention than the clay-pigeon. I knew a man who had a good deal of shooting out of sight of keepers and beaters; after the beat was over—we were covert shooting—he joined the rest of the party and never said a word about having killed anything, and—doubt-less from desire to spare his feelings—he was not asked. Next day quite by accident we found the bodies of no fewer than nine pheasants which would otherwise have rotted, unless some prowling fox had found them.

There are two points in modern pheasant shooting which strike me forcibly—one is that there are too many birds to shoot at, which is bad; the other is that the birds few or many, are made to offer the most difficult shots, which is decidedly good. If there is one thing in shooting which I detest, it is walking up and shooting pheasants in roots or other walkable cover. As a gamekeeper I often have thus to kill pheasants for the larder, but I always feel that I should like to pay someone else to take each shot. The old-fashioned method of shooting pheasants was almost entirely of the walking-up order. And surely the working of their lively, well-trained spaniels or springers must have sup-plied the chief part of the sport our grandfathers enjoyed. Occasionally an old cock who managed to survive the volley fired at him, as he rose with as much fuss as an old gentleman trying to catch a moving train, would soar high and fast over the firing-line to gain the shelter of his favourite covert, and offer a shot comparable with the average "tall bird" of modern methods.

It is an undecided question with shooting men whether the stopping of a fast, high, down-wind, curving pheasant flying with a free-wheel appearance, calls for more skill than the most sporting partridge or grouse. The great error the majority of shooters make is to imagine at least a portion of a pheasant's tail is part of its body.

I do not see how the man who almost day after day takes his stand at a spot chosen for him by somebody else can avoid becoming weary of crumpling up the very best of pheasants; but were I to take my share in planning the beating of coverts and exercising all I knew to make the pheasants as difficult as possible to hit, it would be a long while before I should tire of trying to hit them.

That hand-reared pheasants fly slowly and low, while their wild-bred relatives soar aloft spontaneously, is a popular fallacy. It is the wild birds which love to skulk, and finally glide away a yard or so from the ground. Hand-reared birds can be made by modern management to give far more sporting shots, and with more certainty than wild ones. I do not say that to outwit the wild ones would not be a more difficult task, but the actual shooting of them would be poorer sport.

The question: How can a keeper rear, cherish, and feed his pheasants for months with unstinted devotion, and then suddenly try his utmost to encompass their end? would seem to be rather a puzzle to most people. I think the explanation is that all the keeper does from first to last is with the implied understanding of sport later on, in consideration whereof he is their slave for the time being, and affords them a life of absolute luxury. He never allows his apparent affection for them to merge into love, as he would if he kept a pheasant for a pet.

I have often wondered if those who cannot or will not shoot forward enough, think of the needless suffering they inflict on hares, especially. The absolute duffer can scarcely fail occasionally to hit a hare; and when I hear a man actually boast of having " stuck some shot into a hare " I should like to serve him the same. If any one were shooting with me and possessed a propensity for wounding hares, I should tell him to leave them alone altogether, or go home. To shoot a hare properly, you must fire at it only at a reasonable range, say up to fifty yards if broad-side, and considerably less if running at a far less vulnerable angle. You must never forget that the immediately vital part of a hare is little bigger than the body of a partridge.

A common practice in modern shooting which I loathe and abominate is to fire at all game at ranges which, however accurate the aim, can only mean a clean kill about five times in a hundred, inflicting ninety-five times a wound leading generally to a lingering death—sheer cruelty and waste. The only remedy which would, I think, appeal to shooters who committed such crimes—and they are much too plentiful—would be, after warning, a fine, with imprisonment for repeated offences. I fail to see much material difference in one man who drives a lame horse, and another who continually wounds game by firing at it beyond reasonable range.

No one loves shooting more than myself ; but I detest the man who is capable only of sitting on a shooting-stick, smoking everlasting cigarettes and blazing away recklessly at all game he sees far and near. Let true sportsmanship be the first consideration—always.

XXI

PREHISTORIC MONUMENTS

"Man passes away: his name perishes from record and recollection; his history is as a tale that is told; and his very monument becomes a ruin."—WASHINGTON IRVING : *The Sketch Book.*

THE ancient kingdom of Damnonia, occupying the south-westerly horn of Britain, reveals Nature in her primal garb, stern and wild. Long before the pleasant hills and vales of Eastern England were raised from the ocean, even before their constituent materials were deposited thereunder, this rugged peninsula stood high and dry, though no man saw it. At one stormy period the hard Palaeozoic rocks were riven asunder by subterranean forces, and there was upheaved a molten mass which thrust itself as veins into the dislocated strata. This material cooled and crystallized as granite. Then the superincumbent rocks, which still hid the solidified mass, were slowly denuded away, and the plutonic lava stood out in the huge bosses which now form the knolls and tors of Damnonia.

Aeons afterwards, successive races of Ancient Britons were driven into this corner of the country by surging tribes of new-comers who coveted the richer Tertiary pastures of the Midlands and the south-east. Thus it chanced that the horn was inhabited by a mixed people, who, in the late Neolithic and the early Bronze Age, seeing that the granite was naturally weathered into slabs and " clappers," employed this enduring stone when they raised various kinds of monuments.

These monuments are mainly dotted

for eight or ten miles radially over a wide plateau whose solid foundation and whose superstructure of tor and valley are uniformly composed of the ancient crystalline material. Truly a grim stage for the actors in the prehistoric drama. Bare granite above, green grass-lands below merging into impassable bog, alder-lined streamlets babbling over heaps of granite " clatters," a territory of blinding rain and penetrating fog. That folk lived here is evidenced by the first monuments which we shall examine, the ruins of their houses. The Damnonian hut, as we now see it, consists of rude slabs of granite set on end and closely arranged in a circle a few yards in diameter. An opening, manifestly for entrance, looks towards the east or south-east. The ground within this hut-ring is hollowed out a little, and if we choose to dig there we may discover a primitive hearth, as testified by calcined stones, and fragments of charcoal and pottery. Strewn around the hut, but lying under the spongy turf, are flint flakes struck off by the inhabitants. The priscan settlers of the tableland doubtless roofed their stone house with gorse, heather, and fern from the moor. These flimsy coverings have long since perished, but the substantial framework of the hut endures.

Scattered on various parts of the moors are rude bridges crossing the streams which rise towards the centre of the plateau. These " clatter-bridges," composed of long, thick granite blocks of great weight, supported on dry granite masonry, and placed in position no scholar knows how, are often assigned to the prehistoric age. This is a doubtful question ; the bridges were probably erected for the convenience of packhorses in mediaeval days, but there is a possibility that they are earlier.

More particularly, however, would we speak of monuments concerned with death rather than with life. Here, in a ploughed field, where, in the later times of Domesday, one Drogo held dominion, stands an artificial structure, perfect of its kind, before whose mystery we linger as under a subtle spell. The erection, known to modern archaeologists as a dolmen, or " stone-table," but to earlier writers as a cromlech, consists of three rude granite pillars, more or less flat-sided, arranged in a sort of triangle, with a flat capstone perched on the top. The pillars are worn and rounded by the storms of three thousand years, and the crystals of felspar, as long as one's finger, stand out clean and bright. Resting for a few moments within this old megalithic monument, we ponder over its meaning. Recent authorities teach that most, if not all, of the dolmens were once covered by a mound of earth, that the dolmen is, in fact, the stone framework which supported the material forming a British barrow. On that supposition, this megalith formed the receptacle wherein some old Iberian or Celtic chieftain was laid to rest. Two pictures are immediately outlined in the imagination. The first shows a horde of skin-clad tribesmen, with the serfs whom they have conquered, scraping up, by the aid of stone hoes, the peaty soil of the surrounding moorland, and toilsomely carrying it in osier baskets to the newly-made grave. As the work proceeds, chips of flint are thrown amid the soil to ensure good hap to the dead man. Soon a gluttonous orgy begins, oxen and sheep are slain and eaten, odd bones are dropped into the accumulating hillocks, possibly one or two human sacrifices are offered. The tumult dies away. Fecund Nature in due time covers the mound with green herbage, and unless the barrow is re-opened for future burials its even contours will be untouched, until some prying antiquary of later Britain comes hither with his iron spade. The second picture is a sad one, and the description perforce prosaic. A nineteenth-century husbandman, with no soul for ancient stones, unsentimentally keen about the yield of his crops, carts away the rich earth of the barrow, once collected at such great labour, in order to give an exhausted field a cheap top-dressing.

It has been hinted that the barrow might be re-opened, for it was very common for one mound to be used for successive interments. The stone chamber has, indeed, been considered a kind of tribal ossuary. Though barrows exist in fair number on the bleak heights of the moor, there are, strangely enough, few certain remains of dolmens in this part of the country. Cromlechs proper, that is rings of upright stones, are, on the contrary, very abundant. It is curious that many of the cromlechs roughly measure either 50 or 100 feet in diameter. Stonehenge may be looked upon as a complicated specimen, the most highly developed monument of this type.

The cromlech is a greater puzzle than the dolmen. In some cases excavations have proved that burials were associated with the stone circle, and it is probable that Stonehenge derived its primal sanctity from its being a grave. Were the cromlechs raised as open-air temples, or for early folk-moots ? Were they crematoria, in the days when the burning of the dead had come into vogue, or were they astronomical stations ? Yet again, were they trysting-places where our rude forefathers held equinoctial feasts to the sun-god ? Each theory has its defenders. The discovery of charcoal in the floors of some of the enclosures suggests that the cromlech had primarily a funereal significance. Briefly, and without pre-judging the question too strictly, we may conclude that burial, probably by cremation, was connected with the stone circle. Afterwards some kind of worship was carried on at the spot, though not, one may suppose, by the all-active Druids of the school-book.

Traversing the wilder parts of the moorland, we notice a row of standing pillars, a few feet high, unhewn, merely gathered together and placed upright. These hoary monoliths are pitted and furrowed by age ; the traitorous felspar has yielded to the gentle in-sinuations of long-continued wind, and rain, and frost. Olive and grey lichens, centuries old, have settled on these scarred columns, but they con-ceal, rather than tell, anything of the past. You may follow this stone-row two or three hundred yards, then it stops, to re-appear on the opposite slopes of the valley. With breaks, you may perhaps trace the stones for a mile or two, but according to present-day notions, they will be found to lead nowhere. If we cross the Channel to southern Brittany we may get some light from the stone alignment of Carnac. Comparisons show that the stone-row is connected with burials. Often it is found in conjunction with a cairn, or artificial pile of stones. The facts, learned in Brittany, and illumined by the study of comparative customs, indicate that certain primi-tive races, ancient and recent, have been accustomed to raise these columns when a chief is buried, each member of the tribe setting up his own memorial stone. The explana-tion may be accepted provisionally, though it does not seem to account for the varying periods to which the monuments belong, nor for the dupli-cation of the alignments—at Carnac there are indeed eleven rows. The imaginative moorman, helped by academic influences, says that the stone-rows were Roman guide lines across the waste. This can scarcely be seriously considered. Nor were the alignments the supports of cattle-sheds, mediaeval, historic, or pre-historic. The boundary-line theory, and the ceremonial sports theory, may also be set aside. Again, any one who knows Damnonia will not be beguiled by the hypothesis that some old tin-miners set up the stones at some undefined date, for purposes also unspecified.

There remains the menhir, or isolated pillar, occasionally the sole survivor of a stone-row, sometimes, perhaps, a boundary stone, more frequently, no doubt, the mark of sacred ground. The rugged moorland bears ample testimony that the early Christians recognized the sanctity of such stones. By gentle transitions they developed and even adapted from them their holy cross, gradually weaning the pagan ideas from the monoliths, and replacing them by those of the new faith.

XXII

IN EAST NORFOLK BIRD HAUNTS

"Birds, Birds! ye are beautiful things,
.   .   .   .
Ye hide in the heather, ye lurk in the brake,
Ye dive in the sweet flags that shadow the lake;
Ye skim where the stream parts the orchard-decked land,
Ye dance where the foam sweeps the desolate strand."
—William H. Thompson.

BIRD-WATCHING has become one of the most fashionable of hobbies; and it is certainly one of the most delightful of pursuits. The well-to-do naturalist makes extensive forays into bird-land, pressing steam yacht and motor-car into his service; nor is the working-man debarred from enjoying privileges nearer at home, for convenient trains and handy cycles speedily take him beyond the radius of civilization and dusty streets. Further than a suitable raiment, and a good pair of eyes, and what is scarcely less serviceable, a pair of trusty bino-culars, preparation and expense are very small matters of detail. In my own case an aged punt, a taut little houseboat, and a pair of Zeiss glasses complete my outfit, and provide me with many a chance of watching our rarer waders and wild fowl.

Every naturalist has his restrictive "beats," his own particular and peculiar environment: and under ordinary circumstances he knows the radius of his peregrinations almost to an inch. Many naturalists may have more leisure at their disposal; but few working-men have, perhaps, a more diversified field than my own, an area, I am sorry to say, becoming yearly more circumscribed as drainage and utilization of waste lands goes on, and an ever-increasing population usurps the *habitats* of the old-time *feræ naturæ.*

The scantier one's leisure, the more one learns to economise his time; and in my own East-coast bird haunts I have had to make the most and best of prevailing winds, the state of the tides, and a knowledge of the times and seasons of the various wild birds. It is little use using our beach in spring or autumn when the wind is west, and an ebb tide is usually abomination. Certainly in August the west wind "draws in" the herring syle, and the passing terns inshore. A stiff easterly, or north-easterly gale in winter may bring hither skuas and petrels, and perchance a few rare gulls; a south-easterly wind is fair for spring and autumn migrants. A northerly wind in January is not amiss. Almost any wind suits Breydon; and a "breathless" day in autumn may find it equally interesting.

These, and other considerations, have full many a score times decided whether I should sail up Breydon, or ramble up its northern or southern walls, or take the North River walls for it, or the beach to the harbour mouth, or go north. Any reasonably fine day will do for the Broads. The barometer should be daily studied; and a railway time-table is by no means an unhelpful volume on the naturalist's shelf.

*　　*　　*

A fine July Saturday afternoon invites us out into the haunts of bird and insect. The light wind is S.W. There is a train passing through Berney Arms at mid-noon, and will stop if we let the guard know we've booked there; we will have a fourpenny ride, and a ramble back by Breydon Walls. Will you join us? It is but a few minutes' run across the marshlands, and from the carriage windows we catch sight of Breydon at several points on our left; on our right meanders the Bure, on whose sluggish flood white-sailed yachts and sober wherries are gliding up-stream, looking odd somewhat as they seem sailing in a dozen different directions, as they follow the sinuous bendings of the river. A heron clumsily lifts himself from a marsh-ditch, where he has been seeking a mess of sticklebacks, hoping perchance to fall in with a venturesome water vole; a few peewits start as we rumble along, with querulous pipings, protesting against the noisy monster that has not, however, done them any harm; and we observe numbers of starlings dodging among the legs of the kine that grow fat by hundreds on the rich saline grasses of marshland.

The train slows down at a one-man station ; and one by comparison jumps out at the isolated little station, dumped down as in the midst of prairie-land. We are more than a mile from the nearest house, which we presently reach by crossing the intervening marshes.

Berney Arms is a hamlet of some half-dozen scattered tenements ; and there is a " pub." a halting-place near the confluence of the Yare and Waveney, for thirsty wherrymen and belated yachting folk. It is a one-barrel hotel. We step inside the brick-floored parlour and order some light refreshments, and strike up a yarn with an old smelter whose houseboat lies moored in a handy creek. These sons of the wilds are always a source of much interest and information, for they constantly live in intercourse with Nature, and are not difficult to edge into conversation.

*   *   *

As we strike the " Wall " Breydon spreads out before us, a huge shimmering lake of silver, confined here at the " Narrows," and broadening out beyond. Over to the south, just across the water, stands the solid masonry of

Burgh Castle, the magnificent three-sided enclosure wherein the Romans in times of old camped and deployed. It is worthy a day's exploration alone. Sundry meadow-pipits jump up from the ditchsides as we brush along, the tall wall-grasses sweeping past us knee high, and a pair of pied wagtails spring out from the wall where they have been snapping up aquatic insects from the drift-weed. A row of black-headed gulls margins the flat at the " Dickey-works " (a long ridge of low piles acting as a kind of breakwater), and half a dozen are dozing on top as many pile-stumps. They are enjoying a rest while their mates are remaining upon the nests at Scoulton.

Gulls make small task of a forty-mile flight for a change of scene and diet. An hour back they were snapping up floating fragments thrown out from the shrimpers' refuse—small dead bibs, and broken shrimps, and air-weakened crustaceans, for all the " dross " does not sink that is thrown out from the catches. A few ditch-prawns, and little fry found stranded in the " lows " on the flats, were added to them. Swallows flit by the wall as we proceed, and a number of sand-martins pass and repass. They are very fond of hanging around pedestrians for the insects that take to flight on their approach. " Daddy Longlegs "—the *Tipula*, clumsily lets go his hold on the seed tufts, and lazily wings on ahead, to be disturbed again. The *Hirundines* do not seem partial to the long-legged fellow, or they could certainly save time and wing-power. One " Daddy " would go as far as a dozen small *diptera*.

Three herons are fishing in a drain yonder, near the wall. Let us go below the bank ; our heads will just be level with the top, and we shall not prove so fearsome to the watchful birds on the mud flats. Between us and the herons are several curlews probing the ooze for worm and mollusc. We watch their movements for some time, unknown to them, for our faces are half screened by the grass which overtops our heads. A khaki-coloured cap harmonizes with the colour of the walls and the ripening vegetation ; and too much secrecy cannot be exercised in our methods.

Quite a number of whimbrel have put in a re-appearance ; they left us in May-end, and lost but little time on reaching northern Europe before they started nesting : these may be birds whose parents halted at the Shetlands. They are as noisy as ever their elders were in May, and whose ancestors were known as the " noisy May birds." How restless they are ! On July 28, 1906, I saw considerable numbers here ; and hundreds of black-headed gulls—young and old. The following day I was much interested in overlooking, from out the watcher's houseboat window, a number of great black-backed gulls pretending to dive for shore crabs among the *Zostera*, on an adjoining flat. There was a good tide, and from fifteen to twenty inches of water over it, which lifted the wrack ; and among it the crabs scuttled and quarrelled over their prey. The gulls were hungry, and most industrious in their fishing for " Sea-Sammy." They could not dive, but lifted themselves, with broad feet and flicking wings, sufficiently out of the water to give an impetus to their head-foremost drop. Now and again they secured a crab : now and then one would seize the rooted grass as well, and become moored—anchored in fact, in a most ludicrous fashion, and remained half-submerged until either the fronds gave way, or want of breath made it necessary to let go. Such little tit-bits as these are always very edifying to the onlooker.

On July 30, I rowed past a rook who was doing battle with a stranded shore crab ; the crab shuffled back and sidewards in such a pugnacious manner that before master rook could pluck up courage to a final frontal attack, the crustacean had reached the edge of the flat, and tumbled back into water and safety ! One is always seeing something new : there is no finality in Nature.

Ringed plovers and redshanks, curlews and dunlins are constantly coming within the focus of our glasses : the first were hatched on the foreshore, and are here with their parents—a marvel that any of them escaped alive from the footfall of many strolling visitors ; the second as miraculously escaped the hoofs of numbers of roving cattle on the adjoining marshes, where they were reared ; the third did not nest this year, nor travelled farther than north Norfolk ; and the last-named are little odd families of very young wanderers from their northern moors. As early as July 7 have I met with these small confiding innocents, who will not budge or fly from one's oar that splashes water on their dainty plumage.

It is getting on for four o'clock by the time we reach Dan Banham's mill—half-way homewards. We have a yarn with Dan, who tells us of a spoonbill using his marshes at the present moment with some herons ; but we fail to see it. We clamber up into the old windmill, and from the balcony on top enjoy a magnificent view. We look indoors, too, at a grand male avocet he shot some years ago from the wall. We soon reach Duffell's rond, a goodly-sized portion of the Breydon-enclosed part of the original level, which has survived the laving of the tides of three hundred years and more, since the Dutchmen raised the walls. Herein, in a little creek, is moored Fred Clarke's houseboat—Fred is the last of the semi-professional gunners who once numbered a score big duck guns ; but wild fowling is a precarious occupation in these days of deterioration and close seasons ; and the hermit ekes out a scant livelihood with rough marsh-farm carpentry and smelting, and the catching of his eels. Clarke is out with his eel-pick, or we had been treated to a fund of bird-lore, and much interesting original observation.

We have arrived at our own old boat, the *Moorhen*, and step inside to brew a cup of tea, and dispose of certain comestibles ; and remain awhile to watch various birds scattered over the flats nearer home, and on the right by which we have rambled on our way from Berney Arms. We have a bit of fun with the shore crabs scrambling near our little landing stage, and are amused at the fights they indulge in over the fragments of dinner we throw to them. The spoonbill obligingly leaves the marshes and wings his way over to a flat near at hand, and a second joins him—a new-comer probably, for they curvet, and " flap-doodle " their great flat bills in a ludicrous manner, and immediately after begin to spoon in a zigzag fashion at the edge of the mudflat : their prey must consist of shrimps and mudworms, and I feel sure these and small mollusca—the *Hydrobia* that abounds on the *Zostera*, form their chief dietary. Tiny fishes are not refused, and absurd pains are occasionally taken by them in endeavouring to swallow flounders they could never hope would enter their narrow gullets.

Need we enlarge upon what we observe in a short cut made homewards across the marshes ? We are somewhat tired ; and the New Road is a bleak, treeless, dusty way, made shorter, I'll admit, by pleasant discussion on the journey townwards.

*   *   *

To the pleasant Broadlands ! A fairly fine September morning finds us hastening thither by a tardy train from Yarmouth, which lands us at Potter Heigham. The run along the coast is interesting ; catching here and there glimpses of the sea, and now

plunging into the countryside and directly into the heart of our celebrated Broads. We have prepared for eventualities of weather—the glass went back yesterday ; we have light waterproofs, and trouble not much about the great fleecy clouds, here and there tinged with deep grey, from between which patches of blue sky show with intensified colouring. We hire a boat at Applegate's, and a second-pair of oars ; stow our provender under the seats, and pull upstream, a fairly stiff breeze bowling along behind us. The banks of the river, like others of these lowland streams, are monotonously level, but rich with marsh vegetation until the marshman has mowed the " gladdon " for rough litter at the farm. A few willows are dotted in places, gaily painted houseboats are moored at intervals, and many a yacht lay berthed by the river side. A month ago saw them numerously gliding to and fro. One sees a few isolated marsh mills, around which cluster a characteristic marshland cottage, and sundry out-buildings, and the inevitable clump of willows, with the few red cattle giving dots of brighter colour.

We row past the mouth of Kendal Dyke, push back the heavy pontoon bridge at Martham, and shortly turn into the secluded waters of Somerton

Broad, a well-known resort of wild fowl and big skulking pike. A wild duck or two start up with frightened " quack " at our approach, and that indigenous rascal—the coot—now and again scuttles into hiding. We agree that the Broad is sequestered, but to-day is by no means lively with bird life. We row back to Kendal Dyke, and at the ruins of the turbine mill spread our dinner-table on the grass, from which, how-ever, we hurriedly bolt for shelter inside, to escape a pelting shower. The half-stripped roof forms a regular rookery for sparrows, whose slovenly nests peer from under many a shifted tile. A sedge warbler settles on a reed outside and sings us a short snatch of song, and a snipe goes " visp "-ing by, and high over the adjoining marsh a couple of ducks are speeding.

Rain ceasing, we get afloat again, having first mopped the seats dry, and had our grumble at the moisture. Odd coots, tame enough and heedless of us, dive and paddle around, busying themselves with certain aquatic weeds, on whose succulent stems they seem to be feeding. How nimbly they thrust their way along through the tangled undergrowth of the reed-mace ! At openings in Heigham Sounds, where the reeds grow apart, wide stretches of crystal water are seen tenanted by the inevitable coots. Yonder is a grebe. The great crested grebe is, to my mind, the characteristic bird of the Broadlands, and more in keeping, I think, even than the ubiquitous coot. I like watching this dexterous and accomplished diver ; how with a pert and almost saucy turn of his head he suddenly dashes head first under water, and leaves you wondering how far he is going, and how long it will be before he reappears. He may come up in the direction you expect him, or he may baffle you and come up in quite another place. Maybe he emerges with a small roach in his mandibles, and with a shake he dislodges the last drop of moisture that lags behind on his shoulders, and with a toss of the head, bolts his prey. If he be fishing for his youngsters' dinner the perform-ance is still more amusing. There will be a race for the coveted fish, and the little ones dart along like so many skiffs, flattening themselves to the water and outstretching their long, thin necks, whilst the old one quite as excitedly spreads its crest, and calls to the hurrying chicks.

We come across another grebe, directly, *standing* bolt upright, not sitting on its haunches as so often depicted by artists, and moreover it scuttles to the water on its toes, and

9

not in the shuffling manner of one that I kept in confinement used to affect in getting to its favourite element.

We have reached the Old Meadow Dyke, and pull up its narrow sinuous stream. It is pretty now, but was a glorious bit of Broadland in July when we last visited it ; its green walls were forefronted by patches of the flowering rush, and the yellow iris, and the meadow-sweet, that here and there growing luxuriantly, dotted the uniformity with its white scented plumes, while above them all towered the tufted reeds, and stalwart reed-mace, the " pokers " of the natives. To-day the various colours are absent, while the reed tufts are " woollening," and the pokers are swelled to bursting point. Dodging among these we espy a trio of bearded tits, perhaps the most beautiful of Broadland birds, not excepting even the kingfisher. Their foothold is secure, although the reeds bend to the passing breeze.

*   *   *

We reach Horsey Mere, one of the most delightful of the Broads. Its surroundings are much like those of any other, but there seems a freshness and a briskness so different from them all—even Hickling Broad, with its wide expanse of shallow water : we seem to smell a breath of the sea—indeed, we can see the white sandhills a mile or so away which shield this beautiful spot from the inroads of the wild North Sea. We are much impressed by the great flock of black-backed gulls resting on its bosom, and more so by the hundreds of coots that, like curious black wave crests, beat into the reeds to hide as we row along.

But the day promises to wind up badly : the sky is full of great rain clouds that are hurriedly thickening up and joining forces. Step that little mast and up sail. The wind has been northering—make everything snug. You squat down for'ard and make yourself comfortable with your chin just above the gunnel. I'll take the sheet and tiller. And away we bowl. If we visit the Broads in the fall we can hardly expect to see them under such favourable aspects as in July, when the great ovate leaves of the water-lily lie placid on the sparkling water, and the tall reeds bend over to reflex themselves in its crystal depths. The Broads are well worthy a visit once in every month.

*   *   *

October is nearing its end : it is a hazy and " rafty " kind of an afternoon, the wind, what little there is of

SNIPE.

it, is nor'westerly. Our ramble shall be to Gorleston pier-head, at the harbour mouth, and back. Come along, " Flo," and you. " Flo " is our little spaniel ; we will have eight pen'orth of natural history between us. Mounting the cars at Southtown, a twenty minutes' ride brings us to Gorleston quayside, right opposite the harbour mouth. Flo is eager to get down to the waterside to inspect the lines of the sea anglers for scraps of herring-bait, to which she is extremely partial.

It is supposed to be wrong, by the ferry lessee at least, whose nearest boat is more than a mile upstream, for any Gorleston waterman to put a passenger across the water. They dare not charge, so we hold up four fingers and point to the sand-dunes over there just beyond the river. These hardy fellows know my way ; and we are soon speeding across, and are landed safely, notwithstanding the dashing in and out of sundry steam-drifters, now by hundreds pursuing the great North Sea herring fishing.

As we clamber up the steps of the breakwater a small dark bird flits out from a weedy corner. It is a rock pipit that has been picking up a dinner of small *Gammaridæ* from under the easily shifted fronds of the brown wrack that will lie prostrate until the incoming tide shall again lift and lave it into fresher life. At the harbour mouth a screaming, dipping, twistering flock of black-headed gulls are snatching at, and as often missing as seizing, some floating fragment of fishy matter, with now and again a big " grey " gull dashing in to dispute possession or ever a dainty morsel is grabbed.

A flock of thirty larks now passed over ; they seemed half inclined to alight, but lifted themselves again and passed on ; and a flock of snowbuntings that had been disturbed from the sand-dunes by some pedestrian, comes tripping by with jerking flight and sweet tinkling notes : how the white splashes on their plumage showed distinctly against the dirty-grey sky. They suddenly drop upon a patch of shingle high above the water-line in a close compact flock, looking like a piece of variegated carpet, whose pattern thins as the circumference of it enlarges, and they scatter to feed on the blown seeds of the marram grass and other dune plants. Flo sets them going again by a mad rush into their midst, and comes back repentant rather than disappointed.

Yon two little shorebirds are busily running to and fro, often belly deep in the wash of a nearly spent wave ;

they look almost black. Our glasses reassure us they are purple sand-pipers (*Tringa striata*), irregular visit-ants to our East coast in October and November. You may depend on it they are not fast chums, for they are far too solitary in late autumn to war-rant a temporary companionship that is more than the result of an accident.

A huge flock of mixed gulls, among which are many greater black-backs, fine adult herring gulls, and a few common gulls, ride as at anchor—the majority are young black-backs in the sober grey of youth. They have been gorging themselves on stranded herrings, and are napping and gossiping away the lethargy which so often follows surfeit. We carefully scan the mile-long regiment for skuas, for we have heard of both Buffon's and Pomatorhines among them. We, how-ever, detect none of the robber-birds, who have doubtless also had their fill, and have, like the highwaymen of old, retired from the beaten track to enjoy their spoils in solitudes far beyond.

There are hundreds of dead and de-caying herrings thrown up at the tide-mark which, on examination, we find were bitten by dogfishes, while hang-ing enmeshed in the fishers' nets. The hungry dogfish bites out large chestnut-shaped pieces from the hapless fishes—

often the largest and fullest, and the mutilated carcasses are thrown back into the sea as useless, when the west winds draw them inshore. Quite a score scads (*Trachurus trachurus*) the "horse mackerel" of fishermen, be-strew the beach at intervals. I am never tired of examining the spiny-sided fellow, with his large and lustrous eye. I cannot say that I like his flesh, which is coarse and insipid : he is not as daintily flavoured as he is handsome in appearance. Sir Thomas Browne quaintly describes it— " of a mixed shape between a mackerel and a herring." The fishermen usually throw them overboard again.

But the hooded crows like the scad as they like dead domestic animals, and the guillemots that are, after severe gales, sometimes thrown ashore dead. Both hooded crows and guille-mots are in evidence ; of the former half a dozen are at this moment busily discussing something black a few hundred yards ahead. All save one are deeply interested in the object, the sixth surmounts a " swill " (fish basket) and acts *pro tem.* as sentry. And out just beyond the broken sea float and dive and paddle a number of rock-birds—auks certainly, but whether guillemots or razorbills we cannot define, so alike are they. When

I was a lad I found more dead razorbills washed up than guillemots : razorbills to-day are the exception ; we seldom find them. Yes ! the tidemark is a favourite hunting ground of mine. I've found dead chaffinches, rooks, larks, little auks, birds of prey, and even a woodcock and a French partridge there ; not to mention many a rare fish—Müller's scopelus, the four-bearded rockling, a huge conger that took two of us to carry it, the pear-crabs (*Hyas*), the porcelain crab, as well as *Portumnus*, *Corystes*, and *Pilumnus*. To-day there are stranded many shore crabs (*Carcinus mœnas*) of diversified colours, and a few hermit crabs, not to mention sundry *Echinodomerta* ; we discover also a dead and bedraggled gannet, a northern wanderer, not seldom seen on the herring grounds at this season, that had evidently come to grief by entangling itself in the meshes of a drift-net.

The hoodies take to flight at our approach ; they have been feasting on a poor little porpoise, scarcely weaned, that had got beyond the care of its mother and had met a similar fate to the gannet. A parcel of dunlins flit by : they are kept on the move by ramblers on the beach, but will find quieter, if more *dangerous* quarters farther south ; there are usually solitary gunners prowling in solitary places. Let us wait a while and see these amateur fishermen haul in the draw-net. We do so, and are much interested in seeing the bight of the net pulled in with its hundredweight of broken red seaweed, among which kick and flap and squirm a medley of whitings and flatfish—of no great size—a pound weight eel, a hundred tiny herrings, several lesser weevers, and a host of kicking shore-crabs. The catches are uncertain, and vary somewhat at each haul, and the fishermen are delighted at taking home a goodly fry apiece.

* * *

The cold penetrating drizzle of last night has given way to a brisker but drearier morning. Big broken clouds sweep overhead, as we tramp Broadwards from the all but deserted little station, along the sloppy roadway, where the brown dead leaves from the hedgerows lie soaking in patches in the puddles, and disconsolate chaffinches flit ahead, or turn off, flicking their variegated wings, into the fields as we disturb them in their quest for provender.

" A kind of a rafty mornin', 'bor ! " quoths a passing countryman, shrugging his shoulders, and wishing us " the seal o' the day."

The merriest bird we meet with to-

day is the optimistic redbreast, who
chinks his metallic notes pleasantly
enough from the hawthorns, where he
and his mates are hunting in crevice
and cranny for such hiding chrysalides
and dormant insects as may be not
too carefully concealed. And the
black-headed gulls, white as the snow,
and with feet like crimson, disputing
with the rooks at the heel of yonder
ploughmen, are too busily engaged
snatching up kicking grub and much-
surprised worm to be anything but
jubilant this morning. The bad
weather, that has kept the fishing fleet
at home for a long dreary week, meant
a scarcity of fishy fragments along the
foreshore or tumbling on the broken
waters.

There are not many birds to be seen,
as we press along ; here and there a
thrush or a redwing darts in and out
at the hedge bottom, where they have
been searching for *Helix* and *Limacidæ* ;
and a fieldfare from the topmost
branches, where the ripe red berries
of the hawthorn offer at present a
repast so plentiful, that the wasteful
fellows do not hesitate to fling away
two for every one they swallow ; a
month hence, and they may be mopishly
searching in the snow for what they
are now so carelessly strewing. Thrift
and forethought do not trouble our

little friends in feathers ; " sufficient
to the day " is to them the beginning
and the end of their simple theology.

Over the chilly waters of the Broad,
made dark and grim by the repeating
of the sombre greys of the passing
storm-clouds, sweep short, broken,
foam-edged waves, that push each
other peevishly and fretfully into the
bending reeds, to be checked and lost
among the myriad stems that shoot
upwards out of the quieter depths
beyond. There is no song of lark to
be heard ; and the harsh click of coot,
and fretful note of skulking moorhen,
although less frequent than in the
merrier days of summer, seem more in
harmony with the wildness of to-day.
A large flock of lapwings silently and
steadily pursue their way above-head,
making for the marshy lands beyond
the river way ; they have probably only
just come in from over the wild North
Sea, foretelling a speedy oncoming of
snowy days. The Broadmen yonder
are busy harvesting the reeds, whose
sapless leaves, brown and sere, are
hanging stiff and lifeless, and soughing
a queer rasping melody as the brisk
winds push through the reed-bed.
From their flat boat, moored to the
edge of the bed, a plank is pushed out
and rests on the shorn stubble as the
sickle-bearer proceeds ; he gathers a

small bundle in his left hand, and swings his weapon with the right. Tied in convenient sheaves, the reeds are shocked to dry, and afterwards stacked until required by the thatcher and the plasterer. The broadman grumbles every year of the damage done by the roosting starlings, which people the reed-beds by night in thousands. The sturdier but airier-stemmed reed-mace saw its ingathering in autumn, for the purposes of the maker of horses' collars, lifebuoys and other strange merchandise. Many a broad acre of reed and sedge and rush remains, to break in the wintry storms, and sink and form fresh layers of peaty soil each winter, to the steady but sure " up-growing " of the Broads.

*   *   *

A sharp stinging frost of four days' duration has " closed-in " the broad-land waters ; and a driving snow-storm has laid meadow and marsh and sedgy bank under a mantle of dazzling white. The woolly-topped reeds are white with it, like cotton-pods, and the leeward side of the old elms yonder looks black by comparison. Here and there a wherry mast upstands gauntly against the steely sky, and more than one ice-bound wherryman on the adjoining river is making him-self as content as he can well be ; an

upcurl of thin blue smoke coils out into the still atmosphere from the cabin chimney.

A walk round on the Broad margin, when the snow scrunches crisply underfoot, is by no means un-interesting either to the bird-watcher or to the gunner ; there are small flocks of wild ducks, and occasionally geese, wheeling around in search of likely feeding-grounds ; and unhappy snipes " *visp* " out erratically from cover at our approach. Some hooded crows, and with them a sprinkling of sharp-set rooks, are busy around some object in the open which our glasses reveal to us at once as a dead sheep. By what mishap it died and remained there we can but conjecture ; the birds are in luck's way to-day, and know it.

We put on our skates, and hasten to join in a merry scamper round, with a knot of folks who have come up from town to enjoy a bit of skating on the smooth clear surface, beneath which the waters look black and weird. A big pike now shot from under our very feet ; he knows of a thin place in the reeds close by where there is " breathing space," and will come back to it.

A poor little kingfisher, bright gleaming and distinctly noticeable, lying on its breast at the edge of a reed-clump, needs no epitaph above him to tell us of an untimely end by starvation and exhaustion. What few the unsentimental gunners fail to slay a long sharp winter will often kill off; poor things! We had little need to shorten their brief existence.

Here is a "wake" in the ice right in the middle of the Broad; the almost imperceptible ebb and flow in the channel which runs through it lifts and lets down the ice that would join hands, in vice-like grip, over it. The wild fowl know of and find out these weak places, and perform queer acrobatic bird-feats on them, keeping them more or less open.

Nine large white birds in the middle of yon "wake" we perceive through our glasses to be Bewick's swans, the smallest of their tribe. They are rather fonder of the margins of a stream than are the whoopers; and they are hardly so graceful in their movements. Hard by them float and dive a flock of pochards—"hard-fowl" that do not mind the cold so long as there is open water somewhere. They are busily feeding on the *Potamogeton pectinatum*; and are wary to a degree. The sportsman dislikes

their habit of rising singly, without "bunching."

A brown-headed bird, apart from the swans and pochards, now came to the surface, holding a struggling little roach in its mandibles. It is rather a rarity here, except in hard winters, and rarer still is the male bird, with its glossy green head and bushy crest. Yonder is a female Goosander—the "dun-diver" of the older generation of gunners.

One of our skates has become loosened; we sit down on the Broad margin to re-adjust it; but a flock of small brown birds that come tripping across the Broad and alight on some reed-tufts distracts our attention. We know them at once as bearded tits, "the pride of the Broads"; and we watch them as they scatter the loose snow and peck out seeds from the silken brushes, which please them well to-day, for the small mollusca they snatched from the mace-stems in their creepings above water in the pleasant summer time are now deep buried in the ooze below, sleeping their winter sleep.

It is beginning to snow right merrily again.

THE HERON.

From a water-colour by
Frank Southgate, R.B.A.

XXIII

THE NATURAL HISTORY OF PLACE-NAMES.

"Then, 'twas before my time, the Roman
At yonder heaving hill would stare;
The blood that warms an English yeoman,
The thoughts that hurt him, they were there."—A. E. HOUSMAN.

SUCH glimpses of the past as we can obtain from the names of places still in daily use on county byelaw placards, in "Bradshaw," and in similar most modern surroundings, are of peculiar interest to all who care for the unbroken life of the English people for the past eight or ten centuries, or the even deeper and more mysterious bond of union that links together our own mixed racial stock and those other dwellers in the land, races long absorbed or departed, who lived by the same swift rivers, and saw the same stars rise over the same brows of the hills. If it is really truth that we desire, and not merely the indulgence of prejudged ideas and fancies, a little knowledge of etymology is a very dangerous thing. Yet there is a great deal to be learnt of earlier England by a cautious and discriminating examination of the names of the rivers and hills, the towns and villages and farms, of our own day. This is not merely due to their essentially English character, which means so much to Englishmen whose duties take them beyond seas, so that any week's list of hunting fixtures is full of old delight and familiar suggestions, even to those who have never hunted in their lives. All these names alike are full of the air which blows over the islands which are our home; but yet, if we examine them with a closer vision, we can clearly read in some of them fragments of a bygone antiquity, and glimpses of history more ancient than any which is put connectedly together in books. There are rhythmical, polysyllabic names which no one who knows his country would ever look for outside Devonshire, any more than he would expect to find Llandyssil east of Severn, or Saxilby or Scrooby outside the limits of the ancient Danelagh.

One of the most noticeable features of rural nomenclature is the way in which, while the natural features, the rivers, the mountains, even the woods, are often called by their ancient Celtic names, the towns and villages (that is, the practical centres of life) bear the stamp of the incoming race, whether Saxon or Dane. In the case of the later Norman invasion, social life was already so strongly developed, and the invaders were relatively so few in number, that with the exception of certain feudal or religious strongholds, the Norman tongue has impressed few unmixed traces on our rural geography. Where Norman names occur, they usually mark a later ownership superimposed upon the original title-deed of a Saxon, as in Keynton Mandeville or Kingston Lisle. A large proportion of our present river-names are simple British words meaning " river " (Avon) or " water " (Usk, Esk, Ouse, Exe, Axe and Ock). And such names as Wishford, and Oxford, which is, of course, almost certainly the " ford across the water," and not the " ford of the ox," as tradition and the city arms still have it, seem to indicate that the aboriginal name for rivers was early taken into the speech of the Saxons, just as settlers in New Zealand or the Pacific Islands have adopted certain handy native words in recent days. The frequency with which many different English rivers are called by the same generic, rather than specific or individual, name, is vividly suggestive of the narrowness of the geographical outlook of the ancient dwellers in the land. Clearly, to each isolated community the river of its own immediate neighbourhood was

" *the* river," or even more vaguely, " the water " ; a man might be prepared to admit that other, outlandish folk might have rivers too, but he felt under no sort of necessity to allow for the possibility by any modification of idiom. It was not till people's horizons extended so far that confusion and inconvenience ensued unless every considerable stream had a name of its own that it became necessary to fit each with a separate description ; and thus arose such modern and arbitrarily formed titles as that of the Arun, which was carved out of the name of Arundel only a hundred or a hundred and fifty years ago, or of the Yeo, similarly formed from Yeovil, though the earlier name for both town and stream is known to have been Ivel, or Givel.

In attempting to decipher the meanings of the names of most towns, villages, and hamlets, it is necessary to proceed with the greatest caution ; for most of these names have been so worn down in the speech of centuries, and exposed to such transferences and confusions of shape, that it is hard to arrive at the original form and its derivation. Acute indeed of judgment would the antiquarian be who could profess to say with certainty whether each of our many places whose names now end in " don " and " ton " was derived from the word for a hill or the word for a homestead. " Marsh " and " march, " or border, are another pair of words fruitful in confusion ; so are the Saxon " wick," and the same word as derived from the Norse " vik," or creek. Yet, in spite of many such difficulties, reasonable, sound judgment, joined to a small Celtic and Saxon vocabulary, and a good eye for a countryside, will enable any one to arrive at a number of strong etymological probabilities among the place-names of any district, and the quest is a very interesting one. Bygone natural features take shape again before us, as the mind pierces the mists of time and change, with these ancient names of the countryside for its slowly illuminating light. We see, above all, a land of vast quagmires and forests, now long cleared and drained, except for the scantiest remnants ; and in the midst of this wilderness of marsh and wood, the scattered tracts and patches of dry and open ground stood out with a momentous contrast of importance which has long been merged and lost in the general reclamation of the soil. The " Isles " of Athelney, of Axholme, of Ely, show how their surrounding tracts of marsh once severed them from the habitable main-

land with almost the completeness of the sea. In Fenny Compton and Fenny Stratford, and many other such names, we see how similar tracts of fen once stamped their character on the landscape where now for ages there have spread wide cornlands or firm, hedged pastures. The same story is told by the emphasis of contrast in such names as Dry Sandford, which throws a vivid light on the general conditions of existence at the other Sandford in that region, Sandford-on-Thames. Dry Street, again, is a hamlet on the ridge of the Laindon Hills, that isolated group which gazes far and wide over the great Thames-side flats of the Southern Essex shore. The two plain words speak in the clearest possible manner of the former contrast of this firm hill-top soil with the weltering tidal waste which lay for leagues around, and of the importance, in such days as those, of the natural causeway along this gravelly ridge, which would be followed, as far as the hills extended, by travellers from west to east. In other names, such as the different Strettons and Stratfords, and in High Street, the long Westmorland mountain which bore the Roman road from Windermere to Penrith, we see how the eyes of the English invaders were impressed by the great paved highways of the Imperial era, which ran straight as a bolt through forest, moor and fen, in strong contrast to those more ancient, wavering highways, such as the Icknield track and the road known later as the Pilgrim's Way, which cling to the flank of the high chalk ridges, midway between the perils of the lower forests and the bleak hills' crown.

The traces of the great ancient woods lie everywhere in English place-names, preserved in many distinct words and several different speeches. Wotton, or " wood-town," is an ascription only less common than such bare generic names of human occupation as Ham, or Thorpe, or Stoke ; and other words for the wood, such as " hurst " and " holt " and " shaw," appear continually in different forms and combinations. We have Buckholt, or Buckhold, " the beechwood," surviving in places still true to this ancient element in the landscape ; Aldershot, till the War Office descended upon it a generation ago, was still a lonely waste where the alders clustered in the marshy bottoms ; and Shotover, the big hill over Oxford of which the attempted derivation from " château vert " is a fine example of mistaken methods, still preserves, in the thickets of untouched greenwood which

fringe its slopes, the remnants of the ancient " upper wood," or " wood above." Sometimes, as in Iron Acton in Gloucestershire, the name now recalls both the oak woods that surrounded the settlement, and the primitive ironworks for which they supplied the fuel ; and in other districts of great oak woods, such as the Weald of Surrey and Sussex, and the Forest of Dean, the " Hammer Ponds " recall the rude water-driven stamps of the Tudor and Stuart age, and such names as Cinderford and Coleford the far more ancient workings of which the " cinder heaps," which remained from the incomplete extraction of the earlier metal, themselves supplied the raw material for the still rough but more thorough processes of the Middle Ages. There are other words which emphasize rather the habitable openings or clearings in the forest than the wood itself ; such are the " royds " of Yorkshire, appearing in names (first place-names, and often, later, surnames) like Ackroyd, the " clearing in the oaks," and the " thwaites," one of the many common names in Cumbria which speak of the Scandinavian settlement of that region. Even more common and widespread is the termination " -ley," which also seems to indicate open, grassy land, either hanging beneath high ground, or enclosed by woodlands ; and " slade " is a word which also describes a narrower forest ride or clearing. Probably, in the Cumbrian district, we have yet another word for wood, in the Norse " lund " ; such, at least, is an accepted interpretation of Plumbland, near Aspatria, " the wood of plum-trees," that is, of sloes or blackthorns. Certain it is that the place-names of the whole lake region are so full of Scandinavian speech that it seems that this wild peninsula between the Morecambe and Solway sands was but little occupied by Angles pressing from eastward, and that the sea-rovers and their sons found a land lying virtually empty to their hand. Grisedale and Fairfield, for instance, are almost pure Norse for the valley of swine and the upland of sheep ; " force " and " seat-" or " satter-" everywhere represent the modern Norwegian words for a waterfall and a hill-farm, while Hest Bank, between Morecambe and Carnforth, is still the spot where the " horse " is driven down the shore to traverse the great sands of Lune and Kent, by the stake-marked trail. The outer Scottish islands were another great haunt of the Northmen as true settlers, not only as periodic invaders ; and in Loch Eford, in North Uist, we still find surviving the Norwegian " fjord," though the name has taken on a deceptively English look by the dropping of a single letter.

Where there was so much forest we may be sure that every early settler was keenly on the look-out for tractable, open ground to dwell in and to till. The existence in any neighbourhood of such clear and habitable sites at the time of the Saxon invasion is generally to be traced by the presence of the name of " field." The word in olden days did not carry its present meaning of a single fenced enclosure, but, like the " fjeld," or the " veldt," denoted a wide stretch of free and open country. It is still used in this original sense in certain parts of England, such as Middlesex and Berkshire, where, in spite of their occasional hedges, such bare, open tracts are locally known, for example, as Pinner, or West Hanney, or Steventon Field, each according to the name of the parish to which they belong.

In the furthest prehistoric days, the peoples of the dykes and burial-mounds sought their open, habitable country on the broad summits of the great chalk ranges ; by the time of the Saxon conquest, however, the land was already half-tamed, the British population had already pressed deep into the more fertile thickets of the lowlands, and we find that the " fields " which drew the new-comers are generally situated on lower ground, and often in close propinquity to " hursts " and " holts " and " leys." Wherever they occur, we can almost always trace the position and extent of some rocky or gravelly upland, or bare arable tract, still conspicuously treeless in its general aspect, which accounts for the ancient name ; and it is just in this kind of way that we are helped by still-existing place-names to reconstruct in mental vision the ancient scenes of England.

It is obvious that any striking con-trast or distinction in the landscape must often have influenced our fore-fathers in giving names to the places which they made their own ; and thus we should naturally expect a " wood " or a " field " to be singled out for definite mention rather at its end or its beginning, where it first struck upon the eye, than in its very midst or depth, where there was field or wood all round.   And this is just what hap-pens. From the northern walls of Bristol, for instance, there stretched for centuries a large tract of royal forest, covering the oval plateau that forms a kind of step between the deep Severn vale and the high Cotswold edge, and stretching as far as the hills

themselves. All this was the " King's Wood " ; but it is only at each extrem-ity of it that we find the actual place-name Kingswood, once in what is now a suburb of the western town, and once in a village twenty miles away, at the foot of the first Cotswold rise, and bounded by the limits of the " wood-town under the edge," or Wot-ton-under-Edge. So, too, it has been pointed out that the areas of Windsor Forest and of a large tract of the Weald are each fringed by a remarkable series of place-names ending in " field," and the reason of this seems clearly to lie in the striking contrast of the first clear, open ground with the depths of the great forest on the other side.

In many country places there are names which indicate the former pres-ence of birds and animals now vanished from the locality, or long extinct on British soil. The eagle and the raven have left their record in many places from which they have long disappeared, and testimony is borne to the later date at which the kite, now rarer than either, began its strangely sudden dis-appearance, by the houses of no great antiquity still scattered about the country which are known as " Kite's Nest Farm." The wolf and boar have left their names more certainly and commonly in Highland Scotch and

SAND DUNES.

From a Photograph by
Kenneth F. Bishop.

Irish localities than in England ; but Wolmer Forest is very possibly derived from the wolves' moor, or mere—for both words had formerly the same sense of waste, wet ground. The visits of the crane to the English haunts, where it is believed to have bred up to three hundred years ago, seem also to be perpetuated in such names as Cranmere Pool in the same wild tract, and Cranemoor Lake at Englefield in Berkshire. Much as the names have changed in the course of more than a thousand years, the surface of English earth has changed still more. But by studying the ancient designations given by our forefathers to their homes, we may look through their eyes at the ancient lineaments of the land, and see, though dimly and only in part, how it spread itself then to the view in that primitive and untamed era.

XXIV

RICHARD JEFFERIES

He is made one with Nature; there is heard
His voice in all her music, from the moan
Of thunder to the song of night's sweet bird;
He is a presence to be felt and known
In darkness and in light, from herb and stone;
Spreading itself where'er that Power may move
Which has withdrawn his being to its own;
Which wields the world with never-wearied love,
Sustains it from beneath, and kindles it above.
He is a portion of the loveliness
Which once he made more lovely. . . .

SHELLEY.

AMONG the earliest things which I can remember well is the North Wiltshire country, and the satisfaction of feeling that it was the country of Richard Jefferies. I was proud to find Ramsons in a hollow near Bassett Down—Jefferies had not found it, as he confesses somewhere ; and to hear a labourer call the Marsh Marigold " water bubble " and " crazy " —Jefferies had said that the people were ignorant of so common a flower. Several years passed before I could believe that he was dead, and I remember thinking that a tall, lean man who ran well with the V.W.H. hounds —he had a glorious view halloo—was Jefferies, though that was as late as 1892. I expected to see him as a man might expect to see Pan in Arcadia. Resting sometimes from heat or rain in an old church at Wroughton, or Wanborough, or Lydiard Millicent, I used to think of him, and repeated with funny religious fervour the words at the end of *The Amateur Poacher* :

"Let us get out of these indoor narrow modern days, whose twelve hours somehow have become shortened, into the sunlight and the pure wind. A something that the ancients called divine can be found and felt there still."

Even the "lardy cakes" from a village baker's seemed finer food because Jefferies had known them and deplored their increasing rarity. Anything good or pleasant that I noticed in that countryside seemed to belong by right to him : as when in February, while the roads were heavy, I heard a little village girl say that it would be a good thing when the cuckoo came and picked up all the mud and made a clean Spring. Not many of the people knew his books : fewer still knew anything of the man ; and what they knew was not easily accessible. Country people do not formulate and announce their tastes and affections. They know their native fields, but do not talk of them any more than two hundred years ago men wrote of them. I think that some of them thought of Jefferies as a priest who was not to be vulgarly discussed, but that others held him to be an heretical interpreter who had disclosed too much. I never met one who was ready to make money or glory out of reminiscences or even inventions. One who had been at school with Jefferies would not say a word to satisfy the enthusiasm of a timid and youthful inquirer. Perhaps there were not many obvious things to reveal. Readers of the *Eulogy* guess as much. Jefferies was hardly of a nature that ran much risk of events and adventures. Those who really knew him would probably not undertake to explain or supplement what his books tell us. And now I daresay that is best. He shall be one of the few modern men who have escaped publicity and not renown. He shall be as Sir Thomas Browne is— a man whom only his books prove to have existed—who preserved the mystery of authorship, and may one day come to be as mythical as Virgil seemed to be to the Middle Ages. In mythopœic times he would probably have been a wood god in a few generations, or have had a statue as the genius of the little willowy River Ray. As he says of farmer Iden in *Amaryllis at the Fair* :

"It was his genius to make things grow—like sunshine and shower ; a sort of Pan, a half-god of leaves and boughs, and reeds and streams, or sort of Nature in human shape, moving about and sowing Plenty and Beauty."

And yet Jefferies is a personality. I do not mean that he had a tricky, suave, and apparently intimate style ; he had not : at his best, he was apt and direct ; but he could, and many times did, write abominably without caring at all. Nor do I mean that it is easy to get to know him and like him through his books : it is not easy to know him, and not always possible to like him. But I mean that in reading any one of his books I have always had a sense of a man behind it, of a man whom to know would be to set a higher value than ever upon his work. What is more—readers are always receiving hints that the man is great, and that his work is sometimes hardly more than a faulty gospel by a not always careful or precise listener to the prophet's words. In the end, readers should come to have an admiration for the personality of Jefferies which it is not a simple matter to trace ; and in its turn this admiration will compel them to set a value upon his ordinary work which is sometimes not easily to be justified.

Certainly, this sense of Jefferies' personality is not due to anything I have read by other men about his life.

He was born at Coate (pronounced something like Court and something like Cart), near Swindon, in 1848 ; his father being the last of his family to own Coate Farm. Apparently the family was odd, reserved, independent, and unsuccessful. From the age of four until the age of nine he lived at Sydenham with an aunt, and was at school there. Then he went home, and was at a Swindon school. But all that we know of his childhood is that he " read everything," that he was much out of doors, and that he was sensitive, not strong, but masterful, and of a quick temper that easily passed into tenderness. At sixteen he and another boy ran away, and spent a week in France—intending to go on and walk to Moscow ; returning to England, they tried to get to America, but failed : we have only the pitiful and senseless outline of a good tale. He continued to read and to draw ; one room at Coate Farm was given up to him. It is likely that reading was to him an adventure that was good for its own sake. He liked it ; he must have absorbed much ; but, though Besant says that " it is evident from his writings that he had read a great deal," he became the least bookish of writers. He sought out what suited him rather than the beautiful, and his few quotations and derived passages seem to be entirely his own. He had no kind of literary admiration ; a book was life and it helped him to express his own life. Between the years 1869 and 1877 he became a reporter to *The North Wilts Herald* and other local papers, and did other journalistic work. He wrote a history of Swindon. He wrote stories which were not so romantic as they prove him to have been. He wanted to be a London journalist : he sent novels to the publishers. His health was bad ; but in the worst times he believed in his own " ultimate good fortune and success." In 1872 he wrote his excellent letter on the Wiltshire labourers to *The Times:* in 1873 he wrote for *Fraser's* on " The Future of Farming." In 1874 he married, and in the same year began publishing novels at his own expense. But he went on writing practical country essays, and then suddenly found that it was easy for him to describe the country. From that time most of his work was devoted to the country books which we know. He lived in the country or at Surbiton, moving rather often. He met with a fair literary success—that is to say, he was busy, uncomfortable, and poorer than his neighbours, during the best years of his life—until the long illness before his death in 1887. He had few friends, but of the nature of his intercourse with them there is little sign. He walked and wrote and suffered. Probably he was brought up in a conventional religious way ; but he was apparently a man who had no understanding of religions ; his reported death-bed prayers are only painful, and not surprising, in their irrelevance. This is nearly all that has been told about Jefferies, and it is certainly one of the most astonishing failures among biographies to show us—which is their business—the life out of which the books arose.

If we knew more of the outward life of Jefferies we should have at least one advantage : we should be able to understand *The Story of My Heart* more completely. As that wonderful autobiography now stands, it is somewhat incoherent and imperfectly intelligible. The only English book which can be compared with it is Wordsworth's *Prelude*, and that is simpler and less equivocal by far. Jefferies' book is almost as incapable of thorough analysis as a symphony ; and perhaps it is fairest to read it as a boy reads it at the age of nineteen or twenty, since in that way the excrescences lose their importance and the most difficult pages are volatilized so as to have something like a due part in the result. The most noticeable thing in the book is perhaps the writer's independent emotion and thought, the frank and brave impressionism of his view of life. He claims himself " to have erased from his mind the traditions and learning of the past ages, and to stand face to face with nature and the unknown." He is an isolated human being looking at Nature with the help only of genius and of ancestors who had looked at it incuriously for generations. He does not say, as he might have done, that Wordsworth's view or his contemporary Tennyson's view was this or that, and that he differs from them or goes beyond them here or there. He leaves books behind him, and goes out on to the Downs, a more lonely man than was ever there before. He becomes " lost, and absorbed into the being or existence of the universe," and he prays that he may have something from sea and earth and sky by which his soul may be enlarged. He strives after some secret (which he believes to be hiding there) by which the human form "may achieve the utmost beauty." He wishes to reach a mode of life in which the mind and soul can be more continuously and fittingly em-

ployed than they now are : and " to furnish the soul with the means of executing its will, of carrying thought into action." As a field for this new life, he believes in " a nexus of ideas of which nothing is known." There are passages in his discourse that will remind readers of M. Maeterlinck of *The Buried Temple*. But he is opposed by Nature. Lonely himself, he imagines an equal loneliness for mankind. Nature is " distinctly anti-human " ; many of its parts, as for example, the creatures of the sea, " call up a vague sense of chaos, chaos which the mind revolts from." In his fine, ironical romance, *After London*, the inexhaustible strength and hostility or indifference of Nature are suggested by his descriptions of the relapse of men and fields into barbarism. In *The Story of my Heart* he dreams far forward of man journeying lonely and with his fate in his own hands. And yet his sympathy with the universe is extraordinary. It is no wonder that he was remote from religions of the past, for he seems at times to be on the edge of a religion entirely new. Except Shelley, no one so much as he was aware of the universe. He says himself that he was " conscious of the earth, the sea, the sun, the air, the immense forces working on " ; his soul " was as strong as the sea, and prayed with the sea's might "; and "the earth and sun," he says, "were to me like my flesh and blood, and the air of the sea life." We might almost think that he has

"The cloudy winds to keep
Fresh for the opening of the morning's eye,"

and is indeed a minister of Nature.

He seems to have thought some things inhuman even in the works of men. Pictures are "flat surfaces"; they have nothing to do with the advance of mind of which he dreams. But "the knee in Daphnis and Chloe and the breast "—" the glowing face of Cytherea in Titian's Venus and Adonis" —"Juno's wide back and mesial groove" —"Cytherea's poised hips unveiled for judgment "—these things were related to the forces of the world; they were to him as "the outcry of the hunted hare" to Blake; they called up the same thirst which he had on the grass, in the sun, and by the sea. The marble men and women of Greece had something of himself and of what he longed for.

"These were they," he says, "who would have stayed with me under the shadow of the oaks while the blackbirds fluted and the south air swung the cowslips. They would have walked with me among the reddened gold of the wheat. They would have rested with me on the hill-tops and in the narrow valley grooves of ancient times. They would have listened with me to the sob of the summer sea drinking the land. They had thirsted of sun, and earth, and sea, and sky. Their shape spoke this thirst and desire of mine—if I had lived with them from Greece till now I should not have had enough of them. Tracing the form of limb and torso with the eye gave me a sense of rest. . . ."

The *Venus Accroupie* in the Louvre recalled the loveliness of Nature. He says that the light and colour of summer air were to him "always on the point of becoming tangible in some beautiful form," while the statue in turn expressed the colour and the light and "the deep aspiring desire of the soul for the perfection of the frame in which it is encased." In the presence of that statue, too, the thought of something beyond the old forms of life returns; "the conception of moral good," he says, "did not satisfy one while contemplating it"; and though he cannot name his new ideal good, he thinks that it will in some way be associated with "the ideal beauty of Nature."

The brow of Cæsar keeps him to the same theme. The conspirators destroyed "the one man filled with mind."

They should have tried to keep him alive ; their act interrupted a divine curve of intelligence which Jefferies seems to connect with the progress he desires. It amazes him that in twelve thousand years men have not built a house or filled a granary for themselves, or organized themselves for their own comfort. He still hopes for a time when " no one need ever feel anxiety about mere subsistence," dreaming of great spaces of ease and happiness in which men may capture the beautiful and good. Yet he is himself greedy of physical life, and envies Ninus and Semiramis and Nero, and the American lumbermen felling trees. " Fulness of physical life," he dares to say, " causes a deeper desire of soul-life." He wishes to be always with earth and sun and sea and stars. The contour and curve and outline of an ideal human form " indicate immortality." Death and disease do not sadden so much as they anger him ; yet he hopes.

Such is the personality which we must feel in reading Jefferies, if we are to know the true worth of his books. *The Story of My Heart* is the key to the rest ; for in it he shows us the value which he sets upon things ; it is a lexicon from which we learn the meaning of words in his vocabulary.

He was one of the great ones who now and then rediscover those ancient matters—the mortality of man and the strangeness of the world. All his books are full of them, if they are read aright. A little thought or personal confession comes in the midst of what seems to the careless reader to be dull and undigested observation, and it shows the man and casts a rich shadow over the writing round about. *Amaryllis at the Fair* is very full of them. *Amaryllis* is a fine novel which is probably not much longer to be neglected because it is unlike Besant's. If it is to be neglected, I see no use in all our modern reading of Lamb and Borrow and the Elizabethans. In Jefferies' sympathy with all life, he comes near to Blake ; in his sense of the visible world, of earth and sea and sky, in which men are placed, he is with Mr. Hardy. But nobody so much as he continually reminds us that Nature truly lives. He never condescends to it, never treats landscape as a mere picture, though there are pages in which weariness or necessity has made him appear to be a sportsman or a naturalist. He never intrudes upon Nature in style or thought.

How could he, when he had achieved that harmony with her which gives the opening chapters of *The Dewy*

Morn, for example, a religious sensuousness ? If there is any book in which the rapture of love appears so clearly to be part of the divine rapture of " Earth, ocean, air, beloved brotherhood " as in the passages which I am going to quote, I do not know it.

"She was bathing in the beauty of the morning—floating upheld on the dewy petals. A swimmer lies on the warm summer water, the softest of couches, extended at full length, the body so gently held that it undulates with the faint swell. So soft is the couch it softens the frame, which becomes supple, flexible, like the water itself.

" Felise was lying on the flowers and grass, extended under the sun, steeped in their sweetness. She visibly sat on the oak trunk—invisibly her nature was reclining, as the swimmer on the sun-warmed sea. Her frame drooped as the soul, which bears it up, flowed outwards, feeling to grass, and flower, and leaf, as the swimmer spreads the arms abroad, and the fingers feel the water. She sighed with deep content, dissolving in the luxurious bath of beauty.

" Her strong heart beating, the pulses throbbing, her bosom rising and regularly sinking with the rich waves of life ; her supple limbs and roundness filled with the plenty of ripe youth ; her white, soft, roseate skin, the surface where the sun touched her hand glistening with the dew of the pore ; the bloom upon her—that glow of the morn of life—the hair more lovely than the sunlight ; the grace unwritten of perfect form—these produced within her a sense of existence—a consciousness of being, to which she was abandoned ; and her lips parted to sigh. The sigh was the expression of feeling herself to be.

" To be ! To live ! To have an intense enjoyment in every inspiration of breath ; in every beat of the pulse ; in every movement of the limbs ; in every sense !

" The rugged oak-trunk was pleasant to her. She placed her hand on the brown, stained wood—stained with its own sap, for the bark had been removed. She touched it ; and so full of life was her touch that it found a pleasure in that rude wood. The brown boulder-stone in the lane, ancient, smoothed, and ground in times which have vanished like a cloud, its surface the colour of old polished oak, reflecting the sun with a dull gleam—the very boulder-stone was pleasant to her, so full of life was her sense of sight.

" There came a skylark, dropping over the hedge, and alighted on a dusty level spot in the lane. His shadow shot a foot long on the dust, thrown by the level beams of the sun. The dust, in shadow and sunshine—the despised dust—now that the lark drew her glance to it, was pleasant to see.

"All things are joyously beautiful to those who feel themselves to be ; but it is only given to the chosen of nature to know this exceeding delight. . . .

"With her soul grew her love ; this purest of love, and yet strongest of passions. Her young limbs became stronger, her young chest broader, her shoulders and her back finer : a firmer pulse throbbed in her veins. So the soul enlarged as day after day of musing passed, and those long half-conscious reveries which are to the soul as sleep to the frame. She rejoiced in the morning and the sunrise, and felt the glowing beauty of the day ; she saw the night and its stars, and knew the grandeur of the earth's measured onward roll eastwards, the hexameter of heaven.

"She saw these things because at her birth love was born with her ; the flame was lit with her life, and must burn till the end. . . ."

His immense, simple personality is at one with the oak and the grass as if he were somehow involved in their beauty and life. He seems to be conscious of all life that is about him, down to the plants in the arch of a bridge which is lit by reflection from the water. His merely physical sight is wonderful ; he has confessed that it was sometimes painful not to be able to cease to see. In *Bevis*, the boys' book for all who admit to being or having been boys, he says of Bevis that he never forgot the sun and stars ; he " lived not only out to the finches and the swallows, to the far-away hills, but he lived out and felt out to the sky." Even if that book were not the only boys' book which is without a trace of condescension in matter and manner, it would be invaluable as a proof of Jefferies' observation.

No other writer leaves us with such a sense of his infinite riches as Jefferies. A book like *Wild Life in a Southern County* seems almost to exhaust a broad strip of English country, and yet it exhausts Jefferies no more than the fields. Hardly a sentence is given to anything but fact ; yet the total impression is as rich in sentiment as in fact. If he did not set everything down, I feel that all Nature was at his right hand. But, at the same time, no other great writer surely had a fainter vocation. He was so steeped in life that it was an effort, and a painful one, to write. His Amaryllis envied neither the great musician nor the great painter ; she was " a passive and not an active artist by nature ; " so was he. He says that could he choose, he would go on seeing beautiful things, and not writing. He calls Nature formless ; he likes to point out how many fields an artist could make nothing of ; and often he seems to have deliberately reproduced this formlessness which (out of compliment) he has called inartistic. There are pages, in *The Gamekeeper* and *Nature near London* and other books, which were forced out of him by his need of a certain income. Some of his transitions are inexcusable except on this ground. He must often have been offended by paper and pen, as he tells us that the sun was offended. " The sunlight," he says, " put out the books as it put out the fire." Yet his big, simple moods will seem to a true lover to enchant his least perfect pages.

For he was like the oak tree, which has but three or four moods—when it is bare, when the buds glow, when it is green, when it is ruddy, when it is dead. These moods are all-important to him, and to the tree, and therefore they are beautiful. But the beauty is not always quite human. It is as if he wrote with clay and not with ink. He did not desire the little beauty that is far withdrawn from Nature, and often inspired not so much by its true strangeness as by mere novelty. He would omit nothing by choice. He would seem to have been Nature's advocate, and to have striven to say all. Of course he failed. But his effort is one of the most splendid things recorded in written words, and we have only to read such things as the opening of *My Old Village* to admit that among his other gifts, Nature had given him a great manner, the manner of perfection.

XXV

THE WEASELS: WEASEL—STOAT—POLECAT—MARTEN

> "   . . . And so we sat, and ate,
> And talked old matters over . . .
> Then touched upon the game, how scarce it was
> This season.
>
> —TENNYSON.

ON the desk before me is a weasel's skeleton: the long, sinuous, snakelike body fitted to follow its prey through the labyrinths of any retreat; the flat skull, hard, yet slightly framed to admit of brain capacity for any mischief; the formidable jaws, armed with canines, delicate and keen as rapiers. All the story and terror of the creature are laid bare in these dry bones. I picked it from a fence, where it hung with about a dozen others. Similar little groups adorned the fences round about. Some were fresh, as though killed that morning; showing that additions were being made from day to day.

Such shambles are established as a warning to their kindred to flee from the wrath to come: it is a way keepers have. They are usually confined to one place. Those, I understood, were meant to impress the proprietor, should he pass that way, with the keeper's watchfulness and devotion, to duty. It was a case of eye service.

There was a reason for this raid on the weasels. The rabbits were not kept down, as on other estates. They were allowed free grazing, and expected to pay for their living. Systematically trapped, they proved a regular and valuable asset. Each death was so much loss, each weasel meant so many rabbits saved. Therefore these effigies before me; and the other groups on the fences.

I looked over the grinning heads, with their eternal unconcern—their appetites appeased, their instincts asleep. The abundance of the rabbits was manifest. Their number was legion. At midday, these twilight feeders squirted in every direction. A patch of woodland was honeycombed with their tunnels. To the teeming warren they could return on the least alarm. The security was absolute. Did these dry bones live, and into these gaping nostrils were the breath once more breathed, were instincts and appetites lit afresh within; the emancipated weasels would make no sensible gap.

Already, a complaint was being raised of the destruction of the young grass for the cattle. When the pasture came to be sold, the bidding would not be keen nor the price high, if indeed an offer could be got. Apart from that, the disturbance of nature's little adjustments is ignorant. It is all a huge mistake this pillorying. Rabbits can, and do, overbreed and overcrowd, even to their own hurt. Weasels are present only in such numbers as will neither imperil the abundance of their own food, nor the interests of the proprietor. They are not innocent : they are deadly : killing out of all proportion to their size. Ruthlessly dainty, they sip a little, and go elsewhere.

A rabbit was lying on the grass. The hand stretched down to lift it by the ears was more hastily withdrawn. It was carmine stained. These keen canines had found their way in somewhere about the back of the head, through the soft, porous part of the skull. A wonderful anatomist he shows himself to be, in the knowledge of just where to strike. In fighting with his own kind, he does not bite there. He had sipped, and left the stain.

Another day, the wound had been given. Disturbed, ere he could go further, the weasel had retired into cover. On the approach of footsteps the rabbit rose, and ran ! not straight, but zigzag. The bite into the cerebellum had reached some source of control, had destroyed the sense of direction. So rabbits are known to zigzag, in their pathetic efforts to keep ahead. Partially satisfied, the weasel may let it go, as a cat plays with a mouse, only to follow it up again. In no case, perhaps, is the bite fatal : it bleeds its victim to death. In the draught is a certain Epicureanism. Blood-thirstiness is the badge of all the tribe.

Still, a third day, a rabbit lay there. Mindful of the crimson stain, the hand approached cautiously. The rabbit bolted from under the fingers : this time straight away. Either it was palsied by the enemy on its track ; or the interference came between the capture and the bite. The keeper's case was that almost any day a rabbit might be looked for, which had been under the tender mercies of the weasel. It was impossible to lead him beyond the obvious fact : to convince him that this was in the plan, and it might be better not to interfere. He only shook his red beard from side to side. All very sad, no doubt ; but nature is not sentimental, any more than she

THE STOAT.

From a photograph by
Charles Reid, Wishaw.

is vindictive. Health is in the bite.

With more than the address of an acrobat, and a little of the grotesqueness of the clown, a weasel was disporting itself. Leaping into the air, it curved its lithe body, as though to pass through an invisible hoop. Sometimes it varied the performance by strange, if graceful, contortions. A little distance away two rabbits were squatted, like the spectators at a circus. What did it mean ? One could partly guess. From the undergrowth, the weasel had seen the rabbits out in the clearer part of the wood. Indisposed to a stern chase, and a hunt through the galleries of holes, it adopted another form of tactics. Suddenly, it sprang into the air, returned on its leap, and so entered on its display : varying the performance, as it threatened to lose its glamour. Instead of bolting, as they might otherwise have done, the rabbits sat on. It may be that they were spellbound, or simply curious : we are not sufficiently acquainted with the minds of the lower creatures to say. A series of bounds, ever a little nearer, and the end would come.

The stoat affects somewhat rougher ground, and such was near. None is among the victims. It is larger, with a characteristic touch of black at the end of the tail. These things in themselves are not sufficient to strike the unobservant in the summer, when it is so like the weasel. The main difference is in the change of body colour. In the winter it wears white ; all but the touch of black, which remains. With the coat it changes its name, and is better known as the ermine. Two coats are not uncommon, but it is exceptional in having two names. If somewhat hardly used in its lifetime, it has a blessed hereafter on the backs of the great on state occasions. With a certain delightful irony, this statute breaker appears as a symbol to lend grace and authority at the administration of the law.

On an estate where rabbits are a perennial source of income, the raising of ermine might be another asset. Each stoat permitted to live on, till the winter snows lay on its coat, would more than pay its summer keep. The weasels seldom turn white. The combination of ermine and rabbit would be perfect. In the face of persecution weasel and stoat are there to stay. If they have larger broods than the other wild carnivores, they are set over prolific races not only in the teeming warrens, but under the grass of the pasture land. The proportion is not disturbed. Notwithstanding the difference in size, these two may be classed as the lesser weasels. The wide gap which comes after places them together.

There are, or were, greater weasels— two also. In the traditions of the place, and the memory of the oldest inhabitant, lingers the polecat. This is the only kind of life it now has. If enquiry were carefully made, I daresay it would be found that more than a quarter of a century has elapsed since the last was trapped. The case is typical of other estates, and the condition of things throughout.

If we search for something distinctive of the polecat, we shall find it in what is less pleasant than the snow-white winter fur of the ermine. All the tribe are more or less provided with a scent gland ; but in this is it most offensive. To the unpleasing odour it sends forth when irritated, or in danger, it owes its common name of foumart. The obvious use of such a weapon is for the protection of slow animals against swifter enemies. When it may not flee, it must drive away. It has no natural enemies here, save man, who can shoot : the gland is a survival. The polecat is the slowest among our native weasels.

From its slowness, it is the least destructive—easily overtaken, it finds it hard to overtake. More largely than the rest, it lives on such slow creatures as frogs. It is not good at a stern chase. With larger quarry, it adopts the slow creature's resource of tactics.

Some of its ways throw light on the incident of the weasel in the wood. From the fence it watches partridge or pheasant feeding in the field. To cross the open were hopeless ; much more hopeless in the case of winged creatures than with the rabbit. No stern chase would avail. Therefore, it turns acrobat to the bird ; which lifts its head from searching for grain to see this great sight. A series of leaps and evolutions, so nicely judged as not to excite suspicion, bring the performer near enough for the fatal leap. The polecat is not a prolific breeder. It has but three young at a birth.

The second of our larger weasels differs from the first in everything but size. The marten affects nearness to cover, and may in a sense be regarded as our woodland weasel. When hard pressed, it will climb trees ; should it want a roosting pheasant, it will climb without being specially hard pressed. It is more agile even than the wild cat. It can afford to leave the frog to sing its song of the marshes, and the field vole to pipe to the growth of the young grass, while it presses on after the quicker footed. With no better will, its greater size makes it a match for nobler than the weasel's quarry, its greater fleetness makes it more formidable than the polecat. It is perhaps the most destructive of the tribe.

Soft and pleasing is the toning of its coat : the pure white of the male's breast, sometimes tinged with as pure a yellow in the female. For the foul odour of the foumart, it bears about with it the grateful smell of the green pine wood. In shape and every movement it is infinitely attractive. The wild cat slouches, the fox sneaks, the otter on land shuffles. The marten alone moves in faultless curves, or ripples with grace incarnate.

Yet it is more than a quarter of a century since the last of them moved in the twilight, across the pasture, to reach yonder wood. Perhaps was strung up on some olden fence, to show the proprietor of the time how extremely diligent his then keeper was. Not at any time, nor anywhere, were they more than a check on the teeming life. Where they abounded, prey did, proportionately, more abound. In the four years following 1837, were killed in Glengarry, each year, some sixty martens and twenty-five polecats. These numbers show how great the destruction, and how small the excuse. Glengarry is so large an area, that, unless these creatures had been seen, or trapped, their presence would not have been known, their food never missed. On a small estate like this, the proportion would be two polecats and four martens.

Among the mere fragments of our wild mammals left to us, the weasels are interesting, in that they form a small, perhaps, but a very complete group. The attempt represented in these shambles to get rid of the smallest of them seems to show a very narrow and mistaken sense of self-interest. And what shall I say of the want of taste, which, as far as this and other estates are concerned, has banished the largest of weasels, and most graceful of wild creatures.

XXVI

THE SQUIRREL

"The old fir forests heated by the sun,
Their thought shall linger like the lingering scent,
Their beauty haunt us, and a wonderment
Of moss, of fern, of cones, of rills that run . . .
—EUGENE LEE-HAMILTON.

WHO does not know the squirrel, by sight at least—that jolly little fellow with the beautiful rich rufous fur coat, and plumy tail! How well-groomed he is, always neat, smart, and presentable. And well he may be, for his time is ever abundant; he has no trains to catch, no office to reach ; he scarcely knows a care or a worry, save, perhaps, when he sees the hazel nuts fall with the blight. Yet even in the worst seasons there are plenty for his needs; and the labour of collecting them and sorting the sound from the faulty is surely then more interesting ; for it is the nature of all animals, from man downwards, to prize the more that which is scarce.

The squirrel's life is a round of pleasure and ease. Few are his foes —save men. In fact, I know no creature of the woods and fields which has less to fear from his neighbours. He is able to run for a short distance at a speed which enables him to gain the haven of the handiest tree when pursued, while in climbing and passing from tree to tree he knows no rival ; even a stoat, clever climber that he is, would look clumsy in comparison. Of course, a stoat could easily climb to a squirrel's nest, and the owner would have no chance against such a foe, though I have never seen or heard of an instance of a stoat killing a squirrel in its nest.

When the wild winds of winter moan relentlessly through the woods, and the birds are hard put to it to find a secure roost on the rime-gripped twigs, the squirrels doze in their cosy nests, dreaming doubtless of the days which are coming — promised days when they shall build special nests for their families of blind, naked, rat-like little ones. Yet during bursts of fickle sunshine squirrels wake, and go forth to visit their store-houses, wondering whether spring is come.

Imagine you are strolling through a wood on one of those glorious days that remind one of ideal spring-time, a day when the bees buzz joyously as they flit between the golden palm blooms. Wander where you will, on all sides the hum of the joy of life greets you.

In almost every oak and larch there is evidence of squirrels; here and there maybe the falling crumbs from a meal of Scotch fir-apples expose the whereabouts of the feaster. The frequent nests lead you to think the light-hearted builders are far more numerous than they really are.

The outsides of the nests are woven of moss and lichen, the snug interiors being lined with soft grasses and the inner fibres of bark. If aught of the British boy is still within you, and you have no respect for your trousers, you climb to investigate some of these nests, only to find the majority are no longer used; and if you are not accustomed from the ground to detect new nests, which are of a well-rounded, plump appearance, you are likely to have many a tiring climb before you find a squirrel at home. So soon as one squirrel-house shows signs of a faulty roof—squirrels hate wet—another is built; for the merry squirrels know nothing of ground-rents or the price of land. Besides, many of these dome-shaped nests are simply sleeping-places, and convenient refuges from enemies and the weather. In summer I have noticed that fresh, green-leaved boughs are constantly added to the nests, evidently for shade.

Here are two words of warning to those who would thrust their hands into a squirrel's drey: The yellow, curved, rat-like teeth of an adult squirrel are not to be despised; and, spotlessly clean as they are in all else, squirrels are generally infested with fleas. For all that, they make charming pets when caught young. I know no fairer sight than to watch the playing of a kitten and squirrel, brought up together by an obliging mother-cat. I know, at the present time, a labourer who reared three squirrels, and has made them a beautiful, roomy cage with an exercise wheel, by means of which the squirrels work a clever model of the roundabouts seen at village fêtes. When squirrels are confined as pets they must be kept scrupulously clean; but much better is it to give them their freedom after a time, though it is impossible to insure their staying at home. Not even the regal bearing of the cock pheasant in the full glory of his courting plumage, as he crosses the lawn to the feeding-place, can surpass in attractiveness the frequent sight of squirrels about the grounds of your house.

The cry of the squirrel is peculiar, being used chiefly, I think, as a note of alarm. I have heard but one good imitation of this squirrel note—the sound made by squeezing the hollow, rubber doll with a mouth in its back which memories of childhood will recall.

A squirrel, as a rule, utters this cry when you expel him from his nest; or when you stand motionless, watching his movements, and he runs on to a branch just above your head, as if curious to know what the strange-looking object is. Sometimes he emphasises each utterance with a simultaneous stamp of both front feet, as if to see whether you have the power to move, or will take fright and flee from his private haunts. Probably he thinks you have been spying out the direction of his storehouse.

A glass case containing an unnaturally fat quadruped fastened to a branch, clutching a giant nut in its hand-like front paws, and with cheeks strongly suggestive of tooth-ache, gave me my first introduction to the squirrel. But, unfortunately (as I then thought) the glass case and its caricatured contents belonged to somebody who did not want to part with it, and the longing to possess a similar trophy, which I might call my very own, seized me forthwith. This covetous spirit quickly led to squirrel-hunting. Yet I think that, on the whole, the squirrels enjoyed the chevies as much as we boys, for our weapons were generally limited to handy stones, chunks of half-rotten wood, and catapults which did not come up to the expectations we formed of them during the process of manufacture. In those eager, breathless scrambles through the undergrowth, as we followed the nimble squirrels, half jumping, half flying from limb to limb and tree to tree, we learnt of their instinctive ways of escaping their enemies. Thus, when we imagined we had a squirrel at bay in a small, isolated tree, we found, on one of us climbing the tree, that it would jump to the ground, and always beat us in the race among the hazel stumps to the nearest impossible tree. And when we brought a terrier with us, any squirrel forced to the ground would dive into the nearest rabbit burrow. Their quickness of sight was so marvellous that some of the squirrels seemed to take positive delight in dodging us round the tree trunks till we almost thought they must have vanished altogether.

But as our years increased, and we became possessed of weapons more effective, we came to leave this squirrel-hunting, for the stronger sentiment of sport and fair play asserted itself; we knew that when slaughter became easy, regular, and mechanical, sport was absent—the hunt ended.

Few indeed are the crimes which can be brought home to the squirrels; one only is common to them all—that they decapitate young fir-trees. Now, however, there can be but few localities where the squirrel population is large enough to menace the fir nurseries. I have known individual squirrels with depraved tastes—one which we had caught and kept a prisoner for a week escaped, though we finally ran him to earth in a hole in an old apple-tree. In this hole we knew there was a flourishing brood of tits, the bulk of which this squirrel had slain and some he had devoured. Perhaps his temporary confinement had turned his brain—at any rate, let us hope so. I once saw a squirrel cross a road in front of my feet with a very young pheasant in its mouth, which, however, by no means proves that the squirrel was the murderer of the pheasant. I should say that it had found the bird— evidently about a week old—dead, and thought it would, by reason of its soft down and small feathers, be a useful addition to the fabric of its drey. I remember, too, a squirrel which was seen to visit a pheasant's nest, and to carry an egg away at each visit. These are the only instances of trespassing in pursuit of game or game eggs I can urge against the squirrels. To say that squirrels are injurious to the preservation of game is, I am certain, a gross injustice to them generally. I suggest that the few which have been caught red-handed have not been as other squirrels—why should not they have their delusions as well as higher mammals ?

But though squirrels are the most innocent and least shy of woodland creatures, there is not to-day one squirrel where a quarter of a century ago there were a hundred. Squirrels make no secret of their lives, they like to be admired—at a respectable distance, they love the hours of daylight, revelling in the sunbeams, and cover not their incomparable grace of movement with the mantle of night. No longer can I see the squirrels as in boyhood—we called them " squgs "— basking in the sunshine in the tall larches, swaying in the life-giving breezes of morning, their russet red a soft contrast to the grateful green of the larch tops. But this scarceness of the merry squirrels—why is it ? Nature surely intended them for ornaments, not to be preyed upon regularly by their fellow creatures, nor to be annihilated by man.

With the modern shooting man and his four-figured game-bags came the modern gamekeeper, and as this new host spread over the country-side, the squirrels went before that one, short-sighted, selfish idea—game and nought but game. For all that, I do not say that the keepers of our ancestors were more forbearing to the squirrels than are the modern men. For in the old days there were many squirrels and few keepers, who, in spite of their best efforts, could do no more than force a reasonable check on the increase of squirrels. But when it came about that there was appointed, almost to each covert, a keeper (game only), possessed of a gun and the highly-creditable accomplishment of using it passably against stationary targets, the doom of the jolly little squirrels was sealed. Thus has the modern keeper-man wrought this decimation in the squirrel ranks, more, I suggest, in thought-lessness than in ignorance ; and in his blind greed for game, and the heresy of his creed that every living thing which is not itself game is injurious to game. Ask the majority of keepers why they treat squirrels as the foes of game, and they will make answer, " 'Cause I know they is." Besides, many keepers regard squirrels as suitable and convenient food for ferrets.

For the last ten years I have been carefully preserving barn owls in some woods, where they lodge chiefly in a few scattered spruce firs. The same protection has been given to the squirrels. But while the owls have thriven satisfactorily, the squirrels show no perceptible increase. For a long time I could get no clue as to why this should be so, till I found under one of the owl-haunted spruces the body of a freshly-killed squirrel. Examination indicated that it had been slain by a bird of prey —the owl flew from the tree while I was looking at the squirrel. Considering the resolute way in which owls attack rats, I fail to see why they should not prey on squirrels when they get a tempting opportunity.

Good-bye, and good luck to you, merry squirrels ; for I love you and your larches in the dear old woods.

THE SQUIRREL.

From a photograph by
Charles Reid, Wishaw.

XXVII

OUR VANISHING FAUNA

"You call them thieves and pillagers; but know
They are the wingéd warders of your farms,
Who from the cornfields drive the insidious foe,
And from your harvest keep a hundred harms." —LONGFELLOW.

TO the open-air naturalist our birds and mammals represent Merrie England as typically as do her hills and streams, her trees and flowers. When, therefore, he hears of the steady impoverishment of our fauna, he is compelled to examine the assertion. At once graver fears are banished; the mischief has been grossly exaggerated. Extermination and diminution have not always been caused wantonly. Some species are actually on the increase. Nevertheless, in spite of bird sanctuaries, animal preserves, and the spread of Selbornian principles, there is ground for real alarm.

Taking first the mammals, we find that some have become practically extinct during the present generation. Two or three genuine wild cats have been recorded, and, alas, shot, within the last thirty years; but save in the rocky fastnesses of the Scotch Highlands, there are probably no successors. Sad as this tale is, there was a strong indictment against the wild cat. But for the slaughter of that handsome carnivore, the pine marten or sweet mart, there is no excuse. A few pairs are believed to linger among the fells of Cumberland and Westmoreland, but soon we shall see this brown-bodied, yellow-throated musteline no more. That the animal betimes slew a weakly lamb cannot be gainsaid, but the loss of our largest marten is national, and passing that of mere money. Another member of this family is the polecat, foumart, or foul-mart, the last two names being given because of its foul smell. The North still shields a few foumarts, but one enquires in vain for them in Southern England. The writer has had experience of two specimens only; both were captured in the Lincolnshire marshes, which still contain a few stragglers, sorely pressed. One of these polecats, finding the farmyard poultry securely barricaded, came up a kitchen drain-pipe after a chicken bait, and a spring trap gripped him in its cruel jaws. The other foumart, held at bay among some mangels, turned on a shepherd dog, and fought furiously for two or three minutes. A weasel attacking a collie in the hayfield makes a third recollection,— this was a braver deed, for the weasel is of more slender build than the pole-cat. Moreover, the polecat has a pair of glands near its tail, from which it can emit such a disgusting odour, that the pluckiest dog must by-and-by run away for a moment's fresh air.

That noble fisherman, the otter, whose powerful legs and webbed feet enable him to swim so well, is gradu-ally being exterminated. Pollution of streams may partially account for the diminishing numbers, but the unworthy jealousy of the human fisher and the callousness of miscalled sportsmen demand the larger toll. The reverse tendency is seen with respect to one animal ; the ruddy fox remains, be-cause it is the privileged minion of its own persecutors. Deprive the fox of its free right to steal, cut down its excellent covers, and give it no more house room than the otter, and the creature, with all its cunning, would die out. One cannot altogether lament its artificial preservation, for whoever has seen an old dog fox slinking by a plantation at dusk, or witnessed its anger when, ambushed in a withy bed, in broad daylight, it is suddenly sur-prised, will long retain the impression. Returning to the dwindling species, we notice the harmless, engaging hedgehog, the destroyer of the house-hold cockroach, the victim of the gipsy's savoury feast. Mainly insecti-vorous, the hedgehog sometimes turns to a diet of snails, worms, and frogs, and is, on the whole, of positive benefit to man. Yet man chooses to extirpate his humble ally. He charges it with impossible crimes, such as sucking the cow's udders, or with rare ones, as robbing eggs from the fowl-house. The poor urchin, which will suffer its body to be torn apart by dogs ere it will relax the muscles that control its spines—its only protection, cannot withstand the spring traps and the snares of superstitious farmers. The long-bodied badger, decked in black and white, so stumpy in leg, and so ursine in muzzle that early naturalists thought him a bear, is in similar plight. Yet he is no bear ; a lover of roots and fruits, he stands forth as almost a vegetarian. Entrenched in his " earths," or nocturnally prowling about for food, he is well protected naturally, but false ideas of sport tell against him. Of the black rat, now all but exterminated, this cannot be said, for his foes are his own kindred. Many naturalists have never seen this indigenous black rat outside a museum, yet it was formerly the prevailing, indeed the only, species in England. Nearly two centuries ago, the ferocious and more powerful brown rat, pushing forward from one continental country to another, at last managed to reach our shores. Hidden in the cargoes of ships, it entered Britain by different ports. Carefully concealing itself in corn-laden barges, or in trusses of fragrant hay, the enemy spread from dock to warehouse, from town to village, from rubbish heap to barn and stable. Always aggressive, always winning in the fight with its dusky congener, it passed on, conquering and to conquer, until the more pacific creature was dethroned and almost wiped out. Only in a few old coppices and granaries, isolated from the general currents of animal life, does the old black breed still hold on, and its days are numbered.

Now for the other side of the story. Of the animals which thrive, and perhaps multiply, we may leave out of the reckoning the red deer or stag, the pretty little roe, and the fallow deer. Subject to careful protection, and treated almost like domestic animals, for them there is no noonday terror or midnight arrow. Two of the mustelines also appear to do well. The bold, white-bellied stoat, domiciled in rabbit burrows, hollows of trees, or old piles of stones, has a lust for blood and an appetite for food, neither surpassed nor equalled by its fellows of the same order. Man's hand is against the stoat everywhere; but because the wily animal does not live in colonies like rabbits, nor frequent the open country like the polecat, above all, because it migrates from spot to spot, it appears to keep up its numbers. What has been said about the prosperity of the stoat might be repeated of the weasel. This little, lithe, tyrannical creature, smallest of its tribe, is readily distinguished from the stoat by the absence of the black tip at the end of the tail. Marauder and murderer, it recks not of its own life when hot on the trail. In the silent night may be heard the piercing shriek of the rabbit, as the weasel leaps on its back, and gives the fatal bite in the neck. Many a woodland gallows and many a gibbet on the barn gable display melancholy rows of dried stoats and weasels. They are essentially the " vermin " of which the gamekeeper babbles, fit company for predatory cats, and handsome jays and magpies; all are condemned together, there is no appeal. Notwithstanding incessant persecution, one cannot fairly assert, on present evidence, that weasels and stoats are much rarer than they were twenty years ago.

The mole, or mould-warp, holds its position well. The mole-catcher and the village mole-club do but keep the little velvet beast in check, after all their mistaken efforts. The three voles also show a moderately satisfactory census. The bank vole, unfortunately called the water-rat, is indeed much harried. Boys pelt it with stones, whilst their elders shoot it for practice, or, believing it to be a true rat, beset its path with the deadly gin. Of the other species, the field or grass vole at times becomes so numerous—thanks to the indiscriminate slaughter of hawks and owls—that the Board of Agriculture has to include the creature as a pest. By chance one picks up a field vole in its more casual haunts. It might be passed by as a large mouse, were it not for its stout head and body, its obtuse muzzle, tiny ears, half-buried in fur, and short, hairy tail.

The hawks and owls suggest a rapid survey of our avifauna. The depletion of some kinds of birds will ultimately give us sorrow. The swift sparrow hawk and the hovering kestrel, perfect masters of aerial movements, the moping owl, with keen, lynx-like eye, the brown piratical buzzard, the sable-hued chough with legs and beak dyed in King Arthur's blood, the hoarse raven of the tall cliff, are vanishing, seemingly for ever. Scarcely can the golden eagle get nesting space in all our broad wilds, the St. Kilda wren falls a victim to the collector's greed. Relentless gunners and specimen hunters scour our fens and uplands. The mercenary bird-catcher and avaricious egg-collector thin out hawk-finches, goldfinches, and warblers. Honesty, however, compels the admission that some species tend to increase numerically, whilst of the departing kinds, there are other influences at work besides man's cruelty. The soaring kite, the avocet, the black tern, and the godwit can be no longer deemed resident species, but their extinction was not due to human agency. Subsidiary causes, working together, produced the sad result. Better drainage, new crops, the substitution of hedge-lined fields for open downlands, lost us the great bustard. It is useless to mourn. There is content to be gained from the great probability that kingfishers, jays, magpies, woodpeckers, and a few other species are actually gaining ground. Nevertheless, as a great authority has said, unless England becomes dispeopled and uncultivated, nothing can ever bring back in numbers and variety many of our disappearing birds.

XXVIII

THE BUZZARD

"above the rest
The noble Buzzard ever pleased me best:
Of small renown, 'tis true, for, not to lie,
We call him but a Hawk by courtesy."
—DRYDEN.

THE average ornithologist, were he asked the present-day status of the once-common buzzard in the British Isles, would unhesitatingly aver that it was, if slightly more prosperous, pretty much in the same deplorable condition as the kite. Indeed, not so very long ago, Mr. Dixon, in his book entitled *Vanishing Birds*, or something to that effect, included the bird in his category. Now, as a point of fact, the buzzard is as yet far from extinction, though admittedly it is very local, and (taking our Islands as a whole) quite rare. It would be safe to include it in the first score of regular scarce breeders. Taking England first, a few pairs still survive in the Lake District, where we are told that it is increasing, whilst Yorkshire possibly can still show an eyrie or two, but thence 'tis a far cry to its next regular habitat—the woods and sea-cliffs of Somerset, Devon, Dorset and Cornwall, and perhaps the woods of Hereford and Gloucester as well. The Eastern, Midland and Southern counties know it no longer as a breeder, though till quite recent years it was a habitué of the New Forest.

In the highlands of Scotland, however, things are much better, and a pair or two may still grace the woodlands of North-West Ireland. But Cambria is the buzzard's present-day headquarters, where it still deserves the prænomen "common." A census would show at least a hundred and fifty breeding pairs, and (Anglesey excepted, and probably Flintshire) it nests in every county, though most abundantly in Brecon, Radnor, Carmarthen and Cardigan. The writer can, any year, lay his hands on over three score eyries, and he knows the whereabouts of fully another thirty, and in short, throughout the British Isles, its numbers may be safely reckoned at well over three hundred pairs. So numerous is the bird in certain districts of Wales that the writer has during walking tours of three or four days only, seen as many as fifty; this, too, in early spring: and if the best country is traversed, it is nothing unusual to meet with twenty or more in the course of the day. This great plenty is due in no small measure to the fact that many a pair resort to the barren sheep-walks dovetailing the hills and dales of those rugged solitudes, a region where the man of leisure may during summer wander for days in unalloyed contentment, never to chance on a soul, save the occasional shepherd with his foxy-looking, white-eyed collies. . . . Suddenly rounding an elbow of the bleak hillside, a huge hawk with owlish and somewhat lumbering flight flaps hurriedly from the putrefying carcase of a lamb. It is a buzzard, and the wanderer, even if he be no ornithologist, will surely stay his steps to gaze. As the one climbs the air, another—its mate—joins it from further down the " cwm," and a master display of wing-power begins. Each bird taking a reverse course, both float up with the minimum of exertion in a spiral curve, with such measured rhythm of wing that one is fain to believe it a preconcerted exhibition. The bird's ample wings are raised almost vertically, each primary standing out distinct like digits on a hand, whilst the broad, slightly - rounded tails are spread to their fullest fan. At one time the sun burnishes the rich umber of their backs and scapu-

lars ; next moment, as a half turn is described, the light-coloured feathers of the belly and under the wings glint like silver sheen. Higher and higher they wind, till the eyes are pained with vigil so intent ; further and further away till the watcher begins to wonder if the specks are really animate, or only the creatures of his imagination. That is the characteristic flight of the buzzard in the vernal year, in the early morning and on fine evenings just before sun-down ; and when as many as from six to a dozen (no uncommon event in early spring) all sail round one another in this fashion, it is a spectacle worth going miles to see. Occasionally a single bird will soar, till it is a mere dot in the heavens, for a great time, and a pair will often hang against the wind at a lower elevation especially when hunting. When seen under any of these circumstances, the buzzard's flight is hard to be beaten. But, on the other hand, when it is flapping along, or when disturbed in covert, which it leaves in a frightened, clumsy manner, it does not inspire admiration, for in truth it appears not a trifle ungainly. When descending into or crossing a valley, the buzzard frequently half closes its wings, and with a quicker speed than usual, literally cleaves the void with a mighty rush, resembling, whilst so doing, some monster bolt with barbs each side hurled from a giant catapult. . . .

The buzzard subsists chiefly on rabbits (young ones generally, though in severe weather the adults as well), moles, rats, mice (especially field voles), beetles (chiefly of the genus geotrupes), nearly any sort of carrion and more occasionally grouse, partridges and reptiles, whilst a dead fish is not ignored. Yet when there are young to provide for, nearly everything is fish which comes to net, and they will then catch that which comes readiest to hand ; thus, should an eyrie be in close touch to a grouse-moor, the " cheepers " are remorselessly harried, and the writer has known of pheasant poults, tiny lambs (taken there when *found* dead, for the Boda is no slayer of lambs), the relics of a cock pheasant, crows, pigeons and other birds, including a nightjar, in and around different nests. In the case of the pheasant, crow and pigeon, the buzzard must, in the first instance, have found them dead or at any rate wounded, for though no doubt the bird could, if so disposed, tackle even this " big game," yet it would be quite opposed to its usual habits, for the buzzard seldom makes a quarry of any bird on the wing,

but picks it featly off the ground, and a cock pheasant could put up a good fight, whilst the crow positively revels in mobbing a buzzard on every possible occasion. Occasionally, but very occasionally, a pair of buzzards, even out of the breeding season, will devastate the poultry - yard. On the whole, then, this fine hawk is harmless to game, though it should be remarked that, when one is crossing a moor, grouse lie like stones, as the writer can testify ; yet, given a young rabbit and a grouse, the former will always be selected. Tame birds will eat almost anything ; cats, squirrels, hedgehogs, and practically any variety of bird, but they will not look at a blind-worm.

The usual way of procuring prey is for the buzzard to harry the ground at a fair, sometimes quite a low elevation above it, with slow, noiseless, flapping flight, and it hunts the open moors and enclosures in the valleys far more than the skirts of the former. But sometimes the bird will sit motionless for hours together on a commanding pinnacle or dead branch, till some likely victim comes within the ken of its keen eyes, when down it glides and easily snatches its unsuspecting victim.

Although the buzzard nests alike in

trees and rocks (in Wales, eighty-five per cent. are on the latter), there can be no possible doubt that it is preferably a branch-builder, a surmise which is easily verified, seeing that if there exist in close propinquity a suitable wood and cliff, the former is almost invariably selected, and it should be further noted that its Welsh haunts show far fewer woods and trees generally than crags. Very rarely a pair of cliff builders have their alternative nest in an adjoining covert. It is to be imagined that young buzzards, hatched in either of the two positions, would be constant to the same when the time came for their own breeding.

The buzzard usually possesses from two to four alternative nests, which are generally not very far apart, though in isolated examples they are a mile or even two away from one another, especially in localities where the bird is scarce or where no suitable site exists close to the eyrie tenanted. Some nests assume gigantic proportions, becoming from constant refitting over a yard high and over two feet across. Tree nests, and more rarely those in the crags, are used by individual pairs for from two to six years in succession, but this event must be regarded as abnormal, for generally two nests are occupied in alternate years. One pair came under the writer's notice, which used five different eyries in a like number of years.

When in an oak, ash or beech, the nest is placed either in a fork (more often than not the second or third up) of the main stem, or, just as frequently, in one of a projecting limb. If, however, a fir or larch is selected, it is built close to the trunk on several horizontal branches, on a projecting bough or on the broad, flat crown of the tree. A tree is preferred which is near the edge of the wood, rather than one in the middle, especially if the covert is closely planted. In a " hanger," the nest must, in the majority of cases, be sought in the bottom half. Apart from woods, odd eyries may be found in small plantations, clumps of trees and even in isolated trees in hedgerows and elsewhere.

Cliff eyries, whether maritime or inland, are generally in the upper half, and ninety-five per cent. are built on the broad platform at the base of and behind some tree or bush clinging to the crags, the other five being on unprotected ledges or in some big cavernous recess, but in any case a partiality is evinced for a cliff with trees springing from it, or one covered with ivy. This habit of building behind a tree may be a further indication of the buzzard's tree - loving propensity, for it may remind it, though slightly enough one would imagine, of its original trait. Eyries on almost level, rocky ground are not without precedent, but, be the site what it may, a secluded one with an easterly aspect is usually preferred to all others.

Although the buzzards (for both sexes assist) always make their own nest, crows' and sometimes ravens' and kites' are used as a foundation, in which case the eyrie is smaller and slighter than usual. Very exceptionally indeed, a pair, possessed of unwonted pluck, eject a couple of crows from their *new* nest.

A tree - nest (especially one built amongst ivy), is frequently difficult of access, for the bird often selects one with a huge, limbless bole ; but on inland crags (in Wales especially) the reverse is generally the case. In fact, out of well over a hundred eyries which the writer has examined, only half a dozen at most required a short piece of rope to negotiate ; indeed, to some eyries ladies and children can climb without difficulty. This propensity to build (unnecessarily) in such simple situations proves disastrous to the bird, and many a clutch,

which would otherwise have hatched, either finds its way into the dreaded egg collector's box or is pulverized under the iron-shod heel of some ignorant shepherd. Sheep dogs will, when they can, devour the large eggs, and crows and sometimes ravens are a perfect scourge to the buzzard.

Individual nests differ a good deal in size, but tree eyries are generally the bulkiest and most substantial. In the ground work, sticks (dead and living), twigs, and heather branches find a place, and the normal lining (in fact, it occurs in all nests) is of dried cotton grass (tufts and blades) or wood-rush, but in different eyries, the writer has notes on the following miscellany—pieces of bark about two inches square, fir and larch sprigs, moss, dead bracken, wild thyme, ivy and other green vegetation such as freshly pulled branches of oak, birch and hawthorn. Indeed, the buzzard has a decided leaning towards the artistic, and the writer can scarce recollect one nest which was not graced at one time or another (for material is added daily right through incubation, and until the young have left the nest) with green foliage of some kind, which is frequently woven roughly into the rim. Some nests are lined (over the grass) with a carpet of greenest larch sprays (this usually when the nest is in a larch), or the more sombre tint of the Scotch fir. Now and then a flake or two of wool is to be seen in the lining or clinging to the sticks, but it is more than doubtful if it is taken there intentionally, the probable truth being that it is adhering to some stick when gathered by the buzzard. Usually, however, it occurs when a raven's or crow's nest is built upon, in which case the event needs no explanation.[1] Fragments of white down from the parent birds cling to the nest and its environment in more or less abundance. Tree - nests have a platform of sticks built on to them, after the young are hatched, on which the old birds stand to break up the food ; on cliffs of course there is no necessity for this, as an adjacent ledge serves the purpose. The lining, if of rough material, is nevertheless fairly smooth, but in one instance it was so " ridgy " that none of the three eggs touched. The egg-cup is, normally, very flat, but never so much so as that of the kite. In

very rare cases the eggs are laid on a little dead grass placed on a rock ledge.

By mid-March or even before, buzzards make as it were a pretence of building, and patch up all their old eyries more or less, though nothing is done in real earnest before the end of that month or early in April, about which time the writer has seen as many as six birds over one site, in fact, a social tendency is evinced right through the year. The real eyrie is, however, indicated by sundry droppings all round it, and by the birds frequenting it most and roosting in its vicinity. The nest is sometimes complete long before the first egg is laid.

The buzzard 'ays from one to five eggs, usually two or three; four is a comparatively rare number, five very exceptional, whilst very ancient females produce but one. They differ wonderfully, even in the same clutch ; indeed eggs of one " set " are seldom of the same type, and when three are laid, one is generally spotless or nearly so, and, as often as not, smaller than the other brace. An addle egg is not ejected from the eyrie.

The ground colour of all ranges from greyish white and yellowish white to very pale bluish white (the internal surface is pale green), and the

[1] *Note.*— A recent writer insists that the buzzard frequently pads its eyrie with wool and hair. Does it ? In all—i.e. in trees and rocks — I have climbed to, and closely examined over two hundred nests, yet, except in the above-mentioned cases, I have *never* found either of these substances. The kite, of course, *always* pads its nest thickly with wool, often with hair-tufts as well.—J. W. B.

markings may take the form of bold blotches, smudges, spots, speckles or more rarely streaks and scratches. Their colour is very variable. In one wide area of country, the usual type was light red, yellowish-red or -brown and rust with underlying markings (if they existed) of lilac grey. One egg in a clutch is often zoned at the small or large end, and a hen accustomed to lay this variety always has one like it every year. In another district, dark red and chestnut, sometimes black, were the prevailing tints in the markings, and the underlying markings, lilac-pink or grey. Other types are filmed with a delicate coat of lime over pink, lilac and rusty streaks on a cream ground, and are exceptionally lovely, or are minutely flecked with light brown and purplish-red on a white surface. Usually far more ground exists than markings; in fact, taken as a whole, Welsh eggs, though of fine size, are not richly-coloured, but a clutch from Somerset, which the writer has seen, was as heavily marked as a real good sparrow-hawk's egg. Sometimes all the eggs in a " set " are spotless. The eggs are usually inclined to the rotund rather than truly oval, and the shell is thick and coarse. The buzzard seldom lays again the same year that

she is robbed, but should such an event occur, another nest is utilized.

From three to four days, sometimes as much as a week, elapse between the dropping of each egg, but the first is frequently sat upon as soon as laid. Incubation, performed chiefly by the female, lasts for one egg a lunar month exactly, but some few days longer must be allowed for the remainder to hatch. The young, pleasing studies in grey plush, remain in the eyrie for six weeks, more or less ; at first they grow very slowly, being, when a fortnight old, only the size of a man's fist, but when the pen-feathers begin to show on the sixteenth day, they increase in bulk rapidly. Whilst in the nest they often keep their beaks wide open, and pant as if oppressed by the heat. As they wax stronger, strange bickerings ensue, and it is to be feared that the first hatched, being naturally the lustiest, often bullies its fellow-nestlings most unmercifully, and sometimes one or even two vanish from the eyrie. There are even rumours of cannibalism afloat, and it is conjectured that either the strongest eats the others, or that the old birds, having much ado to keep body and soul in both or more, find a way out of the difficulty by destroying them, only leaving one to be reared. But the writer is disposed to treat this as mythical, for he has known many a brood (both twos and threes) fly intact from eyries situate in the wildest rocky regions to those in comparatively lowland woods. No, what most probably happens is this—the largest bird pushes the others out of the nest *inadvertently*, for the structure is more than a little flat, and to substantiate this theory, it may be mentioned that on more than one occasion, the writer has found a young buzzard in an advanced state of decomposition on the rocks beneath an eyrie, and as a further proof it may be cited (as above mentioned), that material is invariably added round the rim as long as the young are in it.

The writer has repeatedly observed that tree-builders remain brooding far closer than those in rocks, fancying, it may be imagined, that the timber affords them some sort of extra protection or sequestration, and ofttimes these may be approached to within easiest of gunshots, but the crag-breeder, especially if intruded on from the valley below, generally quits her eyrie the moment an intruder has commenced to climb, sometimes the minute in which he is first visible far down dale.

The average buzzard is a noisy bird at the nest, and both sexes (the male, known by his slightly smaller size, often being the most excited) wheel and flap above the haunt, but seldom within shot, mewing distractedly, often most so when an explorer is furthest from their secret. If the eggs are taken, they fly straight away without more ado. In other cases they are not noisy at all, and fly silently away, returning at intervals, or take up a position on some adjacent crag or tree. The non-sitting bird is seldom long absent from its sitting partner.

Very exceptionally a pair (the male particularly) will show fight and literally attack an intruder. Such an event has occurred with several of the writer's friends, but he himself has never been more than threatened, the bird coming within say ten yards of him with outstretched talons and open beak. On one occasion, as he commenced scaling the rocks to reach an eyrie, the female stooped at a ewe and her lamb, causing them considerable fright. But at all times the buzzard is inquisitive, for when lying motionless in heather on the open moor, individual birds have approached the writer within a few yards, doubtless taking him for carrion ; again, when in covert, a passing buzzard has flapped down into the trees to see what strange object was there, whilst on several occasions a male has accompanied the writer for miles, leaving his sitting hen far behind.

The non-incubating bird is usually close to the eyrie, either on an adjacent tree or ledge, or wheeling above the site, and were it not for its senseless habit of advertising the place by flapping down the valley or over the wood to meet an intruder, and squealing persistently, many a nest would escape the greedy egg-looter.

The earliest " set " of eggs the writer has ever seen was complete by April 7, but more usually those eyries in the sheltered woods of the lowlands contain eggs from between April 18–25, those in the hills from that date to May 10, or even considerably later. Sometimes, however, even hill-nests have eggs by April 20, and curiously enough the early record above referred to was in a gorge right up in the mountains. Individual hens commence laying almost to the day year by year. There may be (when the bird is really plentiful) two tenanted eyries within half a mile, and the writer knows one big wood where three pairs breed yearly ; in the Welsh valleys, however, there is usually a pair about every two miles, more or less.

As a rule, the buzzard is a sad poltroon, which any bird may mob with impunity ; ravens, crows, rooks, daws, magpies, all the small hawks and even herons, the writer has seen so engaged. A pair of merlins will make a regular business of it, for whilst one mounts a hundred feet or more above its lumbering antagonist to stoop at it quick as thought, the other waits on its fellow to take up the attack, and, in short, the buzzard, mewing with fear, gets no peace till it seeks a sanctuary in some sylvan or rocky retreat.

The buzzard's usual cry is a melancholy and rather nasal half-whistle, half-mew, thus—" s-e-i-o-u," and it is often repeated, but with an appreciable interval between each utterance. It may be heard either when the bird is on the wing, or when at rest. But in wet, dismal weather a pair often sit on the rocks answering one another with an uncanny repetition of the syllable " mah," thus " māh - māh - māh - māh - māh," whilst nestlings possess a curious, iterated, soft whistle —" whee - ou - whee-ou-whee-ou-whee-ou-whĕŭ."

A certain amount of internal migration, chiefly local, is noticeable during autumn and winter, and in the writer's opinion it is generally birds of the year, which, driven by their parents from their birth-place, seek perforce entirely new quarters. He thinks this for two reasons, firstly, because all the buzzards one hears of as being shot or trapped down country are almost invariably immature birds ; and, secondly, because he has on so many occasions known a pair of these birds frequent their breeding haunt the year round, roosting close to the nest nightly.

The usual Welsh appellation for the buzzard is " boda," plural " bodaod," but the word " bwncath," which means cat, is sometimes used, though it should be noted that this expression is loosely applied to nearly any large bird.

WIND.

From a water-colour by
W. Tatton Winter, R.B.A.

XXIX

THE GEOGRAPHY OF HANDICRAFTS

Dicendum et quae sint duris agrestibus arma,
Quis sine nec potuere seri nec surgere messes;
Vomis et inflexi primum grave robur aratri,
Tardaque Eleusinae matris volventia plaustra . . .
. . . Omnia quae multo ante memor provisa repones,
Si te digna manet divini gloria ruris.
—VIRGIL; GEORGICS.

EVERY one who is closely familiar with any wide area of English soil must have noticed how the outward features of life on the farms and in the villages form a curious geography of their own, which is often wholly independent of the local divisions of modern life. On many journeys of a few score miles through England, we can observe a striking change in the characteristic styles of local architecture, which seldom coincide in their distribution with the limits of county soil. But the same kind of ancient and traditional variety can be seen very strongly marked even in such accessories of rural life as the scythes and the waggons upon the farms, and the milestones which number the stages of the journey. In rugged and upland countries, where cultivated fields are small and roads steep and heavy, the farm waggons are scanty and simple in design, sometimes being but little more than boxes hung over wheels; but among the broad vales and gentler slopes of the south and east, where the produce of the great corn-fields and hay-fields demands ample transport, centuries ago the skill of the waggon-builder was concentrated on producing the most perfect type of vehicle which could be devised, till the farm-waggons of Wiltshire or Berkshire to-day are framed on a traditional pattern which is as perfect an adaptation of means to ends as the lines of a racing yacht. On a journey from a south-eastern county, such as Surrey or Sussex, westwards through Berkshire into the Wiltshire country that is drained by the Bristol Avon, the beginning, the middle and the end of the route will each display a traditional local type, peculiar both in colour and design. Amid the steep hills and thin soils of most of Surrey, and the dense oak-forests and deep clay of the Weald, agriculture did not develop as fully and as early as in many other districts of the south; and it is noticeable that the farm-waggons of those districts, though far ampler and more skilfully moulded than the wains of Cornwall, or Westmorland, or Wales, do not display the perfect development

13

of free and raking curves which enables the wains of the Thames and lower Severn valleys to combine strength, lightness and carrying capacity in the highest possible degree.

It is not till we cross the chalk downs by Guildford, and have traversed the light and hungry sands of the Aldershot district beyond, that we first meet the farm-waggon in its highest development, among the wide and often hedgeless Berkshire corn-lands, through which run the Bath and Oxford roads. The constant and traditional colour of these Thames Valley wains is a light and unobtrusive yellow, so closely akin to the tints of the pale stubble and ripening corn of the wide, fenceless fields over which they ply that it appears to have been evolved in the minds of the villagers by a compelling process of long association. Travelling westwards, whether by the downs and the deep Savernake glades, or by the long, tilted pasture-slopes of the White Horse and Avon vales, as we leave the Berkshire country of chalk and corn for the richer swards of the west, there comes a sudden change in the appearance of the waggons of the new countryside. Though their build is very nearly the same, and they are only a little less huge and roomy than those of the slopes above the Thames,

the uniform yellow which prevailed to eastwards gives place to a bright and cheerful livery of blue picked out with red. All the conservatism and tenacity of rural life centre round such fashions in the gear of the farm ; and the true explanation of why the waggons of the Vale of Abingdon are yellow, while those of the valley of the Avon are red and blue, would possibly take us back to the days of the Heptarchy.

Many prevailing differences in domestic architecture can be directly traced to the utilization of the natural resources of each district, in times before cheap production and rapid transit put Welsh slates and Peterborough or Middlesex bricks within easy reach of every local builder. In the parts of England where there is no natural supply of good building-stone, the old artificers worked out those local styles in timber, brick, tile, plaster and thatch, which are so thoroughly attractive in their perfect adaptation of available means to ends. Chalk is too soft, as a rule, to make a lasting material when exposed to wind and weather ; yet the white, squared blocks can often be found built into the walls of old farms and cottages in the down countries, interspersed with bricks, chipped flints, and fragments of the sarsen stones, or " grey wethers," which the denudation of the former overlying strata has left scattered here and there about the chalk. For pillars and other inside work of churches the soft white rock is used more often ; as the darkness of the winter afternoons falls in the village aisles, the chalk sheds a soft luminousness from its half-seen outlines which adds a peculiar beauty to such an interior. The characteristic chipped flint architecture of the southern and eastern counties involves a degree of preparatory labour which would only be readily undergone in the absence of a free supply of building-stone in mass ; while for rougher and less permanent work, chalk marl or clay is worked up into the wattle-and-daub walls which, when standing in isolation, are topped with a coping of thatch or tile to prevent them from liquefying in the rains. But the most widely distributed and interesting method of construction in the districts where good building-stone is absent, or timber was specially plentiful in more ancient times, is the half-timbered or " post and panel " style, which is so common and delightful a feature of the older towns and villages through a large part of the country. In one or two instances the half-timbered style is also found in existing village churches ; but the cases were few in which churches and the larger country houses were not built of stone, though the material might have to be brought from a considerable distance, and at heavy expense. The half-timbered style is typical of cottages, farm-houses and smaller manors ; and it is this close association with the homely, every-day life of our forefathers which adds a special attraction to the picturesqueness of its varying local forms. There are two large regions in which half-timbered houses form a conspicuous and delightful feature of most of the older villages, and many of the towns. All down the western midlands, from Lancashire on the north, through Cheshire, Shropshire, with Worcestershire and its neighbouring counties, into the lowland part of Gloucestershire on the south, there are to be seen in abundance the well-known " magpie cottages," in which strong black beams are conspicuously contrasted with the white plaster-work of the intervening spaces. In a great part of this district, indeed, the style seems to have been adopted rather because of neighbouring fashion and the abundance of such an easily worked material as wood than of any general lack of good building-stone. The southern limit of this style occurs in the Severn valley, about half a dozen miles to the south of Gloucester. For many miles further to southward there runs the same luxuriant pasture and orchard country, densely shaded with groves of pear-tree and elm. But the magpie architecture is seen no more. Henceforward the typical style of the older farm-houses in this valley is a modification of the famous stone-built and stone-slated style of the Cotswold Hills, that hang above ; but it is less classically pure in design, and the walls are covered with white rough-cast, that gives a footing to the western roses.

The Cotswolds form the south-eastern limit of these half-timbered dwellings of the west ; and it is not until we pass beyond these borders, and leave their beds of yellow limestone and the incomparable domestic architecture which was fostered by this free supply of material, that we come, in Berkshire and Hampshire, to the borders of a second great district in which the half-timbered style is constantly seen in the villages. This district includes at least two prominent varieties of the style ; and both of them are conspicuously different in external appearance and minor detail from the magpie cottages of the west. Kent and Sussex are the headquarters of the most fully developed southern type ; and here the white plaster and intricate, almost barbaric, ornament of the western woodwork are replaced by red brick and hanging tiles, while a thoroughly typical specimen shows rows of closely set perpendicular beams, divided by plain strips of brickwork, hardly, if at all, wider than the beams themselves. This arrangement gives the half-timbered villages of the Weald of Kent and of Sussex a more restrained and sober architectural beauty than is seen in the strangely-fretted front of some ancient Shropshire or Worcestershire manor house, but one which is certainly no less deep and enduring in its charm. Beyond the Kent and Sussex borders there is a wide strip of country, roughly including Hampshire, Berkshire, Middlesex, Hertfordshire and Essex, in which brick and tile are still used in combination with timber beams, but the beams divide the brickwork into rectangular panels, rather than close parallel strips, and the whole effect is at once more irregular and more ornate. In the Berkshire cottages the brickwork, for instance, is often set in a herring-bone pattern, or a series of zigzags, while the hanging tiles are curiously varied in form. These local differences are, of course, not absolute or invariable, and features which are proper to one style may often be found in the territory of the next. But the bygone builders were strikingly consistent in the main ; and there is often a curious hint of some obscure ancient frontier of the peoples, in the way in which a predominant characteristic of the style will suddenly cease at no boundary which is explicable from modern causes, when, so far as the supply of material is concerned, it would seem quite as natural for it either to extend twenty miles further, or to cease twenty miles before. It is extremely interesting to trace the leading features of local fashion in these beautiful old buildings, and gradually to form a map in the mind of where the herring-bone or zigzag Berkshire patterns first become prevalent as we go westwards from Kent, or in what other districts of the Home Counties we may find the long, oblique beam cutting athwart the rest, which is a notable feature in Essex.

In all the more northerly and westerly districts, where the rock is seldom far from the surface, stone was regularly used in old days for many needs which were elsewhere supplied by timber, or in modern times by cheap cast or galvanized iron. In many western counties, the wanderer in England will note the great slabs of stone set edge-ways in the wall, or in a solid frame of masonry in the hedgerows, that form the stiles on the footpaths in the fields, and are so strange to the eye of the native of the chalk, sands and gravels of the south and east. In certain parts of the country, as in Westmorland, where a common formation of slaty rock splits easily into large, thin slabs, obelisk-like posts for slip-rails are constructed of this stone, by piercing four or five holes in them with a chisel and setting them up on end at each side of the gate or gap. Stone troughs are seen in every old farmyard in many districts on the great belt of older and harder rocks which runs through the western and northern counties ; and modern haste and impatience wonder at the labour which must have been expended on chiselling and hollowing such masses of native stone, when the farmer of to-day simply chooses an iron pattern from an illustrated agricultural catalogue. There is perpetual interest in the utilization of the local resources of nature, which links the soil and the life upon it into a distinct and coherent whole ; and the mind of the observer is filled with a sense of admiration and respect at the solidity and lasting efficacy of such products of ancient labour.

One of the most distinct and interesting of the bygone local crafts which have left their traces on the country of to-day was the iron-working industry of the Weald, which at length succumbed, after a quiet prosperity of many centuries, to the growth of the great iron towns of the Midlands and the North. In all the wooded tract which lies in Hampshire, Surrey, Kent and Sussex, between the sundered arms of the North and South Downs, the land is still full of the traces of the ancient smelters and smiths, both in the numerous " hammer ponds " which perpetuate the memory of the rude, water-driven stamps, and in ironwork which supersedes in this country-side some of the ordinary uses of wood or stone. Most curious, perhaps, of the existing relics of the ancient smiths are the cast-iron slabs of the sixteenth and seventeenth centuries, which in some of the old churches take the place of tombstones or brasses on graves. They bear a close similarity in style to the iron firebacks which were produced in the same Wealden foundries ; indeed, an instance occurs in which a duplicate cast from the mould of a sixteenth-century grave-slab is still to be seen as a fireback in a farmhouse near the church. Among these deep clays of the Weald, or even on the ridges of " Kentish rag " and kindred building-stone which overlook the wooded vales, there is no solid bed of rock suitable for work in bulk ; for part of the value and convenience of Kentish rag for purposes of building is that it occurs in thin layers, unlike the virgin rock of the north and west. Milestones, therefore, in this county are generally not stones at all, but meagre wooden posts ; on the other hand they are often faced with a rude iron plate bearing the distance in Roman numerals, which is another product of the old Sussex smiths. Here and there, again, in the fields of the same region the rambler will still come upon a rude and solid iron pipe, taking the place of an ordinary earthenware drainpipe or brick culvert, and carrying the water of some ditch or runnel under a path or cart-track. Here iron ousts stone and wood from familiar uses, just as wood prevails over stone in the cottage architecture of the same Wealden region, and stone preponderates, in its turn, among the villages of the north and west.

There are many instances of local crafts which were peculiar to a single district or village, and were carried on by a single family, or an association of two or three. Some of these industries have become only a memory; of others, probably, not even a memory

PUFFINS.

From a photograph by
Oliver Pike.

survives ; but there still exist one or two of these curious local monopolies, built up, in some cases, on a closely-kept trade secret which depended on a single life. Even to-day those solid wooden bowls which are used for holding bath-soap all reach the market from one rustic cottage on a wooded Berkshire ridge. Yet, interesting as are all these isolated handicrafts, there is a still wider fascination in noting the local diversities in the make of some one familiar instrument, or in the minor details of some general process, and in tracing, or at least conjecturing, the causes which have led in so many cases to an almost infinite variety and gradation as the centuries went by. The make of such a universal implement as the scythe, for instance, seems to answer as sensitively to the nature of the soil and its agriculture as the crops or the farm-buildings themselves. Only in the widest, deepest and richest vales of the south-west is the scythe seen in its highest development of power and balance and curve. In hillier regions, or those where agriculture is a less age-old and flourishing industry, it shrinks sometimes to little more than a short pole fitted with two handles and a blade. All these differences in country use are like the old local dialects, which in their purity are vanishing so rapidly. They have their roots deep in the history and antiquity of our land and race, and they deserve and reward the attention of every Englishman.

XXX

ENGLISH COUNTRY SONGS

Dire per rima in volgare tanto è quanto dire per versi in latino.
—DANTE, V.N. xxv.

THE first feeling which a casual mention of our country songs will arouse in any one who takes a keen interest in the subject will probably be tinged with melancholy. And this not for artistic reasons, or because the particular songs he may be thinking of are depressing : our folk music has moods at least as gay as that of any other nation. It is a feeling of regret for a beauty which has almost passed away from the land, and at the present minute can only be caught now and again in out-of-the-way places, where—

" Extrema excedens terris vestigia fecit."

It is fairly safe to prophesy that in a few years our traditional music will have become a closed chapter of history, and those who would rescue what fragments they can from oblivion have great difficulties to contend against. For the people who can remember the old songs are generally aged, and almost always extremely shy about singing them, and many suffer from varying degrees of loss of voice. The generation now growing up takes no interest in the songs which used to be the delight of the older people. Owing to the vulgarizing influence of the large towns it has learned to relish the imported sentimentality of " The Old Folks at Home " and the thoroughly urban humour of " Father keeps on doing it." Probably the only traditional unpublished songs which still hold their place in the hearts of the youth of the present day are those which can be heard as easily in the town as in the country—I refer to those songs which are sung on occasions when men are met together in the names of temperance and celibacy, to celebrate the coming of age of one of the party, or some such important event. Some of these are of easily proven antiquity, as the curious may see for themselves by consulting the volumes of Playford, Ritson and similar collectors. But with these ditties we are not here concerned ; for, in the first place, they are not in danger of

perishing (and, were they to do so, there would be few to mourn them) ; and, secondly, they are not in any special way typical representatives of our traditional country music.

It is, I suppose, impossible to check that mysterious thing called the March of Progress, and it would be rash to impeach any particular class of people as responsible for the change which has come over the musical taste of the country populations. But for allowing the old music to be forgotten before it was recorded, we (speaking retrospectively) have only ourselves to blame. The songs of the English country lay within easy reach, but our educated men, affected by a strange sort of intellectual presbyopy, neglected them and looked further afield. Yet we have always been willing to allow that other nations had their folk music. We believed that the Sicilian and the Neapolitan sing naturally. We accepted masses of German " folk songs " without questioning which of them were genuine and which of recent fabrication. It would not have surprised us to learn that the infant Spaniard relieves the monotony of the hours devoted to the feeding bottle by intervals of inspired improvisation on a diminutive guitar. More than this, we have lauded the

Scotch popular songs to an almost sentimental extent; we have been courteous to the Welsh, and should never have denied that the Irish could sing. And yet a good number of these songs, Scotch and Irish at any rate, are English in origin, but could not gain admission to polite circles at home until they had left their native land and returned clad in an unseemly kilt or stammering with an infantile brogue.

Even nowadays our songs are sometimes introduced to us by our neighbours as their own. An Irish woman of reverend age, who for some years has been selling flowers (and sometimes gold collar studs at two a penny) in London, once took me so far into her confidence as to consent to sing me some of the songs which she had heard in her youth in the country not far from Dublin. The four songs which she sang were a curious selection. The first was " Lord Rendall." This, of course, is a song of which many variants are known in England, especially in the West country, and it has travelled as far as Scotland, where it is known as " Lord Ronald." The tune was very nearly the same as the first of the two printed by Mr. Cecil Sharp in his *Folk Songs from Somerset*. The second song to be re-introduced was a form of " Dabbling in the Dew," beginning—

" ' Where are you going, my pretty little girl, O?
Where are you going, my pretty little maid ? '
' I'm going a-milking, kind sir,' she said to me,
'Rollin' on the dew makes the milk-maids fair.' "

It will be noticed that, while this is cast in exactly the same mould as the Somerset version, the second line—

" With your red rosy cheeks and your coal-black hair,"—

has been dropped, its place being taken by the repetitive line given above. The English origin of this song will not seem very doubtful if we bear this comparison in mind, and remember, too, the famous nursery rhyme, the motive of which is the same—

" ' Where are you going, my pretty maid ? '
' I'm going a-milking, sir,' she said "—

and of which we find an echo in the sailors' chanty—

" 'O, where are you going to, my pretty maid ? '
' O, away to Rio ! ' "

The tune to the Irish version was quite uninteresting, and had no relation to the rhythmical and characteristic melody printed by Mr. Sharp. The third song was still more startling. It was nothing more nor less than an incomplete form of " All round my Hat." Now the origin of this is frankly and indubitably cockney. Whether it was sung in the streets before it was sung at Vauxhall Gardens, or whether Mr. Valentine, the composer, and Mr. Williams, the singer, were responsible for popularizing it in its first and loathsomely vulgar form, seems doubtful. But certain it is that, however it was begot, it was, in its original form, the song of a costermonger whose sweetheart is in prison for stealing. Still, the tune was built on a very beautiful theme, and it has been converted, with very little alteration of words and melody, into a graceful and tender song by Mr. F. H. Sheppard (*see* his note on page 27 of *A Garland of Country Song*). The fourth and last song might very likely be able to establish its claim to be of Irish stock. It began—

" Sure, I'm always drunk and I'm seldom sober,
   And constantly rovin' from town to town ;
And when I'm dead and my days are over,
   Come along, mavourneen, and lay me down."

The tonality was certainly interesting, but of its origin I can say nothing.

It has become a sort of traditional saying, generally accepted without contradiction or investigation, that the English are not a tuneful race. No sober man is expected to sing unless he be specially trained for the purpose, and standing with gorgeous gleaming belly beside a piano, facing rows of people specially met together to hear him, or unless he becomes a sailor, in which case he is expected to sing chanties at his work. But it is evident, from what has been taken down by modern collectors, from casual references in old books, and from the evidence brought together by enthusiasts such as W. Chappell, that up to a fairly advanced date in the last century England must have been ringing with melody from end to end. And, precisely because it was so common, no notice was taken of it. There lay the treasure before men's eyes, yet no one would stretch out his hand to take it. It was not in the fashion. People wanted foreign songs, or songs composed by Englishmen whose ideas were derived entirely from foreign sources. Some of our native melodies were too antique in structure to be easily caught or appreciated, and all were too easy to get at. Even those who kept alive the reverence for Nature and the love of the country neglected this aspect of country life. Yet what interesting and valuable work could have been done by an enthusiast in this field, in the days before the music hall type of song came roaring through the country with its coarse, heavy voice, and, overstepping the modesty of the rustic music, caused the latter to hide its head for shame! There must have been as many men then as there are now with sufficient leisure and knowledge to enable them to undertake such a search. The difficulties attending it would have been infinitely less, the harvest infinitely richer. Perhaps men had not then developed the historical spirit in all its fulness. Perhaps they were not very ready to see the value of antiquity as represented by unlettered tradition. Another fact which may also have inclined those who heard the old songs to neglect them is that many of them are not composed in our modern scales. Owing to the recent revival of the study of ancient music, we now recognize that they are pure modal melodies; but up to a comparatively short time ago they were regarded as simply incorrect.

Still, enough has been preserved and printed to make an extremely attractive study, even to one with but a slight knowledge of music or folklore. Apart from the intrinsic charm of many of the songs, one of the most obvious interests connected with the subject lies in comparing the many variant forms, both of music and words, in which a number of them have been taken down. Not only do we find what is substantially the same song, though of course with considerable local modifications, sung in counties as far apart as Somerset and Westmorland, but in many cases songs have been taken down quite recently from the mouths of the peasants which are clearly descendants of songs which were in manuscript or in print two or even three hundred years ago. There is something highly satisfactory and gratifying in a discovery of this kind, at any rate to a bookish man or to one who loves continuity and tradition. It is not possible to think without a feeling of affection, and perhaps of reverence, of these songs which, like the unconquered Klephts of the Greek mountains, have held their own in their native country-side in spite of all the foreign influences with which England has been flooded. A good instance of such survivals is the old ballad of " The Over-Courteous Knight " (1609), which has been taken down recently in a form known as " Blow away the Morning Dew." The story is as follows. A knight (or, in the modern version, a farmer's son) rides out in the morning and meets a " bonny lasse " : they talk, and she invites him to come with her to her father's house. When they arrive there she slips in, shutting her would-be lover outside, and ridicules him for not having taken advantage of her when he had the chance. Now in the two forms of the ballad, separated by nearly three centuries, the tunes are entirely unlike and the metre is not the same ; but the likeness in phraseology is very striking. Take, for instance, these two verses from the song of 1609 :—

"He set her up upon a steed
    And himself upon another,
And all the day he rode her by
    As though they had been sister and brother.

"When she came to her father's hall,
    It was well walled round about,
She yode in at the wicket gate,
    And shut the four-eared foole without "—

and compare them with the version taken down by Mr. Sharp :—

"If you come down to my father's house,
    Which is walled all around,
There you shall have a kiss from me
    And twenty thousand pound.

"He mounted on a milk-white steed
    And she upon another,
And then they rode along the lane
    Like sister and like brother.

"But when they came to her father's gate,
    So nimble she popped in ;
And said : *There is a fool without,*
    And here's the maid within."

So tenacious is the memory among people who neither read nor write. Again, one of our most popular West country songs, " Young Herchard," or " Richard of Taunton Dean," though its descent cannot be traced directly from one forefather, has two obvious

ancestral relatives, dating, one from the middle of the sixteenth century, and the other from the early years of the seventeenth. The two songs in question are " Quoth John to Joan " and " I have house and lands in Kent." Both are the utterance of a boorish country wooer to his lady. There is not much verbal resemblance between the two ancient and the various modern forms of the song, yet such lives as—

" Twopence halfpenny is my rent "

(showing the country lad's idea of wealth), and

" I've corn and hay in the barn hard by,
    And three fat hogs *pent up in the sty*,"

are suggestive of lines in the modern versions, such as—

" The old mare's keep be corn and hay,
    And I earn my ninepence every day " ;

and—

" For oi have a peg *poked up in a stoi*
    As'll come to us when Granny do doi."

Finally, in every case the wooing, whether successful or not, was at least rapid. For both the old songs have the refrain, " I cannot come every day to woo " ; nor do the modern forms take us beyond the day on which the wooing commences :—

" Dick's compliments were zo polite,
    He won Meess Jeeun avoor it were night ;
An' when her'd got no moor fur to zay,
    Whoi he gee'd her a kiss, and her coom'd
        away."

Another song which has lived long and travelled far is " Who's the fool now ? " dating from the end of the sixteenth century. It is commonly taken, as Chappell says, to be " a satire on those who tell wonderful stories," and simply relates a string of impossibilities :—

> " I saw the man in the moon
> Clouting of St. Peter's shoon.
> Thou hast well drunken, man,
> Who's the fool now ?
>
> " I saw a hare chase a hound
> Twenty miles above the ground ! "

and so forth. Two centuries, at least, later than the composition of this song, Dr. Alexander Campbell took down a version of it in the Highlands and published it in his *Albyn's Anthology* (1816–18). In the Scotch version, though the number of lines remains the same as in the old English song, the tune and rhythm are utterly unlike those of the original ; and it has been altered for the better. It contains the curious couplet about the man in the moon, but, for the rest, it is infinitely more full of fun and verve than its predecessor :—

> " I saw a hare taking care
> Of twenty greyhound pups, and mair !
>
> " I saw an eel chase the Deel
> Round about a fishwife's creel.
>
> " I saw a snail drag a whale
> And a ship tied to her tale "—

and its refrain is more genial :—

> " And I think ye're a' blind drunk, sirs,
> I'm but jolly fu', my jo ! "

Equally triumphant, it yet lacks that touch of bitterness contained in the words, " Who's the fool now ? "

These country songs belong, in a sense, to the past. The period of creation is ended, and they will no longer be kept alive by oral tradition. But there is good ground for hoping that those which have got into print will not be forgotten. Though conditions have changed, the genius of the people remains the same, and wherever our native music becomes known it makes an appeal. As Mr. Kidson says, speaking of the old nursery rhymes as compared with those of modern composition, " Their age and popularity have ever made them welcome in all nurseries, and a new generation is constantly demanding those selfsame rhymes which have been in a like manner continuously demanded by their ancestors from a remote period. They can never by any chance be superseded by others seemingly more fitted for the child of to-day. Children have always sung and repeated them, and in spite of the many substitutes offered, will continue to sing them." So much for the first stage of musical education. As for older children, the experiment, which has been tried in some schools, of teaching the old country songs in class, shows that they are not only more immediately welcomed than the more modern songs, but more easily learnt and more accurately remembered. And the interest which has been taken in the various collections published recently seems to indicate that our traditional music has something to say even to those who keep abreast with the latest developments of the art.

XXXI

TREES

Through launds, and by sweet-smelling underwoods,
Which guirlanded with honeysuckle locks ;
Where windflower blows, and dew-dropt daffodillies,
With robin, medléd in the thicket grass ;
And loved maylilies, most of heavenly grace,
And pure ambrosial breath : where vermeil-white,
Are blossomed boughs, of cherry and the thorn ;
And strew wild-apple blosms, their forest path.
Be these wild garden-grounds of Britain's woods. . . .

—CHARLES M. DOUGHTY.

Hæc nemora indigenæ Fauni Nymphæque tenebant.

—VIRGIL.

IT is a curious question, whether the human race could exist without trees. A race of beings of some kind might, but it would not be the human race. Besides the easily provable necessity of trees to make the world physically habitable for us men and women, there is the æsthetic necessity. For my own part, so thoroughly has the idea of " trees " entered into my soul, that I cannot even think of a landscape—natural or painted—without thinking of trees. Of course, I exclude sea pictures and arctic pictures, which are not landscapes, and represent places only collaterally, as it were, habitable. Architectural views may also be excepted : though the mere architect, when he draws an elevation, seldom refrains from attempting to suggest a garden or " grounds " by sticking in a tree or two at the corners of his drawing. Of course, also, there are landscapes without a vestige of a tree : but these I refuse to consider as exceptions to my statement. I assert, without reservation, that all genuine landscapes make me think of trees. Paradoxical as it may appear, the landscapes which have no trees are just those which suggest the " trees " idea most vividly. If one analyses the compound emotion which one feels on looking at a perfectly barren desert, or at a picture of one, it will be found that the utter absence of trees is the most salient factor in the emotion. In such a view, trees are emphatically conspicuous by their absence, and you cannot forget the fact. It is the same with a picture of a rolling common or of a moor or of a vast grass prairie. Trees haunt these pictures as invisible ghosts. Artists know this ; and they know also that it is this conception of the trees that are not there which makes the desert look so thoroughly and impressively a desert. Sometimes the artist puts in a palm tree or two, with the result that the desert is thus made to look much more of a desert than it did when it was drawn as absolutely treeless.

I cannot separate my æsthetic self from trees. It does not seem to be difficult to discover several reasons for this. Perhaps the underlying, congenital, instinctive reason is that we men and women are still the subjects of an hereditary sylvan taste derived from our very-far-off arboreal quadrumanous ancestors. When we are in a wood we seem—at any rate, I can speak for myself—to have got home

again. The muffled noises, a kind of audibly-breathing silence, the glints of light and shade, the only half-seen movements of the coy wild things of the wood, the strong motionless stems and the ever-waving boughs with their infinite variation of curve and colour— have we not some kind of indefinite recollection of it all, as in a forgotten past ? We throw ourselves down upon the mossy mound at the foot of a quincentennial oak, and were never more children than we are then. We may not own an inch of land in the world ; but the wood, while we are in it, is ours by a kind of right of inheritance. In a word, we are at home again.

Whether all this is mere fancy or not—it may be mere fancy to many— there are other reasons why trees, massed as forest or woodland, impress us. Most of us have a multitude of acquired woodland associations, which have given to trees a special charm. But when the rare incident happens of an adult discovering himself or herself in a wood for the first time in his or her life, besides the inevitable sense of novelty, there is called forth equally inevitably a vivid emotion of admiration and, in a larger or less degree, of wonder and awe. Without troubling ourselves with the question whether beauty is in the mind or in the object, we none of us refuse to admit that trees have the power of compelling admiration; and, when they are large or thickly massed, they compel an admiration which we yield to them alone. We probably attempt to give verbal expression to our admiration by comparing the vistaed clusters of the tree-stems to colonnades of columns, the over-arching and intertwining higher boughs to the arches and vaulted roofs of cathedrals, the chequered light and shade to the " dim religious light " admitted through richly storied church windows—but it won't do. Our metaphors do not help us. The woodland details are more to us than the metaphors, they are simply what they are, and they take hold of us more despotically than do the things from which we derive our metaphors. If the woodlands do not belong to us, at any rate we belong to the woodlands, willing thralls, spell-bound happy victims of the *genius loci*. If neither Pan nor the dryads, nor Oberon and Titania, are visible, they must be not far off, and we may catch sight of them at any moment. If we had never heard of either classic or Celtic or Norse myths, we should be tempted incontinently to invent myths of our own. To indulge in metaphors drawn

from other sources is to allow the real charm to escape—the woodlands are the woodlands, and there is nothing more to be said.

We have to go very far afield from civilization, nowadays, to find any good representative of the old German Hercynian forest. We know too much about forests to feel all that must once have been meant by such expressions as " horrida silva." But it is still possible to lose one's self all day long in European and even in British woodlands. Some of my pleasantest, and certainly some of my most vivid, recollections of a residence in a quaint old German university town, are those of my woodland rambles. From early morning until evening, sometimes guiding myself through pathless tracts by the direction in which my shadow fell, either alone or with a merry-hearted German student, making an hour's halt at midday for refreshment at some curious old water-mill or at a pleasant Forsthaus in the recesses of the wood, where the best refreshment might be a chat with the genial intelligent, highly-trained forester himself.—If those times could only come back again!

As the past glides farther and farther away, it breaks up into its more salient details and loses its continuity.

One of these details belongs to an Easter tramp my student-friend and I made through a part of the Odenwald. It was late at night, the full moon was already high in a cloudless heaven. On the ground lay an inch or two of crisply frozen snow, which glittered in the moonbeams. As we dropped down towards a valley from the open hill-top, we came into a pine wood, in which were only large trees standing twenty or thirty feet apart, nearly ready to be cut. We had no camera with us, and could not have used it in the moonlight ; but the scene is photographed in my mind. The dark tree-tops, the black shadows of the stems on the snow, the great patches of glistening moonlight on the snow : simplicity itself, but it made us stand at gaze. It was just such a scene as compels a recollection of the well-known passage in Heine's *Harzreise* :

" Like a great poet, Nature knows how to produce the greatest effects with the fewest means. Da sind nur eine Sonne, Baüme, Blumen, Wasser und Liebe." The last sentence sounds best in German : let the original flavour cling to it.

Another detail, or associated group of details, is connected with a spot in a forest to which I always happened to go alone. The journey meant a few miles by train to save time, and then a walk into a remote part of the woodland, where, on a lofty hillside, was a small clearing. The ground in the clearing sloped sufficiently to allow me, sitting on a boulder at the highest edge of the clearing, to look over the trees below and around. Before me and on either side spread out a wide and distant rolling country absolutely covered—in the perspective, at least— by forest. Here were tracts of oak and beech, there tracts of fir and pine and larch, old plantations and young ones, all shades of green, and masses of varied contour : but everywhere trees. It was as if I were sitting on a mountain top and looking down upon layers of green clouds. The scene had an endless charm for me, and often since I have made it the imaginary locale of my daydreams. In fancy, into that magic solitude I have conjured great-souled men, and held refreshing intercourse with them. Though one day I discovered, in the far distance among the tree-tops, the quaint point of the spire of a church belonging to some small village which was hidden from me, that only intensified the sense of retirement and solitude. I was not " where no man hath been since the making of the world," but I was temporarily dwelling apart, in a sacred place, alone with the Great Mystery. And I had but to turn to that tiny spire in the distance, if the solitude became too oppressive, and then I could add to the emotions which my surroundings called forth the last word of Heine's in the quotation given above, human " Liebe."

The witchery of trees is by no means confined to woodlands. As I go about in our beautiful England, I am ever thankful for the hedgeside and scattered timber which the taste or the policy of our people has planted, and to which our propitious soil and climate have given such noble proportions. The roadside elms, the ancestral oak in the middle of the pasture, the ashes with the graceful sweep of their boughs, and the many other trees of this promiscuous fellowship, affect me as if they were conscious of their utility of beauty, breaking the horizon line or giving a superb variety to our hillsides and river-valleys. How grandly they shape themselves in their isolation or semi-isolation, toning the uniformity of green undergrowth with their shadows, or enhancing the beauty of distance by half-hiding it with their own beauty ! Age adds another charm if it takes away that of lusty vigour and early symmetry. The grotesquerie of shape and the jagged remain-

ders of lost limbs seem to demand a reverent admiration. I often haunt an ancient park where stand many venerable oaks which, centuries ago, were spared because they were even then too old for use as ship-timber. Two of them I have measured, and have found that the bole of each has a girth of more than thirty feet. These monsters still possess flourishing limbs, each of which is large enough to make a fine tree of itself. Then, scattered about all around, are others which, if a little less in girth and more decayed, are all the more picturesque. If these were but " Talking Oaks "— nay, they do talk, and I loiter among them and listen.

If there are any dwellers in our latitudes who regret that the climate compels us to have a majority of trees that lose their leaves every autumn, I am not in sympathy with them. Can there be any one who makes a claim to good taste, yet has not recognized the unique beauty of our winter leafless trees ? Certainly, no lover of Nature. The giant bole, the sinewy arms, the graceful boughs, the feathery twigs, what a picture they make ! There is nothing else like it in Nature. Let such trees be silhouetted against the splendour of the sunrise, or against the gold and orange and red and lemon

SEA GULLS.

From a photograph by
Messrs. Gibson & Sons.

tints of sunset, or against the dark transparent azure of the star-sprinkled night, or against the moon slowly gliding up the heavens! If we had never seen this before, and came upon it suddenly and unawares, is there a dictionary that could give us words by which we could do more than imperfectly suggest our emotion?

Trees are a part of us. Each one of us is himself, plus his environment. And for most of us, trees are so important a constituent of our environment that, without them, our lives would be maimed indeed. Surely, every one who has read the following most deliciously human quatrain of Omar Khayyám's (one must suspect that there is as much of the Western Fitzgerald in it as of the Eastern Omar Khayyám) has felt that it would be far less perfect than it is without the suggestion of trees :—

" Here with a Loaf of Bread beneath the Bough,
A Flask of Wine, a Book of Verse—and Thou
Beside me singing in the Wilderness—
And Wilderness is Paradise enow."

Here we have Heine again—"Baüme" and " Liebe." Both—neither without the other.

XXXII

WILD-FOWL SHOOTING

" The mallard, borne on swift and powerful wings,
Seeks reedy marsh, or boggy lowland drear,
Where river to the sea its waters flings,
Its surface mirroring the sky's blue sphere."

—GREATREX.

TO-DAY there may be said to be two kinds of wild-fowl shooting —the pursuit of genuine wild-bred fowl, and the killing of wild-duck reared much as are pheasants. At any rate, there is one form of shooting duck which, I rejoice to say, has become practically a pastime of the past ; at least, no one who indulged in it now could hope to sustain his reputation as a sportsman untarnished. This is " flapper shooting," the slaughter of young wild-duck whose power of flight is yet so limited that a short stick, used after the manner of a boomerang, would be a more sporting weapon than a shot-gun.

To-day you hear of magnificent bags of duck in localities from which the wild-duck of our grandfathers have long since been driven away. Perhaps you go to inspect one of these modern " duckeries," and you are probably disgusted at the idea of any man calling himself a sportsman shooting the crowds of duck which waddle over the feet of their keeper. Though at first sight it may appear paradoxical to say so, the tamer are hand-reared wild-duck, the better the sport they give. "But, surely, birds so tame and confiding can afford sport scarcely superior to the shooting of barn-door fowls," is a comment I am always hearing. The uninitiated townsman invariably imagines that a heavy fusillade is directed against all hand-reared game as he sees it. He either does not know or forgets that this very tameness is encouraged with the direct purpose of controlling the birds, be they ducks or pheasants, so that each bird may offer a shot ten times more sporting, ten times higher, and ten times more difficult than does a mallard rising from a ditch or a pheasant kicked up in turnips.

Many men who shoot nowadays are not naturalists, but they may be good sportsmen for all that. That the man steeped in business should insure as much shooting as possible during the few days he can snatch for sport is only human after all; the leisure to shoot and to study the ways of birds and beasts is a privilege not given to all.

Not the least advantage of combining pheasant and duck rearing on the same shoot is that, should the day chosen for pheasant shooting be wet—which means failure, for pheasants cannot rise if wet—the duck show at their best, and provide more difficult shooting than ever. Each shot at duck in a storm of wind and rain is so sporting that no man need turn his back in disgust at its simplicity, or be ashamed to miss it. Sometimes duck are turned into the coverts with pheasants, with whom they live, feed, and find their fate.

To shoot flighting fowl at dusk or dawn is the most fascinating of sport, though it has its drawbacks; for howling winds, driving sleet, and cold feet—I can hear your mere mechanical shooters shudder—are the price at which you get the full cream of shooting. Besides, to him who loves to hear and to see the busiest hours of Nature, there is no more delightful time than when wild life says "Good morning," or bids "Good night" to the world. The honck-honck of geese, the quack of duck, the whe-oh of widgeon, the wild piping of curlew, and plaintive plover notes form an orchestra which rouses the numbed soul of the wild-fowler. Having reached the spot from which he knows he can best command the line the fowl take to and from their feeding-grounds, morning and night, he and the old retriever who has been his familiar companion from puppyhood wait in silence. At first there is no sound save the moaning of the distant sea, but soon a host of life stirs on all sides. And so time flies. A warning whine from the old dog tells his master he must be up and doing. Though at the finish the game-bag be empty, there is reward always in an appetite for breakfast or dinner which is beyond the power of gold.

But to my mind the great charm which the shooting of wild-fowl possesses, no matter whether your prey be geese, duck, teal, snipe, or woodcock, is that you can enjoy sport which is quite difficult enough to stimulate the keenness even of shooters above the average, without that feeling of restraint from which the ordinary, formal shooting party is never free ; and which is so often spoiled by making it more or less of a social function.

When I go shooting, I like to shoot, not to treat the sport as a means of passing another day. If your object is to kill time—go in for croquet or golf. But this reminds me of a story : A certain shooter, more famous for his classical learning than his skill with the gun, was assigned the place of honour, in front of the other guns, at a good pheasant beat. The day was gloriously fine and the beat long. At any rate, a stream of birds flew finally in his direction, but never a shot greeted them. When the rest of the party came up, there lay the scholarly sportsman on his back, deep in Horace.

I have a peculiarly vivid recollection of shooting my first wild-duck. I shall never forget it, for—I must confess that I shot it on the ground ; and, in those days of boyish exuberance to kill, I certainly should have shot at its fellow also on the ground with my second barrel, but it did not wait. But, though my heart was thumping like a dozen motors, I steadied myself for the shot, and two fat duck were mine. To stalk within range, I had to crawl over a long, sloping manure heap, by no means dry. But what cared I, so long as I bagged my first wild-duck ?

Even in these less ardent days, I would trudge ten miles to get a " right and left " at wild-duck. Often after a formal day's shooting at other game have I turned out into the chill winter twilight on the chance of getting a duck, and more often than not, have got none ; though to hear them quack was some recompense.

With a congenial companion, and a

brace of retrieving spaniels, there are many worse ways of spending winter days than in tramping along winding, sedge-fringed streams, trying here and there a withy-patch, or rushy pool for wild-fowl, here to-day and to-morrow gone. The charm of such hunts is that you never know what each day, or each step, may bring forth. The bag may contain at the finish anything from a jack-snipe to a wild-swan, even though the total of the reddest-lettered day may not exceed ten head.

There is no doubt that our wild-fowling would be the better, if decoys, punt-guns, and—vile recent inventions, when used against anything but vermin—automatic guns were strictly prohibited. And yet I do not remember ever to have seen even wholesale decoy-slaughter made a target for the shafts of paragraphists whose pens oscillate between the "butchery of game" and "the battue."

So far snipe have escaped the improving hand of man; nor do I think the time will ever come when one will receive invitations to big snipe drives, with a postscript that so many hundreds have been turned down with the idea of insuring a bumper bag. There is something so inexpressibly wild about the "scape scape" of a rising snipe—a sort of hall-mark which guar-

antees the bird above suspicion of coops and broody hens, maize and keepers' whistling.

I fear that woodcock have much to answer for in the way of being the innocent cause of shooting accidents. In most parts of England this fascinating bird is so rarely met with, that, in their frantic efforts to bag it, men who are ordinarily cool, careful, and self-possessed, completely lose their heads at the imminent risk of blinding their companions. As a means to an end, the advice of a practical sportsman, that when you hear furious shouts of "Mark woodcock!" you should fling yourself flat on the ground, and there remain till the tumult has abated, has never been improved upon.

There is a little story attached to the first woodcock I *ought* to have shot. I was taking part in my first covert shoot, and my ears were ringing with various admonitions bearing more or less (some of them a good deal less, at least so thought I) on the etiquette of the occasion. I had noted a plea of the keeper on behalf of some rather backward pheasants alleged to be in the wood we were shooting. I was standing in a broad ride, and just as the beaters had come almost to its edge, up fluttered two small, brown birds, as I thought, immature pheasants. I restrained myself—which at that time was in itself no small feat— and let them go, only to be upbraided in terms which made me feel very young—though I was quite fourteen— for failing to cover myself with im-mortal fame by bagging a right and left at 'cock. I must admit, how-ever, in mitigation of my misdeed that I had been assured that the flight of woodcock was so tortuous and swift that none but an experienced shooter could hope to hit one. But I soon had the pleasure of atoning for my disgrace by stopping the next woodcock after it had flown the gauntlet of seven cartridges.

To the man who has patience and no wild-fowl, I recommend the pursuit of wood-pigeons. There are few locali-ties where pigeons cannot be found in plenty ; but the difficulty is to get at them. So wild, shy, and keen-sighted are they that I consider I have done well to make a fair bag once in ten attempts. One of the cleverest accomplishments of a wood-pigeon is the rarely forgotten trick of putting a branch of adequate size between its body and your shot, whenever it makes the unusual mistake of dashing out of a tree on the right side for the shooter. And I have yet to meet the man who can say with truth that wood-pigeons are easy to hit, even when they give you the chance.

XXXIII

THE ENTOMOLOGIST'S METHODS

> " The virtuoso thus, at noon,
> Broiling beneath a July sun,
> The gilded butterfly pursues
> O'er hedge and ditch, through gaps and mews ;
> And, after many a vain essay
> To captivate the tempting prey,
> Gives him at length the lucky pat,
> And has him safe beneath the hat ;
> Then lifts it gently from the ground ;
> But, ah ! 'tis lost as soon as found.
> Culprit his liberty regains,
> Flits out of sight, and mocks his pains."
> —COWPER.

TO capture a butterfly with a net, of even Brobdingnagian pro-portions, is not always the soft thing it seems to any one who has not attempted the feat. The insect has settled on a tall thistle blossom ; you approach stealthily until, as you judge, you are within striking distance of the object. With a grand sweep the net travels rapidly in the direction of the quarry, but although it has decapitated the thistle it does not enclose the butterfly. It was just that elegant sweep that lost the fly; next time get the net rather higher than the thistle head and then strike downwards and obliquely.

Two collectors are busy among the butterflies in a clover field. One has taken up a position and quietly nets the right kinds as they come within range. The other is rushing about hither and thither; he does not catch much, but he is taking plenty of exercise, and incidentally doing some damage to the farmer's crop. Again, in disturbing moths from their resting-places in hedgerows, bushes, etc., one collector will slash away right vigorously, but he seems anxious all the time to push on as fast as he can. Insects leave their retreat in response to his summons, but he does not see them because he has passed the spot when they emerge. Most of those moths will return to cover and be secured by the collector who, working methodically, has lagged behind his companion. He gently taps the twigs here and there, pokes his stick well into the hedge and stirs up the vegetation growing below, but he faces his

work all the while and very little escapes his wary eye. There is, too, this further difference in the tactics of the two; the collector in a hurry boxes or kills outright everything he succeeds in bagging, whereas the slower worker carefully examines all his catches and at once liberates anything he does not require.

Although it is always well for the collector to have the implement with him when on an entomological foray, the net is not the all-important article it may be considered. There are collections of butterflies which for the most part comprise only bred specimens. In some cases the net may have been used to capture female butterflies from which to obtain a stock of eggs, but the majority of the specimens contained in such collections have been reared from eggs, or from caterpillars obtained by searching or beating among the food plants of the various species. It would be possible, too, to acquire a very respectable collection of moths without using the net at all.

Searching low-growing herbage by day, or by the aid of a lantern at night, is a bit trying at first, no doubt, and some collectors may think the business too wearisome. Success in this kind of work is probably a matter of temperament. A good stock of patience and a sharp eye are the essential requirements, and being armed with these the egg or caterpillar hunter will find that practice overcomes seeming difficulty and leads to proficiency.

To obtain leaf-eating caterpillars from trees or bushes, the collector with one hand holds an open umbrella under the branches, whilst with a stick in the other he strikes from above in the direction of the receptacle held below. Sudden sharp thumps on the thicker part of a branch are usually more effective than any amount of indiscriminate thrashing of the foliage and smaller twigs. Some collectors, however, prefer to search the leaves and twigs for the caterpillars and rarely bring the beating stick into action.

Two friends, one an advocate of forcible ejectment, and the other an expert in the more gentle art, decided to test the two methods when on an expedition for caterpillars of the Large Emerald, which feed on birch, hazel and alder. At the close of the trial the searcher had eight caterpillars and the beater only two. Seven moths were subsequently reared from the eight caterpillars, but neither of those that fell to the beating stick reached the chrysalis stage.

It is the habit of many kinds of moths to sit during the day on tree-trunks, rocks, palings and other sorts of fencing, etc., and the collector often secures a goodly bag by simply walking about a wood, or by the side of a long stretch of paling. Some moths are rather conspicuous objects when resting in this way, but others seem to so closely match whatever they are upon that their detection is at first somewhat difficult. Many collectors become such adepts at the sport that they can not only see a moth on a tree several yards away from them, but very often they can tell whether or not it happens to be of the kind they want. Such efficiency is, however, only acquired by considerable experience. The bulk of the moths found in this way may be boxed without much trouble, but some kinds are rather skittish and fly from their perch on the approach of the collector. In such cases the net comes in handy.

The collector will need to familiarize himself with those plants whose blossoms are attractive to insects. Of these sallow, which blooms in early spring, and the autumnal flowering ivy are especially to be located, so that each may be worked in its season. Isolated bushes of the former, when growing in or near woods, are more remunerative than large and dense masses. Swarms of bees and flies visit the yellow catkins, the so-called "palm," during the day, but at night moths gather together from all quarters, and carouse on the nectar drawn from the blossoms. The method of collecting the moths is similar to that employed in beating for caterpillars just referred to. The tapping, however, should be even more tenderly done. The insects fall readily and will remain perfectly still for a time. When they arouse themselves they crawl quietly towards the edge of the umbrella or whatnot. There is always plenty of time to examine the inebriates by the aid of a lantern, and to select such of them as may be required. Ivy is worked much in the same way, but sometimes, as for instance when the plant grows on the sides of a wall or house, the lantern will have to be turned on and the moths boxed from the flowers direct.

In most woods that are more or less open to the public it will be noticed that the trees on each side of the rides, and on the edges of the wood, have blackish vertical patches on their trunks. These marks do not indicate that such trees are to fall under the woodman's axe. They are the signs manual of the collecting craft, and result from frequent applications of the saccharine composition which the collector uses to attract those moths that have a partiality for sweets. Although the basis of the mixture is either brown sugar or treacle, or both, reduced to a workable consistency by boiling in beer, there are various recipes for the preparation of the bait. Very often the compound is finished off by the addition of a modicum of rum, and some collectors put in a drop or two of the essence of jargonelle pear or ribston pippin. Not infrequently it happens that the moths are not to be tempted by anything in the way of sweets that the collector may prepare. What the meteorological or other conditions should be exactly is not clearly understood, but certain it is that on some evenings, ordinary treacle spread on the tree trunks will allure moths by hundreds, while on another night equally favourable so far as one can judge, not a single moth will put in an appearance, even although the most cunningly concocted mixture has been put on. When, however, the moths do attend the feast provided for them, the collector's heart is glad, and he enjoys an hour or two of considerable excitement moving from tree to tree, selecting a specimen here and another there. As

THE OWL.

From a Photograph by
Oliver Pike.

each patch of sugar is approached and the light of the lantern allowed to fall upon it, the collector is on the tip-toe of expectancy, for what grand prize may the flash reveal! A Small Mottled Willow, perchance, or perhaps a fine example of the Blue Underwing or Clifden Nonpareil. Even among the things of less rarity there are many which give the collector pleasure to see at the banquet. When the attendance of insect guests is large, what a scrimmage there is between those already feeding and the new arrivals anxious to obtain a share of the entertainment. Some of the larger kinds, such as the Dark Arches and the Yellow Underwings, are quarrelsome fellows, and delight in rowdyism, much to the discomfort of the quieter sorts. At the foot of trees that are frequently sugared it is not uncommon to find a well nourished toad seated and patiently awaiting whatever may fall from the festive board above him. Centipedes also get to know of the moth gatherings, and find that a supper is easily to be obtained on such occasions.

XXXIV

THE STUDY OF BOTANY OUT OF DOORS

"Come forth into the light of things,
Let Nature be your teacher."
—WORDSWORTH.

IT may as well be stated at once that in order rightly to appreciate a ramble in search of wild flowers, some knowledge of scientific botany is necessary. Unfortunately, the study of plants is usually accounted a dull and uninteresting occupation, and it may be admitted that the rudiments of the subject are not of an exciting character. Yet it is only with the study of botany, as with all other branches of learning. There is no royal road to knowledge save that of strenuous and intelligent study. The main difficulty, however, with regard to botany seems to be the strange and unfamiliar terms in which the science expresses itself. This again may, to a certain extent, be admitted, and yet, when the intricate and delicate structure of plants is taken into consideration, it may well be doubted if any simpler mode of expression, consistent with scientific accuracy, be possible. And, after all, with the aid of such excellent textbooks, as Oliver's *Lessons in Elementary Botany* or Professor Henslow's *Botany for Beginners*, the difficulty of learning the A B C of the science should not be insurmountable, and once mastered, the study becomes henceforth one of increasing fascination and delight. A little steady work during the dark days of winter will overcome the initial difficulties, and enable the student in the first beginning of spring, when the celandines are starring the mossy banks, and the hellebore is in blossom on Selborne Hill, to say with the poet Chaucer, " Farewel my boke, and my devocioun," and to hasten to the " mede," to " here the foules synge," and to see " the floures gynnen for to sprynge."

In the olden times, before any English Flora was written, and botany as a science can hardly be said to have existed, the study of plants was carried out almost entirely in the open air. The species themselves had first to be discovered before they could be classified and described. And so the early herbalists, as they were wont to call themselves, made " itineraries " or " simpling-voyages " into the country for the express purpose of ascertaining what plants were to be found in Great Britain. A botanical expedition in the far-off days of the sixteenth or seventeenth centuries, in company with old Gerarde, or Thomas

Johnson, or Mr. Goodyer, or John Ray, must have been an experience of rare interest. It was then that the knowledge of our indigenous wild flowers was being gradually accumulated, and hitherto unknown species were being constantly added to the list of British plants. " What wonderful scenes," as Richard Jefferies says, " old Gerarde must have viewed, when our English lanes were all a tangle of wild flowers, and plants that are now scarce were common, and the old ploughs, and the curious customs, and the wild red-deer—it would make a good picture, it really would, Gerarde studying English orchids ! " It is still possible to make out from his *Herball* some of the routes this good " Master in Chirurgerie " took in his herborising expeditions, and to compare the flora of to-day with what it was in the reign of Queen Elizabeth. The county of Essex was clearly a favourite and familiar district, especially in the neighbourhood of Braintree and Colchester, and along the coast from Tilbury Fort to Walton-on-the-Naze, and many rare and interesting plants, such as the Sea Cotton-weed at Mersea Island, and the Wild Asparagus " at a place called Bandamar lading," he chronicles for the first time. To Thomas Johnson, however, who after Gerarde's death brought out an enlarged edition of the famous *Herball*, we owe the first local catalogues of British plants ever published in this country. Johnson, it appears, kept a drug-shop on Snow Hill in the city of London, " where," we are told, " by his unwearied pains, advanced with good natural parts, he attained to be the best herbalist of his age in England." His " unwearied pains " consisted in part in undertaking botanical expeditions " two or three times a summer," in company with like-minded friends, into various parts of the country. On one journey, of which he has left us an account, through Oxford, to Bath and Bristol, and back by Southampton, the Isle of Wight, and Guildford, he collected upwards of six hundred species, several of which had never been discovered in England before. He was also among the earliest botanists who visited Wales, where he found a large number of new plants, including the Rose-root (*Sedum Rhodiola*, DC.) on Snowdon, and " the yellow wilde Polly of Wales."

To the illustrious naturalist John Ray belongs the honour of collecting together the botanical knowledge of his time, and of bringing out the earliest systematic Flora of our indigenous plants. He published the first edition of his *Synopsis* of British plants in 1690, which may fairly be regarded as the foundation of every subsequent English Flora. The book was the result, not only of strenuous work in the study, but also of a personal knowledge of plants in their native localities. Indeed, Ray is said to have himself examined every species described in the *Synopsis*. Like the other early botanists he made extensive excursions into various parts of England and Wales for the purpose of observing rare and interesting plants ; and an account of some of these " Itineraries," written by himself, remains. Only last summer, I experienced the pleasure of following in his footsteps in South Pembrokeshire, and of finding most of the choice species still flourishing in the very places mentioned by him two centuries and a half ago. Moreover, some years ago, I made a pilgrimage to Ray's cottage (now unfortunately burnt down) at Black Notley in Essex, in which he wrote the famous *Synopsis*. It was a most interesting visit. I stood in the very room " facing south "—the one warm room in the house, which he speaks of as cold, and " exposed to the north and northeast winds," and " inconvenient to one who is subject to colds and whose lungs are apt to be affected—floored with wide oaken boards, and with a dark heavy beam running across the ceiling, the window fitted with the leaded casement of the seventeenth century, in which the great naturalist worked, where he examined his botanical specimens, and where he wrote his scientific books. Cupboards of all shapes and sizes were to be noticed in the house, planned, no doubt, by Ray himself—for he built his " house on Dewlands "—for the purpose of storing his scientific specimens. For rare plants and other curiosities were constantly arriving, by the Braintree carrier, at Dewlands, sent by one or another of his many friends. One especially, Thomas Willisel by name, a professional naturalist of humble birth, " employed by the Royal Society in the search of rarities, both animals and plants," "for which purposes," says Ray, " he was the fittest man in England, both for his skill and industry," seems to have supplied him with a number of choice specimens of rare plants. Thus, by personal observation, and through the researches of others, carried on in the open air, Ray was enabled to write his *Synopsis* of British plants, which henceforth, for a long period, became " the pocket companion of every English botanist."

It is now over two hundred years since the *Synopsis* first appeared, and since then the researches of botanists have rendered the British Flora practically complete. It may be taken as almost certain that there are no new indigenous species left for modern enthusiasts to discover. Still the charm of botany remains. There is a strange fascination in the search after rare plants, especially in localities rendered interesting by the " record " of some early observer. The purely scientific student may carry on his investigations in the laboratory, the field-botanist seeks the open air. With Izaac Walton he sallies forth into the meadows " chequered with water-lilies and lady-smocks," or along the " high honey-suckle hedge," or " under the willow-trees by the water-side." With John Ray at Black Notley he knows the " habitat " of every rare plant in the parish, or like Gilbert White he visits season by season every choice species in the neighbourhood—the mezereon among the brushwood at the top of the Hanger, the herb-paris in the Church Litten Coppice, or the marsh cinquefoil in the bogs of Bin's-pond.

In this way only is it possible to become acquainted with the growth and habit of species. A dried specimen in the herbarium is not the same thing as the living plant in its own surroundings. *Scilla verna,* be it never so carefully pressed, is but a sorry likeness of the exquisitely beautiful Vernal Squill as it may be seen in thousands on the short sandy turf above the magnificent cliffs of Cornwall and South Wales. It is difficult to recognize in the dark, mummified specimen labelled " *Ophrys apifera, Huds,*" the splendid Bee-orchis of our Hampshire downs. Hence many teachers of botany have given instruction out of doors as well as in the lecture-room. Professor Henslow of Cambridge regularly made " herborizing " excursions with his pupils into the Fens that they might gain a practical knowledge of plants in their native haunts. So Charles Kingsley, when he was Canon of Chester, was wont every week during the summer months to give his botanical class what he called a " field-lecture " ; and these natural history rambles became so popular, and were so largely attended, that on one occasion, a person meeting the party outside the city walls supposed it to be "a congregation going off to the opening of a Dissenting chapel in the country." And the charm of such expeditions can hardly be exaggerated. The more we know of botany—the scientific structure of plants, their ways and habits, their relation to insects, their adaptation to environment, the folk-lore associated with many of them—the greater becomes the pleasure of the pursuit. " To a person uninstructed in natural history," said Professor Huxley, " his country, or seaside, stroll is a walk through a gallery filled with wonderful works of art, nine-tenths of which have their faces turned to the wall. Teach him something of natural history, and you place in his hands a catalogue of those which are worth turning round." " Surely," he adds, " our innocent pleasures are not so abundant in this life that we can afford to despise this or any other source of them." And as we grow older—" The coarser pleasures of our boyish days, And their glad animal movements all gone by," —the charm and interest of natural history remains. We find that " Nature never did betray the heart that loved her." Wild flowers to us, as to Dr. Arnold of Rugby, are our music. They are as unfailing a source of delight and recreation as they were to George Crabbe at Aldeburgh, or to John Stuart Mill at Avignon. We are still, with the poet Wordsworth, lovers of " the meadows and the woods and mountains, and of all that we behold from this green earth."

XXXV

THE OTTER

And deer-skins, dappled dun and white,
With otter's fur, and seal's unite.
—Scott.

BY highland streams—the Teith and the Leny; and on the lochs which nurse them—Vennachar and Lubnaig, the otter lives and fishes. The tenure is of ancient date. Amid the rude adornments of the sylvan hall on Ellen's Isle, Scott mentions an otter's skin, presumably from the investing Loch Katrine. The stream is rough, boulder-strewn, with fretting currents, and sudden shimmering pools. The loch is riven shored, and remote. Solitary all winter long, save for the stag which comes down to drink; silent, save for its own heart-beats. As the trout are not the same, so may the otter of the loch differ from that of the stream.

Running water makes a wild element even in a tame scene. It frets its banks into holes and galleries, and scores its channel ever deeper, laying bare the stones round which the current swirls. In times of spate it bites yet lower, opening mysterious passages among the tree roots. Sedges margin the stiller reaches with an impenetrable forest. It piles its débris until the shallows become islets, and the islets jungles of stranded tree roots and coarse vegetation. And so it takes a character to itself on no plan save its own, and works out a home for its tenant. In such environment the fauna remain wild. The fox of the covert may be pampered, but not the otter.

Hard by is a lowland stream pure and simple. It has no rough reaches. Two igneous heights of some fifteen hundred feet on one flank are its sole claim to highland kinship. For the rest, the source is lowly. It is fed by the drainage of a sloping country. On either side throughout it is gentle and uniform in its flow. For several miles its waters are tidal. Any rudeness it has is here, for there is ever a certain untamableness about tidal reaches. It ends in a small but picturesque estuary across whose mouth is drawn a shallow bar fretted by the winds into a watery chevaux de frise. It is an otter stream. If not of the most promising kind, still it has done some of its sculpturing work well, made the most of its chances. In a certain pleasing way it is wild and has some wild places which wild creatures know about. It is sufficient for the purpose. Where are otters at all, one may study them. And the nearer to one's present point of view the better.

In fact, the stream is a tributary of the Tay; in form, it is not. Just where it is bending northward to meet the parent river it flows out of sight. The sea comes in and hides the rest; nor does the lowest ebb lay bare the junction. Now the Tay is queen among the rivers for the multitude of her subjects. This distinction, in its measure, the disjointed tributary shares. Perhaps it has rather more than its share, since the fish running up the coast from the south-east strike it before they reach the mouth of the Tay. Seals are never absent from the estuary. As they are after the salmon, they give a sufficient hint of the constant run and the abounding life.

This act of the sea in blotting out the junction has dowered with independence. This happy stream is under no fishing laws save those imposed by a common interest. In this respect it is perhaps exceptional. No one is turned away : all rub shoulders on its banks. Where freedom is, poaching has no meaning, save for that miserable crew who prefer to do things in a crooked way and so spoil the sport of their betters. Its side paths remain open : its trout are his who can get a bite or a rise. Its salmon belong to the shabby-coated angler. No one may lessen or spoil the sport without his consent. No tacksman nets the tidal waters for his profit. Nor does any riparian proprietor use the upper reaches for his own pleasure. Nor is there any manner of trifling with the free play of natural forces in this people's water. Thus free from the interference which has so altered the complexion of other streams, choking the life at the mouth or making them into so many preserves, it is all the more favourable for the study of its wild forms.

On the whole the otter leads a pleasant and uneventful life. It is not persecuted ; if it were it has a fine faculty for looking after itself. No traps are set. It thrives in this republic of the waters, nor does it find the people to be a hard master. The only disturbance is the periodical visit of the otter hounds ; but that sounds worse than it really is. These occasions are interesting rather than eventful. There is always music to keep a pleasant ripple of excitement in the sport. Sometimes there are hot dargs ; but seldom a kill. In the three visits this year no otter was a penny the worse.

Seldom, almost never, are the otters seen by day. In the evening they come out to fish, if from some water-sealed holt below they may make their first catch before they appear. Like others they prefer to have their private dwelling at a distance from their place of business. They generally travel down stream. The fishing pool is below. They fish close in, swimming up and down under the water-grasses which float out from the bank. To the observant the habits of one wild creature lay bare the secrets of another. At that hour the bigger fish must be feeding near the edge : the otter knows best. The rings are seen to be breaking there. In lakes and other open waters their mode of hunting is different and more like that of a cat approaching a bird.

The night angler is sometimes startled by a sputtering blow beneath his feet. If curious enough to bend forward he may see a glittering object in the mouth, and envy the creature a skill so much greater than his own. The diet may vary according to the resources of the stream. The other day one was caught in an eel trap trying to get at the captives within. In times of stress it may even visit the ditches and marshy places to sup on frogs.

Sleek from the bath, and shedding the drops in a run of liquid notes back into the still pool, the dark form crawls up the bank among the water grasses. She looks about as though expecting something to be there. Laying down the trout she sends her strange whistle out into the twilight. The whistle searches everywhere, down among the sedges, across the pasture to the pine strip, up the stream to the weir by the mill. She waits—seldom has she to blow twice—and anon two heads appear. The pups had gone away on some little excursion of their own. Gravely playful, she has a romp with them after the meal and before she returns to the water.

Yet the trout do not suffer—probably benefit. The raiders do not seriously deplete the stream while they add to the virility of its fauna. What are taken can be well spared, and are represented in the size and play of those that are left. The true sportsman prefers a water with pike because he finds the trout ever so much more worth hooking, and would frown on the man who would kill out the less deadly otter.

Enough are left for the hook and to fill the net of the human poacher who unfortunately takes by so much the biggest share. Old anglers sigh for old days, but that is common in other pursuits. And even those who complain the loudest of lighter baskets are never heard to blame the otter. "Traps by all means," drily says a grizzled cynic, "but not for furred animals."

Certain it is that these unmolested otters of the stream do not increase. That prince of raconteurs, the old angler, has tales to tell of the otters of long ago, from which, with the needful pruning, it appears that in number they were much as now. Only another instance of a phase of wild life becoming increasingly familiar to many.

Animals of prey do not become a nuisance. We do not know altogether why. Much of the working is hidden, but so it is. We can see that it is wiser in their own interests; and when these things are left alone, few suicidal mistakes are made. They are always checks, not scourges. Only the ignorant think them many, nor pause to wonder why they are not more. Only the greedy blame them for taking so much instead of thanking them for taking so little. Nature begins with the breeding—so far we can follow. She allots —at least to the larger of them—a smaller number of young than to other creatures. Certainly than the creatures they prey on. To the trout she gives legions, to the otter she gives two, or at most three. Even so, the young should sum up with the years. They do not. There are other checks than the obvious ones. These appear not in themselves, and lie in wait in the path of those forms which are too strong to fear natural enemies.

Obscurity greater than that which rests on the lives of wild land mammals hides many of the doings of the otter. This is partly owing to the mystery of the medium in which it lives. It keeps no calendar, yet it knows when the spring salmon run, when the summer grilse and sea trout are due, and when the autumn visit of gravid fish draws near. In view of these events, it remits its evening swim under the floating grasses and seeks a change from its daily dish of trout.

Past pool and current, it drops down to the last dyke which checks the up-running tide, there to choose another holt against the coming of the migrants. Of an evening, it passes the mile or two of tidal water, to where the stream broadens out to the estuary. This vantage place commands away to the white bar running across the shallows by the edge of the sea. Thence it can watch the diving of the seals as they come up after the droves. When the hurrying salmon pass into the narrows, it falls in behind, and follows on the trail.

Finding it good to be there some elect to settle. On the banks of the tidal waters is always a fresh scent for the hounds. On the more generous diet the otters fatten, cast healthier cubs, and wax bigger. Excited by the play of the herding seals they go forth to join in the fray. They remain on the estuary nor seek to cross the bar. This is the nearest approach to a marine type, this intermediate form, this brackish water otter.

We have not, as on the west coast, the sea otter : that is, the otter which like the salmon has taken to a wider life. For that is all, it seems to me, that sea otter means. The difference in size is more than equalled in the salmon, and both fish and mammal have a like appearance of being over-grown. The inveterate marine habits are accounted for by the glamour of the sea, which possesses that which goes there, once and for all : its abundance also.

Even so, there are hints of an earlier life, however distant. It keeps inshore partly because its forebears were accus-tomed to a near bank on either side. Also to be in the path of the migrants seeking the river to which it has lost the way. If the vision of the dyke where otters wait for the run has faded, the olden taste for sea trout and salmon remains. In the sense even in which the seal is, the otter can never be a sea mammal.

The absence of dipping shore and deep water by the edge keep the east coast otter to the stream for a haunt, and to the trout for a living.

XXXVI
SOME COUNTRY BOOKS

In the cool of the evening, when the low sweet whispers waken,
  When the labourers turn them homeward, and the weary have their will,
When the censers of the roses o'er the forest aisles are shaken,
  Is it but the wind that cometh o'er the far green hill ?
                                        —ALFRED NOYES.

READING Lamb the other day, I could not but envy his pure love of the country and contrast it with our own, and especially when I came to the conclusion of "Blakesmoor":

" Mine too—whose else ?—thy costly fruit garden, with its sun-baked southern wall ; the ampler pleasure-garden, rising backwards from the house in triple terraces, with flowerpots now of palest lead, save that a speck here and there, saved from the elements, bespake their pristine state to have been gilt and glittering ; the verdant quarters backwarder still ; and stretching still beyond, in old formality, thy firry wilderness, the haunt of the squirrel, and the day-long murmuring wood-pigeon, with that antique image in the centre, God or Goddess I wist not ; but child of Athens or old Rome paid never a sincerer worship to Pan or to Sylvanus in their native groves, than I to that fragmental mystery. . . ."

Call it a passing tenderness or what you will ; but where in modern books can we find an attitude as happy, sincere, unquestioning, and intelligible as that ?

We protest too much to-day. We have reached, perhaps, the edge of a great mystery, and we are querulous and chattering as swallows before dawn. No class of books is now exempt from announcements of our affection for the country, but there are, excluding the scientific, two classes, not very well defined, which contain little else.

The first class is composed of books by naturalists and sportsmen, who may write very well, but pretend chiefly to share their knowledge, and incidentally their love of the country,

with their readers. The second class is composed of books by literary men and women, who may know much of natural history, but aim chiefly at expressing their own emotions in the presence of wild life. The best of each class approach one another very closely in character.

Knowledge of the country life abounds ; never more so, if one may judge from the number of sandwich papers found lying in the remotest parts of the earth ; but men seem not to have progressed so much as might have been expected in the art of setting down observation. Dull records of facts that mean nothing when they are dull are multiplied continually. But even they have their beauty when compared with the similar records which are garnished with jaunty sentiments and hastily chosen words. A sense of arrangement is very rare. A clear motive is rare ; thousands rush to inform the world that they have found a bird's nest or seen a vole climbing the tender shoots of young ash trees. In mere bulk such books are remarkable, and a proof that many persons of modest talents become well acquainted with the country to-day. But at the head of this class there is a small number of books which stand high, as literature, in comparison with any other books of our time. In the best of them, the modern attitude reaches something like its best expression. They have a sound knowledge of the facts of Nature, coupled, as it has hardly been at any other time, with a deep and sometimes passionate and mournful love of all that takes place in the open air and in the human mind under its influence. They have, too, a curious interest in character— the character of birds, for example, of snakes, of places. Thus, at their best, these books add considerably to pure knowledge; and (by the sense of the poetry of life) appeal to any one with an intellectual and spiritual life, whether naturalist or not ; and they give an interesting view of the mind of our age, and continue the revelation which Jefferies began in " The Story of My Heart." To this class should be added the gardening books which abound in information, but, in spite of much sentiment and quotation from Bacon and Marvell, hardly succeed in rising out of the rank of guide-books, to which rank they do honour.

The second class is equally large to-day, for it includes half the essayists and half the writers of verse. In their work, form is less the result of accident than in the first class. Observation,

for its own sake, is less conspicuous, and the mind of the author expresses itself rather through the moods which certain objects produce, than through a careful record of the objects themselves. The worst of this class are worse than the worst of the other, because they are derivative in form and manner, and without any fresh observation. There are also a number of considerably gifted people who do nothing but continue or weaken in verse the attitude of Shelley, e.g., or of Keats, sometimes with the addition of a vaguer mournfulness and a less intelligible choice of words, which may mean that they write for posterity.

In prose, these writers have their equals in some very sweet-voiced persons who use material already well known to us through Jefferies and Kingsley, and the rest, in a manner which differs little from theirs, except that it has less sincerity, more whims, and a much more poetical vocabulary. On a somewhat higher level than these, but not very high, stand those of a frankly town-bred attitude, who tell us, with some wit and some felicity, the joys of walking, of fishing, of country inns, and thus produce a literary form of bread-and-cheese and ale.

Higher in aim, but not always successful, are those men of reading and much musing, who express a mystical attitude in lyrics and songs which use Nature as a symbol, as a background, as a pigment for use in self-portraiture. Even these at the best are apt to write after Wordsworth and Thoreau, or to differ from them chiefly in a wilful use of the pathetic fallacy or in a vague religious sentimentality. Here, as in the other ranks of country books, too many writers give infinite attention to detail, but no thorough kneading to the whole, a weakness which seems to be due to the lack of a philosophical or individual attitude in minds much influenced by books.

Higher still are the books which really show, in verse or prose, the inseparableness of Nature and Man, with an inevitable tendency to dwell upon the power which Nature derives from her mystery—a romance like "Green Mansions," the supreme example ; a poem like "The Rout of the Amazons."

In these the differences from nineteenth-century work are not always easy to define. But I find in them subtler rhythms, a diminution of man's importance in the landscape, the use of the visible and tangible things as symbols of the unseen, and a great love of detail that is perhaps due to a belief that if only a scene is clearly drawn in words, the effect of the scene will be gained. Knowledge, love and art are not wanting. But one may conjecture that scientific discoveries and theories, while they feed and in no way impede the outdoor literature, yet tend to break it up, to confuse its aims, and to make impossible a grand concerted advance like that which accompanied the French Revolution.

It is not surprising, therefore, that many go back with a high zest or a great sense of peace to the old books that reveal a sensitiveness to Nature that is quite unlike our own, and to some later books between whose lines we may insert our dreams, like rose leaves, undisturbed. There is nothing in books, for example, to surpass the tale of Guiscardo and Ghismonda, read on a hot May morning, when you have just caught enough trout in a little chalk stream. It might be argued that, under those circumstances, the book does not matter ; but he who could argue so is no true lover of joy or of books. A page of Chaucer, of Parkinson, of Temple, of Malory, of Goldsmith, of Keats, will please this one or that, as well. And, for my part, I have found myself pretty often in May going back to a passage in a certain famous book, which begins thus :

"To take a boat in a pleasant evening, and with musick to row upon the waters, which Plutarch so much applauds, Aelian admires upon the river Peneus, in those Thessalian fields beset with green bays, where birds so sweetly sing that passengers, enchanted as it were with their heavenly musick, forget forthwith all labours, care and grief : or in a Gondola through the Grand Canal in Venice, to see those goodly Palaces, must needs refresh and give content to a melancholy dull spirit. Or to see the inner rooms of a fair built and sumptuous edifice, as that of the Persian Kings so much renowned by Diodorus and Curtius, in which all was almost beaten gold, chairs, stools, thrones, tabernacles, and pillars of gold, plane trees and vines of gold, grapes of precious stones, all the other ornaments of pure gold . . . with sweet odours and perfumes, generous wines, opiparous fare, etc., besides the gallantest young men, the fairest virgins. . . ."

It is not easy to like our modern authors as well, however gracious in spirit and in body rich.

A MARCH EVENING.

From a photograph by
Mary Cottam.

XXXVII

THE ATTRACTION OF BIRDS

For now when they may hear the small birds' song
And see the budding leaves the branches throng,
This unto their remembrance doth bring
All kinds of pleasure mix'd with sorrowing ;
And longing of sweet thoughts that ever long.

—CHAUCER ; *Wordsworth's version.*

IN England, where wild animals are comparatively rare, and wild birds exceedingly familiar and abundant, it was natural and almost inevitable that a close interest in the living bird in its haunt should pass into the blood of the people, and emerge into a conscious and often lifelong pre-occupation with a frequency which is rare elsewhere. Many centuries ago the wolf and boar and bear, which still gather round themselves the attention and folk-lore of other northern peoples, passed among ourselves into a fable of old times. The place which they once held as presiding spirits of the wild has for ages been occupied by the great company of our native birds, some, like the bittern and the eagle, themselves already but legendary in the heart of many of their former homes, but most of them still plentiful to gladden with busy life the diverse kinds of scenery in which each is adapted to thrive. It is the birds which to human eyes and minds are the master-spirits of the English countryside. In diversity, in bright vitality, in their free-dom over the ways of the air, in their poignant powers of song, they seem to reach a keen pinnacle of being to which man and the higher animals have somehow missed the way in their ascent, and yet to reflect, in smaller and clearer scope, so many of the absorptions and passions of human life.

There is an endless resourcefulness and precision visible in the adaptation of birds to their haunts which impresses itself more and more deeply on the mind as experience widens and observation grows. No one can fail to be struck with a kind of wonder and delight at the first view of one of the rarer marsh-birds, such as the stilt or avocet, with its marvellous specialization of form for wading through the deep, watery ooze, or detecting and seizing beneath the surface the minutest form of life on which it preys. But it is only familiarity which is apt to obscure the equally wonderful adaptation of the tree-hewing bill of the woodpeckers and the submarine litheness of the dabchick, or to miss the meaning of such points of structure and development as the robin's large crepuscular eye, and the free activity at birth of those young birds which are born in bare and unprotected nests upon the open ground. This precise adaptation to special surroundings leads in turn to that constant association of certain birds with certain places and types of scenery, which adds so much to the distinctness and vividness of the pleasure which we gain from their life. The wagtails flashing yellow through spray and rowan-shadow where the torrent sparkles down its gorge ; the call of the wandering curlew, down-borne from the air and the moorlands above ; the murmur of the hot June turtle-doves, pulsing from the white-hung elder-thicket that skirts some vast corn-land of the southern chalk ; or the faint, shrill pipe of the brown rock-pipits, wavering between the spray-clouds of a thundering shore-line—each bird's voice and presence seem to give the final stamp of expression to the indwelling features of its home, and are bound up lastingly in memory with each haunt of English soil.

The first introduction to a sense of the wider citizenship which birds enjoy may come, perhaps, when we first meet some familiar migratory species established far from our shores, in its summer or winter home. In earliest spring on the Nile, the swallow's wings are viewed with a curious sense of familiar strangeness, circling round the palms, and past the dove-cotes, with the same familiar motion which a few weeks later will sweep them over the gold of the Midland buttercups in May. In Norway, again, there is no accompaniment of a summer journey more quietly interesting to a bird-lover than the sight of our winter redwings and fieldfares, scattered in small nesting-parties through the forest, or picking about in the birch-scrub by the wayside post-houses, like the black-birds and thrushes in our own home gardens. The interest of bird migrations is enormously amplified and deepened when the other end of the journey is also brought into the mental picture, and we begin to regard the birds' visits to our own island, not merely as happy interludes of active life, to be contrasted with vague periods of homeless exile, but simply as one phase of a great yearly move-ment, in which both our own lands and others far remote each play their part. Nor does the increased interest of a wider and more accurate know-ledge involve any lessening of the old mysterious charm. The fascination and deep natural wonder still remain unweakened of that bare March morning when the chiff-chaffs are first heard and seen in the garden larches, bearing on weak and tiny wings the mystery of Africa and redoubled leagues of sea into the quiet acre of English soil where the winter's life has revolved in so narrow a round. The exhilaration and awe do not grow less of that other and rarer moment of the waning year, when the wind pulls into the north, with a smell of the fog-breath and snow upon the seas, and the air at midnight is loud with the throngs of the north-breeding birds, packing downward from the Arctic to unfrozen lands. For these winged creatures, questions of distance hardly exist, in the degree in which they affect and limit the movements of even the most powerful and roving quadrupeds. They are formed, as a race, to take advantage of abundant supplies of food either for themselves or their young, in whatever latitude it is to be found, from far within the Arctic circle even to the equator, and beyond it. Yet it is marvellous to see how some of the feeblest-winged members of the order join in these great world-journeys with an energy of racial impulse from which their organs and habits of flight would at other times seem

wholly to preclude them. We cannot discern the compulsion which impels the sluggish-winged landrail twice a year at passage-time over so many miles of land and sea, or urges the minute but hardy golden-crested wren to dare in such vast numbers the storms of the German Ocean, in order that it may change one forest for another at different seasons of the year. Our knowledge fails again, at present, to give us any full or adequate explanation of why in spring the fieldfares and redwings are driven northwards and eastwards, to bring up their young in regions of which the climate is intolerable to them after the frosts of middle autumn, while of their own near relations, thrushes and blackbirds are found with us all the year round, and the ring ouzels are a degree more sensitive yet, and visit our island moors and hills for the breeding-time alone. A very little knowledge of birds suffices, of course, to teach us that nearly every species, and not merely the so-called "birds of passage," is to a great extent migratory in its habits. Many of our home-birds, such as larks, robins, and other familiar winter species, wander in autumn towards the south, while their place is taken by roving immigrants from Germany and the lands beyond.

The species which we are accustomed to call definitely the summer or winter migrants are merely those of which the extreme rearguard is carried altogether beyond our borders by the great movements to the south in autumn and to the north in spring. But the problem of migration is very far from being solved by proving it to be a much wider and more general principle in bird life than was earlier supposed; and the curious differences which detailed study begins to show in the routes chosen by the different species, and the size and constitution of the parties in which they travel, do not foreshadow that "the way of a bird in the air" will be robbed of its fascination and hidden attraction as the sum of our knowledge expands.

The mere power of flight possessed by the bird, in conjunction with the play and expressiveness of its vitality, has inevitably won it, to an unusual degree, the regard and admiration of man. Yet we grow so easily accustomed to this disproportionate fulness of life in frames so small that it needs a conscious and deliberate comparison to realize with adequate truth how greatly birds exceed the four-footed creation in self-expression and ardour of character, just as they stand apart from all winged insects in their responsive attitude to man. We can understand better the fulness of their song's appeal by imagining the volume of the universal chorus if similar powers of singing were possessed by our British four-footed animals in a degree proportionate to their size —if all the voles and shrew-mice of the woods, fields and watersides, whose voices are rarely heard as a thin, shrill pipe, had the utterance of our blackcaps and thrushes, and every rabbit-warren were to clamour with the insistent tumult of a colony of sea-birds at nesting-time. Yet the vitality of birds is displayed hardly less by their joy in motion than by their wonderful songs and cries. Their native activity in three elements gives an almost limitless sense of freedom to their movements which perpetually delights and refreshes our wingless and slowly-moving human race, and seems to realize that ideal freedom of the spirit which is the goal of aspirations and dreams.

The high development of family life among most well-known species of birds is one notable feature of their existence which greatly helps to increase their interest and charm in human eyes. Not only do the successive stages of courtship, nest-building, the laying of the marvellously varied and beautiful eggs, and the emergence of the young from these delicate chambers of birth make up together a history of singular and exquisite detail, but there is a direct appeal to human sympathy in the way in which the male bird, unlike most male animals, takes, as a rule, a prominent and vigilant part in the protection and nurture of the young. There is an inner circle of bird acquaintances which appear to seek man's neighbourhood at nesting-time with a genuine comprehension of his nature, and a deliberate trust in his goodwill. The swallows and sparrows, robins and flycatchers of our gardens seem to establish themselves easily and naturally on a footing of friendliness and familiarity, which we find it much more difficult to secure in the case of the more highly organized and timid mammals. How real and attractive to ourselves is this conscious familiarity of the birds can easily be realized by comparing the demeanour of grown-up titmice or robins with that of the round, wide-eyed fledgelings, just emerged from the protection of the nest, which haunt in such numbers the depths of our shrubbery paths at midsummer. The young birds have no more consciousness of our human identity than a bee has, or a butterfly; they will hop from our knee to the chair arm and back again with a complete inability to distinguish between the human figure and a stock or stone. It has been noticed that humming-birds, curiously insect-like in intelligence as in appearance, never seem to develop the adult bird's sense of the nature and identity of man. There is all the difference in the world between the blank indifference of the young robin at three weeks old, with the utter gulf which its ignorance interposes between our life and its own, and the shrewdly companionable confidence of the same bird three or four months afterwards, when his breast is kindling to full brightness in his first autumn season. But over and above all these direct and sociable traits which give rise to such natural companionship between bird and man, bird life offers the readiest and most attractive of all fields for acquiring some first-hand familiarity with the nature of the great biological principles which have so profoundly enlarged and modified man's conception on his own human position. Deep in the play and passion of bird-life, as we watch it in woods and fields, we come little by little to discern the dim but living rudiments of many far-reaching and conscious forces and instincts in our own developed natures. Reverence deepens as the sense of our vast relationship grows ; and from the kindling of a far fellow-feeling with the tremors and joys of the wren, we return with a vision enlarged, and a wider sympathy with the concerns and affections of man.

XXXVIII

NATURE IN ENGLISH POETRY

Gold have I of corn and field-cup ;
Of the warm breast of bee and bird ;
Of autumn leaves and sunset sky.
Silver have I of the dawn ;
Of the breeze-blown grass ;
Of the aspen, birch and willow-tree ;
Of the broad-minted moon

And O ! rare evening star ;
Of the sea uncoined.
Bronze have I of all the fields and trees ;
The tumbling jewels of the air
And simple pebbles in the brook are mine ;
Also a treasure of eyes ; kind eyes
I meet in man and animal.

—JAMES GUTHRIE.

AS we passed up the valley to the dawn we found a strange small wilderness surrounded by the richest of the lower fields ; neither copse nor common, fen, brake, nor moor, but a rough hollow of rocks, bent-grass and stunted trees. We wondered indolently to see this waste amid the best pastures of the country-side, until we realised, silently yet together, that here was the last space of primitive earth by which we might know what ancient men had regarded when Norsemen came to break the soil for their steads, monks to succeed to their labours, builders of peel-towers (half drovers and half knights) to turn from their feuds to their farms.

Afterward we spoke of the changes of aspect in the most familiar English landscape, and regretted no school of English painting had persisted from the illuminators to Gainsborough and Morland that we might realise as clearly how nature had appeared to bygone men as, by the progress of English poetry, we know its varying importance in their lives.

When the short day was over we sat by candle-light in a lonely house among hill-side woods. Thyrsis interrupted a silence with that song of " Sumer is icumen in " which always springs anew as effortlessly as it must have done for its inventor : the clear melody stirred thoughts of the innocent nature of English folktunes, in which every curve is characteristic of an untroubled joy in bright air and flowery places, and of an ignorance of the subtleties of life and vision bred by towns.

In passing, by the verses which accompany these tunes, to the first nameless English poesies, there is an initial impression that nature alone impels man to artistry and grants him expression of gladness or tenderness ; yet a farther examination shews these beginnings of poetry possessed by the beginnings of the year ; the coming of Spring is the only moment that stirs a sense of beauty or of song.

> " Lenten ys come with love to toune,
>   With blosmen ant with briddes roune,
>   That al this blisse bryngeth ;
>   Dayes-eyes in this dales,
>   Notes suete of nyhtegales,
>   Vch foul song singeth ;
>   The threstlecoc him threteth oo,
>   Away is huere wynter wo,
>   When woderove springeth ;
>   This foules singeth ferly fele,
>   Ant wlyteth on huere winter wele,
>   That al the wode ryngeth."

" Lenten ys come with love," and in these songs love-makings too suggest Spring, from the singer who praised Alison

> " Bytuene Mershe ant Averil
>   When spray biginneth to spring,
>   The lutel foul hath hire wyl
>   On hyre lud to sing : "

to James of Scotland looking from his casement at Windsor with

> " Worschippe ye that loveris bene this May,
>   For of your blisse the Kalendis are begonne
>   And sing with us, Away, Winter, away ! "

Even the devout, singing of their God's wintry nativity, must exemplify its beauty by thoughts of April.

> " He came al so still
>   There his mother was,
>   As dew in April
>   That falleth on the grass. . . .
>
> " He came al so still
>   There his mother lay,
>   As dew in April
>   That falleth on the spray."

In some nations the dawn of poetic impulse was tribal, a chant of epic deeds transmuted from one generation to another ; with these nature is seen to have had little influence on the medieval mind. Throughout the Icelandic sagas Gunnar's farewell stands alone as a poignant realisation of the earth ; and even this is not the regretful joy which Autumn has stirred in the modern world, but an exile's desire for his home.

With other nations the dawn of poetry was, as in England, lyric and personal ; and here the more spontaneous form, the single impression, were favourable to a farther inclusion of mood and observation of circumstance. The apparently greater appeal of nature is, however, no more fundamental than in tribal epics ; the merry friendly companionship is seen to be joy at the vanishing of dark nights and rough weather, delight in the warm shade of woods, the fragrance of green things, the softness of grass, after months of harbouring in dwellings yet rudimentary.

Europe was blinded to the power of the earth by the desire of an ideal world : St. Bernard was its type as he passed through Switzerland, ignorant of its mountains and of the lake-shore he followed awhile.

Perhaps early England came near the creation of an epic cycle with the ballads of Robin Hood and such allied idylls as *The Nut-Brown Maid* ; but no great ideal unified these, and they remained disjointed romances, personal productions. This makes their slight contact with nature the more noticeable : the forest life they celebrate might seem to implicate a farther recognition of nature, yet in its essence it was but an expression of the individual's desire to hold fast an ancient vanishing freedom amid demands of an increasing social consciousness. Again the coming of spring is Little John's point of sensitiveness to natural things. . . .

> " To se the dere draw to the dale
>   And leve the hilles hee,
>   And shadow him in the leves grene
>   Under the green-wode tree. . . .
>
> " ' Pluk up thi hert, my dere mayster,'
>   Litulle Johne can say,
>   ' And think hit is a full fayre tyme
>   In a mornynge of May.' "

In other ballads the deeds of men are even more completely seen to be men's preoccupation—

> " For Witherington my heart was wo,
>   That ever he slain should be ;
> For when both his legs were hewn in two,
>   Yet he kneeled and fought on his knee."

And in such apparent exceptions as the *Three Ravens* the fierce birds come but to make human death and grief more piteous.

The spirit of the more elaborate and cultivated poetry is not different : when Piers Plowman has set his scene on a hillside of Spring he turns to the evidently more serious business of his allegory ; and in Chaucer the gnomic or the dramatic wait but for such a Springtide moment as in the opening of the *Canterbury Tales,* or such a pause as that in Criseyde's bedchamber when

> " A nightingale, upon a cedre grene,
>   Under the chambre-wal ther as she lay,
>   Ful loude sang ayein the mone shene,
>   Paraunter, in his briddes wyse, a lay
>   Of love, that made hir herte fresh and gay.
>   That herkned she so longe in good entente,
>   Til at the last the dede sleep hir hente."

If the inference be thought fanciful, the poet's testimony in the prologue to the *Legend of Good Women* shows clearly the extent of nature's hold upon the medieval mind—

> " On bokes for to rede I me delyte,
>   And to hem yeve I feyth and ful credence,
>   And in myn herte have hem in reverence
>   So hertely, that there is game noon
>   That fro my bokes maketh me to goon,
>   But hit be seldom, on the holyday ;

Save, certeynly, whan that the month of May
Is comen, and that I here the foules singe,
And that the floures ginnen for to springe,
Farwel my book and my devocioun !
Now have I than swich a condicioun,
That of alle the floures in the mede,
Than love I most these floures whyte and rede,
Swiche as men callen daysies in our toun : "

Then came those Wars of the Roses which crowned so many with thorns, and English poetry must have seemed at an end.

Not until the Tudor settlement did the art revive in any degree ; and a greater restoration than any of Lancaster or York was needed to bring it to maturity.

Chaucer had been conscious of the early ardours of the Italian Renaissance ; yet it was by Spenser that Virgil and Theocritus first touched English verse with the life and passion of the earth— unless Stephen Hawes had turned to them in a brief pause of his pursuit of vanishing medieval allegory. Englishmen may pardonably hope that Hawes knew no Virgil ; for only thus might we believe that Virgilian harmony with events of nature, which is the source of one great fascination of English poetry, to be inherent in our race.

" The end of joy and all prosperitee
Is death at last, thorough his course and might :
After the day there cometh the dark night,
 For though the daye be nevere so long,
 At last the bells ringeth to evensong."

A dim earth, a fading sky, a church-tower, a bell—much of Milton and Gray, Arnold and Wordsworth are implied in these lines ; yet possibly none among Hawes' first readers saw that a new order was at hand.

The modern feeling for nature, however, did not follow this first hint. Spenser learnt his art from the recent Italian rather than the ancient, and perhaps still more immediately from his French contemporaries with their joy in a garden-earth—always man's first step towards nature.

In the landscape of the *Faërie Queen* the influences of Spenser's life in Ireland are said to be manifest ; but the aspects of Ariosto-land are more manifest. Magic wood and Bower of Bliss are not so much Italian as a sublimation of Italy to a poet's garden.

The Shepherd's Calendar, despite Spenser's declaration

" Lo, I have made a calendar for every year, . . .
 To teach the ruder shepherd how to feed his
  sheep,
 And from the falser's fraud his folded flock
  to keep."

cares more that shepherds should be poets, kinsmen of the shepherds of Greece and Rome ; yet here the influence of Virgil and Theocritus ensured a fuller conception of nature, a constant and familiar observation of seasons and rural occupations. The authority of the most admired of all civilizations had added a new category to English art.

Young men desirous of poetry were assured that natural aspect was a serious addition to their resources; love-songs no more lingered over Spring, though the poet's joy in his lady has never forgot the propriety of a garden as her associate.

" Say Rose, say Daffodil, and Violet blue,
    With Primrose fair,
  Since ye have seen my nymph's sweet dainty
    face,
      And gesture rare,
  Did not (bright Cowslip, blooming Pink) her
    view
      (White Lily) shine—
  (Ah, Gillyflower, ah Daisy !) with a grace
    Like stars divine ? "

Such nosegays are endless, and endlessly delicious.

This enlargement of limits must have added confidence and freedom to envisage other portions of life as subject-matter; thus preparing a divine way for the succession of the dramatists whose preoccupations, radiating in many directions, preserved the art awhile from a later assumption that contemplation of visible nature and an unwarrantable transference of sympathy could constitute absolute poetry.

In the great array from Marlowe to Johnson the treatment of nature is perfected as the treatment of life is mature : by scene and simile alike the only life that men can know is enforced and enhanced with a harmonious setting of the external world; and, when music must sublimate the dramatic movement, by a subtle instinct each writer often chose to add it to a song concerned with those things—birds and water and rustling trees—the faintest idea of which is implicated with sweet sound.

Thus Webster, in one of his few lyrics, writes

" Call for the robin-red-breast and the wren,
  Since o'er shady groves they hover,
  And with leaves and flowers do cover
  The friendless bodies of unburied men."

With Shakespeare this harmonious and proportionate governance of natural aspect is complete ; the poet's conception of the life and function of nature is part of a perfect equilibrium, free from obsessions or interested statements ; the tempestuous, desolate wastes that enhance the significance of *Macbeth* and *Lear*, the river of Ophelia's death, the sea-shore of Prospero, testify that a poet had at last fully realised the part possible to nature in man's existence ; a farther intimacy, the comprehension of animals' idea of themselves (not man's idea of animals), is apparent in the creation of Caliban ; yet in no place can there be seen a falling away from the true creator's impersonal attitude to his work—

the import of elemental things is the theme, not the side one man chances to take regarding them.

If this subordination of nature be thought an accident of the dramatic form, the conditions of the sonnets and lyrics should prove no less unmistakable ; as in

" That time of year thou mayst in me behold
When yellow leaves, or none, or few, do hang
Upon those boughs which shake against the
      cold—
Bare ruin'd choirs where late the sweet birds
      sang."

and

" Come unto these yellow sands,
      And then take hands :
   Courtsied when you have and kiss'd,
   The wild waves whist,
Foot it featly here and there ;
And, sweet Sprites, the burthen bear : "

Implication and suggestion embody in the latter as true a landscape as any inventory could contrive ; and by some unnameable magic the association of human actions adds detail to it ; yet the emotion is central, and no uneasiness of personality distorts nature with its own attributes, or projects its own local truth in order to take it back translated.

Such art must be found classic in both governance and significance.

The progress of painted landscape suggests that impressiveness of contour and large disposition of light and shade have more power than have knowledge and detail of natural things to render the essence of nature. If this is so, literature must always be at a disadvantage in landscape work— as though the art of using man's words must deal in the first place with man's deeds.

Certainly landscape is most potent in literature when it accepts this experience of painting ; so that perhaps its finest manifestation in English words is Traherne's setting to his recollection of childhood—

" The corn was orient and immortal wheat, which never should be reaped nor was ever sown. I thought it had stood from everlasting to everlasting."

In the age when this was written the large dramatic energy was expiring ; but the lyric impulse passed by Johnson, in whom it outlasted the ossification of the dramatic, to another generation. By this the Jacobeans' large sane outlook upon nature was preserved—even though Herrick, the greatest of the younger men, concentrated his art upon the country life in a manner not seen before.

" When now the cock (the ploughman's horn)
   Calls forth the lily-wristed morn,
Then to thy corn-fields thou dost go,
Which though well soil'd, yet thou dost know
That the best compost for the lands
   Is the wise master's feet and hands.
There at the plough thou find'st thy team
With a hind whistling there to them....
This done, then to th' enamelled meads

Thou go'st, and as thy foot there treads,
Thou see'st a present God-like power
Imprinted in each herb and flower ;
And smell'st the breath of great-ey'd kine,
Sweet as the blossoms of the vine . . .
O happy life ! if that their good
The husbandmen but understood !
Who all the day themselves do please, . . .
And lying down have nought t'affright
Sweet sleep that makes more short the night."

One page is almost as pertinent for quotation as another ; even his courtier-compliments to ladies take another grace from country airs. (The stirring of Puritan intention did not immediately hamper poetry ; though a consciousness of the Fall of Man made Marvell uneasy in his garden until he had remembered Eden and felt justified.)

The specific assertion, however, of the life of nature as the most perfect condition of human activity came from the youth of a poet of greater reach and dignity. Though Herrick and his companions had again accepted the authority of the Classic poets for their attitude to nature, the whole purpose and intent of Virgil first matured in Milton ; in him the power of earth and sky and light to answer and enhance man's elemental moods was shewn with greater intimacy, if not with greater passion, than Shakespeare had thought needful.

" Together both, ere the high lawns appear'd
Under the opening eyelids of the morn,

We drove a field, and both together heard
What time the Gray-fly winds her sultry horn,
Batt'ning our flocks with the fresh dews of
  night,
Oft till the Star that rose, at Ev'ning bright
Toward Heav'ns descent had slop'd his
  westering wheel."

or again

" Oft on a Plat of rising ground,
  I hear the far-off Curfeu sound,
  Over som wide-water'd shoar,
  Swinging slow with sullen roar ; "

in many passages as famous as these the Shakesperean harmony was extended ; with such proofs of the nameless spirit that wanders through the association of nature with human needs (as an unbodied voice seems to slip between the instruments of a symphonic orchestra) the part nature may have in poetry was determined.

A change of tendency in English poetry has often come by France ; and with the Restoration the return of refugees brought another conception of verse. Although the silence of Milton's middle life obscures any native tendency to such a change, the mightier verse of his last years shows its existence ; the accident of blindness, indeed, is answerable for the gradual withdrawal of nature from his pages—until he remains conscious only of Light also withdrawn,—but the impulse to regard man alone came from the revived religious passion for another world.

This Puritan achievement had an unforeseen outcome. The return of the Stuarts was essentially the Restoration of an aristocratic ideal; the example of France made the arts seem implicitly an affair of courts, and possible only to a well-bred culture and leisure; poetry was ascertained to be almost a kind of statecraft, a suitable training for diplomatists. The importance of man became nearly spurious in the guise of the importance of affairs: towns were the source of every air, and the country was only worthy to supply variations.

Perhaps the transition is visible in Randolph and Cowley, who desired nature, yet thought of it as but a place of retirement and abdication, never one of activity. When their generation would translate the Georgics it treated them as if Horace had been their author.

The most delicate and dignified of living essayists has argued a love of natural things from the eighteenth century poets' references to sylvan groves, shady bowers, crystal floods, rustic mirth: yet the facility with which such epithets were conventionalised surely makes of nature an occasional pastime. Writers who remembered the classic pastoral thought it elegant to emulate it, but would have been at a loss for even an opening stanza had not Spenser's initial error of conceiving English shepherds to be poets because those of Greece were aided them.

The first sign of a return to nature appeared when James Thomson went to live idly in a remote place and believed poetry might come to pass in a record of the only aspect of life at hand. A sluggish digestion failed to assimilate his inventories of observations; but the pleasing catalogues had restored nature's authentic material to other men's hands.

Afterward a desire of Virgilian emotion may have led Gray to discover nature's ability to produce it; but the influence of affairs still diluted nature's appeal for him, and a more unreserved trust in the nobility of the emotion's cause took Collins to the source of the effects Gray longed for.

" Now air is hushed, save where the weak-eyed bat
    With short shrill shriek flits by on leathern wing,
      Or where the beetle winds
      His small but sullen horn,

As oft he rises, 'midst the twilight path
Against the pilgrim borne in heedless hum:"

has in it more of the power of the evening hush upon men's hearts than have Gray's better known deductions from that passionate hour.

Though Blake was almost contemporary with these men he remained too long obscure to influence the course of poetry in his time ; but the possibility of his simplicity of vision and utterance, his disconcerting freedom from traditional usages, prove to our later sight that men were ready for poetry to be made whole again.

In Wordsworth this consciousness became explicit ; to such a seclusion as Thomson's was added an obstinacy of nerves and moral power resembling the heated resistance some metals offer to the passage of electricity ; this brought about that fusion of unfamiliar material which Thomson had failed to accomplish, and the mould filled again.

It is conceivable that if Wordsworth had lived in an earlier age we should have had in him a Dryden of a more terrible energy and range. Sympathy with nature was not his natural means of expression ; he has recorded that the magical far light man may cast upon nature could not hold him :—

" Such happiness, wherever it be known,
  Is to be pitied for 'tis surely blind.
  But welcome fortitude and patient cheer,
  And frequent sights of what is to be borne !
  Such sights, or worse, as are before me here.—
  Not without hope we suffer and we mourn."

The mad world of his youth perhaps reversed such an energy upon itself and drove him into lonely places, where his bony rectitude dwelt upon the life about him until it produced a singular quality of naïf observation and insisted on a vocabulary of a corresponding literal innocence. A new freedom of material and a purged speech came by consequence ; in his use of them, honest even against his will, Milton's enchanted sense of nature returned. Wordsworth's need of moral purpose led him to believe the desires of his heart were reflected by the earth visible to him ; his pantheism and unjustifiable attribution of human purposes to blind elements were no worthier than Landseer's infusion of human pathos into animals' eyes, and are responsible for recent beliefs that the description of natural sights and sounds legitimises any verse as poetry ; but at one point of his career the natural dignity of his life and perceptions restored the harmony of nature with poetry.

Fortunately this restoration came at the opening instead of (as with Milton) the closing of an age ; and the practice of the art has since remained authentic and whole. Poets such as Coleridge and Rossetti, possessed by supernatural possibilities, intensified their effects by contrast with sudden observation of external things ; such poets of the senses as Keats enlarged their subject by looking out upon the earth ; Shelley looked down from his intellectual ardour and saw the earth as a bird of Paradise might see it ; Tennyson and Arnold built white shrines to the Virgilian sense of things —though Tennyson sometimes thought garlands of real roses more fitting than seemly sculptures.

Perhaps Morris reached most nearly Milton's feeling of natural places as the most perfect for human life ; but he manifested it only in brief pauses in misproportioned narrative.

In such passages as

" Far out in the meadows above the young corn,
The heavy elms wait, and restless and cold
The uneasy wind rises ; the roses are dun ; "

and

" The Earth and Heaven through countless year
    on year,
Slow changing, were to us but curtains fair,
Hung round about a little room, where play
Weeping and laughter of man's empty day."

earth has become one with the essence of life; and Morris' virtue may have been so to escape the pantheistic solution.

Though the nineteenth century had become completely sensitive to nature's place in poetry, an enfeebled theological tendency clung to the pantheism latent in its acceptance : the priestly function resident in poetry awaited more logical realisation.

In Mr. George Meredith's work the elemental forces are seen to require no justification outside themselves :—

" I walked to observe not to feel,
    Not to fancy, if simple of eye
One may be among images reaped
    For a shift of the glance as grain :
Profitless froth you espy
    Ashore after billows have leaped.
I fled nothing, nothing pursued :
    The changeful visible face
Of our Mother I sought for my food ;
    Crumbs by the way to sustain.
Her sentence I knew past grace."

And again

        " the man descried
The growths of earth, his adored, like day out
    of night,
Ascend in song, seeing nature and song allied."

He naturally reverted to the only mythology in which natural things had divinity inherent : in the poem of *Melampus* nature's purposes are restored and its divinity is perceived to be no antagonist of man for man's benefit.

The unusual mythologic instinct of a more recent poet, Mr. Sturge Moore, manifested in both verse and plastic design, assures us that nature is at last freed from all interested and partisan schemes against it : while such verse as

" Smiling at evening's silence or the noon's,
Then, thinking that he hears a distant bird,
Half reeling with delight,
Impassioned for that voice of simple joy
Whose easy triumph over sweetest words
Makes him afraid his mother hears it not,
(Although he sees she hears)
Because she is less shaken than himself,
Less new to pleasure,
Less ignorant of pain ; "

shows not less that a majestic and great poet is among us again than that in his hands the harmony of nature with poetry is still kept perfect.

XXXIX

NATURE IN ART

For don't you mark ? we're made so that we love
First when we see them painted, things we have passed
Perhaps a hundred times nor cared to see ;
And so they are better painted—better to us,
Which is the same thing. Art was given for that ;
God uses us to help each other so,
Lending our minds out. . . .   —BROWNING.

THE beginning of the arts was concerned with the deportment of manlike gods ; and, when another worship brought about the modern revival of the arts, a humanised God-head again ensured the persistence of man's instinctive preference for himself, his habit of interpreting nature's heart by his own.

The Elizabethan stage had not fewer requirements : men and a platform were all the early painters sought, and it was long before the consciousness of where feet are set became insistent enough to stir Angelico to leave his Virgin in a walled garden of lilies even yet symbolic.

A lily for Gabriel to offer, a dove to descend, the differentiation of angels by an imperfect observation of the anatomy of wings—these were all the care of the early Sienese or Florentine painter when his men and women were placed. In the miniatures of a Book of Hours first appears the child's curiosity in the construction of blossoms, the poet's knowledge that a Flight into Egypt passed among blue hills set in blue night.

It has been thought that when the aspects of the earth at last made some proportionate demand upon painters' eyes, when there began a knowledge of atmosphere's effect upon the objects it contained, the theatre of an action might still have been depicted by suggestion and symbol had it not been for the inventories of town and river and tree-girt meadow with which the early Flemish painters filled their back-grounds as the illumination of books had taught them. By such suggestion Oriental painters had already avoided the unending and disproportionate demands of an irrelevant realism : certainly the heightening of the Flemish conscientiousness of warehouse and counting-house to more serious purposes at that moment has often obscured the needs and purposes of art to succeeding generations.

It is notable that in its first stage this enlargement of vision was still most concerned about the works of

THE FERNERY.

From a photograph by
Henry Irving.

man ; for some time town and palace and bridge showed a greater intimacy than river or meadow ; and when at last man advanced to perception of the earth he remained true to himself, and conceived it to be no more than the garden he had made from it. The wood where Botticelli saw the masque of Spring, the lonely shore where he alone saw Venus leave her waves, are choice and chosen places, and not less suspiciously sympathetic to the figures they environ than is Perugino's slender and pensive valley in tone and contour to the languid and gratifying Cruci-fixion in its foreground.

Perhaps the earth was not made for man ; but the early painters had no such misgiving, even in their treatment of other animals : when Giovanni Bellini must paint the Conversion of Saint Paul, he was content with a rudiment of horses, and untroubled by any thought that the burden of his subject was as much implicated with the actions of horses as of men. Only isolated men such as Piero di Cosimo were curious enough to discover the wisdom and faith of a hound, or to discern animals' knowledge of them-selves sufficiently to create a centaur (still half man) or an abnormal monster for Perseus to slay.

Balzac, in his *Histoire des Treize*, speaks of " that faculty of observation in which nearly all human genius consists," and certainly the progress of the arts has been by continual enlargement of the scope of such observation.

The pursuit of human anatomy was the first stage in the vitalising of church-painting ; but it was not until the dead theology of Greece gave, in rediscovery, a basis of fertile legend uninvolved with responsibilities of dogma that research of the unclad body might reveal all its possibilities. The most significant thing amid those years of wonder is surely that when Giorgione and Titian first found the virginal beauty of flesh they found also man's relation to earth, sky, and atmosphere —as if the study of man in his natural condition had been necessary to arouse complete perception of the rest of nature.

Italy took the art no farther, yet in the centuries which followed the nations sought Italy as if painting were its language ; and by this the land saw one more advance.

The French Claude found in Italy the place of his mood ; if events of man were still required from him, his reply was an evasion which set puppets in the foreground of a landscape to prove them negligible. His work may be thought too singly the repetition of one mood to involve the elemental greatly ; yet the research and intimacy of his sketches hint that here also he was subject to patrons unaccustomed to too great an admixture of nature.

The Flemish Rubens found his masters in Venice, yet not their logic : his studies of flesh were at first as little concerned with their surroundings as were Angelico's hazardings after spirit ; his landscapes were backgrounds to be put in by journeymen. Yet the Venetian way proved its elemental relation again ; though it was far from Italy that Rubens' Cæsarian conquest of the visible world ended in those great landscapes where for the first time the contours and values of tree, cloud, and water were proved capable of the imaginative and emotional content once thought inseparable from the shapes and situations of men.

When the creative vision thus passed from Italy to the heritors of van Eyck and Memlinc, the landscape art became finally authentic in the hands of Rembrandt, Ruysdael and Hobbema ; and while art was potent in that more northern place it proceeded to its last conquest of the sea.

Since that time of landscape's final justification, its pursuit has alternated between the amount of observation compatible with perfect processes of picture-construction, and a mordant observation pitiless to its means of expression.

The rise of artistic activity in England, the land of conscious conscience, was bound to farther the art by this dilemma ; and the growth of a water-colour convention based on the blue-white tonality of paper instead of the yellow-white tonality of oil confused the issue for a time sufficient to ensure the final development of the observation of nature.

The fascination of an exquisite surface and a delicately poised brush led Wilson and Gainsborough to be satisfied with the moderate amount of nature attainable in a summary act, yet here there was already a greater power of consideration than had satisfied Van Dyck in the no more summary plumes which passed for trees in portrait-backgrounds ; while in Wilson the tender quality of paint was in itself indicative of subtler regard, and the mood of Claude reached a more vital realisation.

Soon afterward Crome and Cotman found Norwich adjacent to the Low Countries ; they surmised painting from the existence of Ruysdael and Hobbema, and, never losing the discoverer's rapture of attention, overcame for their successors the Italianate seduction which was perhaps Wilson's first knowledge of inspiration.

Yet at all times the aspect of the picture is apt to impose a standard and a test upon nature ; the authority of many generations had deduced the nature of the envelope of paint too strictly from the practice of the previous ; and Constable and Turner were needed to reassert the potentialities of natural colour and to disinvolve the miracle of light from the good taste of academic tone.

Here the sentiment of Italian grandeur had yielded far to evolution of an impersonal elemental ; the simplicity needed to complete the distinction came by the pre-Raphaelite ardour heralded shyly by Blake and the early work of his disciples Palmer and Calvert.

The pre-Raphaelites, desiring the innocent aspects of tempera, losing consciousness of the power and restrictions of any medium, sought the familiar liberty of water-colour in the handling of oils upon a white ground— finding a narrow dissonant brilliance suitable for a feverish insistence upon natural effects and appearances, though often without consideration of the purposes of a picture. Their intention was attained immediately ; their recaptured knowledge could not be used until their position was abandoned.

But the men of France, already adept in the conduct of revolutions, governed by a greater passion of reason, were able to trace a similar instinct to surer bases—following natural aspect to a consciousness that its essence was in the condition of light, that " light was the only person in a picture." Regardless as the Englishmen of their means of expression, they followed their idea with the ardour of scientists ; and, if at this moment the subject of the picture is again more valued than its object, the means of expression and the power of nature are no less enlarged for ever by their faith.

At the close of each succeeding age of research emerges the same fundamental sense that the purpose of art is not imitation of nature, but a newer act of creation by which may be perceived the quality of the divine. That a thing has happened perfectly in some gracious confederacy of place and hour is essentially a reason that it should not be done over again ; the reproduction of an ecstasy need not be an ecstasy, and if all art is in a way an art of portraiture, yet the study of external aspect may do no more than teach the artist true shapes for the expression of his sense of the elemental in nature and man.

XL

SEA BIRDS

No. 2

"A sportive pair
Of seafowl, conscious both that they are hovering
Within the eddy of a common blast,
Or hidden only by the concave depth
Of neighbouring billows from each other's sight."—WORDSWORTH.

SURFACE divers are to the manner born. They rest on the water when they are satisfied, and go under when they are hungry; so their days are passed. They know their way in the still depths beneath the jabble. Their wings are short; they were not designed for flight. Heavily, and with much beating, they pass from place to place. The legs too are short, and far set back. They are clumsy in the air, and awkward on the land. The sea is their natural home.

The ducks are shallow keeled to float, and not for flight. They fly, but they fly with a whirring beat. They do not sail nor rest with the easy mastery of birds, whose medium is the air. When they cease to drive themselves on, they pitch down. On the ground, where they are seldom seen save at breeding-time, they waddle. The representative forms on our waters are the eiders, or white drakes, and the scoters, or black drakes.

Eiders are summer visitors. They nest wherever is a stretch of moorland; their absence tells of no near breeding place. In April they appear from somewhere; for it is hard to tell where they have spent the winter. Into the voes of Shetland the sober ducks sail on the tide. The next tide bears in the brighter drakes, as though this were the trysting-place. So they mingle and pair in the bays and firths off the moors, further south. In September they vanish. Scoters reverse the order. For all save the extreme north they are winter visitors. Some nest in the Caithness or Sutherland lochs. Most of them go further away. After the breeding season they spread south; and remain till April.

The mode of diving is of the simplest, and adapted to their mode of feeding. They live on still food, or creatures whose motions are slow, almost to stillness. It is mainly molluscan, crawling and spiralled univalves; or fixed and gaping bivalves. Needs but to know the kind of bottom their quarry affect. This their parents taught them, while they were yet ducklings, and may be seen teaching a new generation any late summer day. Tide by tide, they visit the same feeding ground : there is no need to shift about. A straight drop, through as many fathoms as the water is deep will serve. An unconscious use of elementary physics will help them down. They have but to make themselves a little less in bulk, a little heavier for their size : then they will no longer float, but sink like a stone. So they pass to the sea bottom. They do not help themselves down in any way. For as long as they can do without air, they feed. By making themselves larger and lighter, they float up, and appear very much where they went down.

A look into their gizzard will tell of their different tastes. Powerful gizzards they are—meant for shell crushing. Yet they have their limits, and are, mainly, filled with the young and thin shelled. The common scoter affects the univalves, the velvet scoter prefers the larger and more fragile shelled bivalves. Quite an interesting collection of deep sea forms in the young state may be gathered of those which have not yet been crushed in the mill.

After the ducks, come a group of four ; all alike in their hues—black above, and white below. The legs are set far back Out of the water, they move with extreme awkwardness. At rest, they have the look of sitting birds. Some are grotesque. Their diet is no longer still food. It is not enough to drop to the bottom. Fish are restless : move from place to place : are easily startled, and dart away, or double on their course. Pursuers must beat them at their own methods. They also must strain and double ; and be in the water as the hawk is in the air. So these black and white birds do ; and very expert they are. Their flapper-like wings, only equal to short, heavy, straight flight, serve for paddles. This would seem to be their true use, inasmuch as it is concerned with the prime necessity of life. There is no restraint in their movements, less even than when they move on the surface. Their feet, dropping out behind the short tail, serve as tiller.

This, it seems to me, is to be a sea bird ; this life under the surface, this free motion through the dim blue medium. This heaviness in the air, this awkwardness on the land, this mastery over the depths. These paddles which beat the water ; these wings which fly through the wingless spaces. And an art in the use of them which seldom fails in its object.

Rare, indeed, is it to find one not stuffed to the mouth.

The little auk is the most northerly species. It overlaps the rest ; it is of the arctic regions. It tends south in the winter ; more or less in numbers, according to the weather. It travels with a quick, whirring flight. It keeps well off the coasts—only storms bring it ashore. Seated on the sand, in an almost upright pose, it looks funny in its gravity, and almost appealing in its helplessness. The puffin is more southerly tending. It is more generally distributed over the North Sea ; though by no means everywhere, nor seen every day. The storm which drives it ashore is often the first revealer of its nearness. It is extremely self-sufficient. The stranded bird makes no appeal. Grotesque on the water by reason of its great mask-like bill, it is absurd on the land. The grave aspect broadens the contrast. The bill is resplendent in brilliant streaks of colour.

A ridged, sharp-edged beak gives the name to the razorbill. It has the appearance and impression of a Roman nose. Not sufficiently exaggerated to be absurd, it lends the bird a knowing look. It seems, but is not really, cleverer than those which go before. Like many among ourselves, puffin and auk are much sharper than they look. In the shape of the bill, in the shortness of the wing, in all but name, the razorbill is the nearest living representative of the extinct great auk. The name has been given to the little auk.

Commonest of the four is the guillemot : a straight-billed bird with no accretion to hide the predominant air of sharpness. He is the fool who talks about the foolish guillemot. It is seldom out of sight. It dots the inshore waters between the horizon of black ducks, and the terns above the ripples or the gulls on the sand. It rides in on every tide, after the young green fish ; and out on every ebb. So it see-saws from day to day. It is a busy bird, and tells where the shoals are ; diving eagerly, and not coming up at the same place. The changes of the unseen life may be followed by movements of the birds.

In winter, the whole underside is white. This swimming bird shows a white front. On the coming of spring the space between the base of the bill and the surface of the water is filled up. The approaching bird shows a black throat : he swims on the white. The margin between the two shades may be called the swimming horizon. This dress he wears in the merry time of courting, and during the weeks of married life. As in many other seabirds, the adornment, if such it be, is worn by both sexes.

The change comes about very much as in the hood of the black-headed gull. At the water mark, a dark line starts from either side to meet in the middle and define the area. The bird swims on this line, while the lake of white still shows on the approaching bird. From the angle of the wing, at the base of the pillar of the neck, a second ring narrows this lake, or breaks it into two. The enclosed space fills up.

A few birds wear the black throat throughout the winter. These, I imagine, are past the breeding stage, and may have stopped moulting. They moult in autumn ; and will stop while the wedding garb is still on. It is quite common for old birds to be gay. Those which wear their white throats in the spring when all the rest are changing are immature. Nor do they leave the open waters with the others for the breeding place. Individuals, in the proportion say of one to a hundred, have, around the eye, white rings sending out a streak behind. These are named ringed guillemots. The distinction seems needless. All have the circular grooves into which

the white is sometimes run. The claim of another form is more assured.

The black guillemot is smaller. The spring colour, or wedding dress, is black. On either wing is a patch of white, not unlike that of the velvet scoter. It is a more northerly species, seldom seen so far down as the Forth. I associate it with the Shetland voes ; where I have felt its meaning, and its magic. Days and weeks pass. It becomes familiar as the native crofter, and more characteristic. " There's the Tyste." And behold a vision flies low. On the nearer side it bears a tiny moon, whose pale sheen is alternately eclipsed and revealed, with the swift raising and lowering of the wing. The far moon shows as a crescent. The lot of the Shetlander is bare. From his dry stone heather thatched croft, the sombre outlook on the voe, shaded at noonday, and fateful in its strange and often fantastic beauty. The lamp-bearer lends a final touch to the weird spell.

Statelier than those black and white birds are the divers proper. In number they are three. All are northerly birds in summer, but spread when the breeding is over. The most southerly and familiar is the red-throat. It goes about singly, but is freely scattered. It fishes close inshore, among the breaking water. It dips in the long shadow of the gathering wave. One knows not where to look for its rise, save that it will be some two or three hundred yards away. So far it has gone, in so short a time. It drives out behind its powerful legs, opening its great webbed feet to hit the water, and folding again to draw them back for the next stroke. Legs are propeller and tiller in one. It seeks refuge as well as food below. It dives on the least alarm. The sea is its element.

Still larger is the black-throat. In smaller numbers it is found in the North Sea. In winter both show a pure white throat above water mark. Each wears his pillar of red or black in spring. In bridal dress they are found in Sutherland, the red-throat on almost every sheet of water, the black-throat here and there. More boreal in his summer range is the great northern diver.

Puffin, auk, and razorbill lay one egg for each pair. Such is the provision against risks, and to keep up the number of the species. These forms show little sign either of gain or loss. The divers lay two eggs, which seems to imply an increased risk, and the need of a wider margin. The common guillemot lays one egg : the black guillemot two. Both manage simply to hold their own.

The solan goose with the aerial dive has one egg. Its near kindred, the two cormorants, which are surface divers, have four eggs for each pair. As gannet and cormorant build on the same rock ledge, the risks of incubation seem equal. In what phase of the life the greater waste happens were hard to say. If speculations are vague, the facts are plain enough. The one egg maintains the number, the four do no more. Nature is far-seeing, and shrewd of calculation.

XLI
THE HOMING INSTINCT IN BIRDS

The crane o'er seas and forests seeks her home ;
No bird so wild but has its quiet nest,
When it no more would roam. . . .
—SHELLEY.

I SUPPOSE the three greatest puzzles of ornithology are the migratory instinct common to so many species, the vulture's detection of carrion miles removed from him, and the homing faculty of the racing pigeon. Neither speculation nor dissection has ever explained any one of these secrets

—they remain matters of very timid controversy to this day. Some years ago it occurred to an ingenious student of my acquaintance that they might be varying manifestations of some sense, or physical faculty that is not common to man ; that all birds possess this sense, and that the scenting of carrion, the periodic migration and re-migration, and the returning of the homer pigeon to its birthplace might all be effected by one and the same faculty. It is perfectly reasonable to suppose that the continued concentration of such a sense or faculty in a single direction would ultimately confine it exclusively to that special channel or direction.

This theory was no sooner enunciated than three of us desired to make such rough and ready tests of it as alone were possible to unscientific amateurs. Dissection we were incapable of, and in learned hands it had failed. We decided that the only accessible test was to ascertain, if possible, whether the migratory birds possessed the homing instinct in any degree, and returned by preference to the locality where they had nested in a previous year. This would, if successful, open up a resemblance to the homing pigeon which has not hitherto been recognized. The method of the enquiry was the first difficulty. We resided in a district where birds were exceptionally plentiful, both in number and species, and to hope to identify, say, a particular hedge-sparrow, in a neighbourhood where the hedge-sparrow nested by hundreds, would be too uncertain of success. The experiment, therefore, was commenced with a comparatively rare bird. This was absolutely necessary, although there was the fear of annoying it by our methods, and inspiring it with a distinct prejudice against the locality. However, this had to be risked, and a peculiarly easy subject was selected to begin with. Some miles from the village was a large piece of common land, with a small outstanding rocky formation jutting up amidst a partially overgrown clearing of long standing. On a particular stone in this rough natural pyramid, a nightjar annually appeared. The cock bird might be seen on this stone in the warmest hours of any fine day with certainty, and his eggs had once or twice been discovered within a hundred yards of the favoured perch. We designed to mark the hen bird as well, after liming her at the nest, but in the summer in which the experiment began, all efforts to find the eggs were unavailing. So a small T-shaped twig was early one morning carefully fixed in a chink of the rock just where the cock was wont to sit. He appeared on the scene about ten o'clock, and for a time entertained obvious suspicions of the intruding twig. The twig was probably a mistake, as the nightjar certainly prefers a broader perch. At any rate he ended by mounting it, but was never comfortable, and frequently jumped off it, and perambulated the surrounding rocks. He was left to reconcile himself to the twig for several days, and finally compromised by spending at least a portion of his time on it. Then the twig was well limed with fresh lime, and he was a prisoner. As rapidly as possible, an indiarubber ring was slipped over his toes—a most delicate operation with a small clawed bird—and relieved of most of the lime he was freed, and the obnoxious twig removed from his perch. We went home rather crestfallen, conscious that we had given the poor nightjar the fright of his existence, and that even if he conquered remembrance to the extent of returning next summer, he would probably suspect that perch for all time, and so compel us to search for his new haunts—no very easy or certain task. But to our delight, when next afternoon we cautiously reconnoitred from a distance with a

powerful glass, he was fast asleep on the old perch. We were so ashamed of the fright we had given him that we were content with a single experiment for that summer. Winter duly passed, summer returned, and with summer came back the nightjar to the familiar perch. I say " the " nightjar, because when we breathlessly limed him, there was our old rubber ring safe on his leg. On this second occasion we did not put a twig for him, but a piece of rotten wood, with some black waxed twine loosely wrapped round it. We released him with a fresh rubber ring, the old being somewhat the worse for wear and weather, and the operation was repeated for three years in succession, till we left the vicinity. Some day I must go and see if there is still a nightjar on the perch, and if he is wearing that unusual adornment for a self-respecting bird, namely, an old rubber ring on the left ankle.

This first experiment was sufficiently successful to warrant our persisting. While it did not prove much, it certainly proved this ; that the nightjar possessed some sense of travel so unerringly certain that he could find his way to Central Africa and back to a particular stone not a foot high in the centre of a country which presented no very striking feature within a large radius. What this sense was, we were as far from discovering as ever. It must surely be compounded of sight and memory, whatever unknown factors it contains in addition. But our very success contained a new puzzle. How was this sense— the " homing " sense—modified in his progeny, for in none of those years did we trace a single additional nightjar in the vicinity. We desired to mark his mate and young, but we never saw a sign of either.

Encouraged by this first success, which would never have come to us in so striking a fashion if we had selected a commoner bird, we enlarged our plans for the summer which gave us this early reward. We obtained some smaller rings, some grey and some red, some smooth and some corrugated, and pursued a similar plan with three nests of nightingales and two nests of robins. In each case the young were ringed just before they left the nest, and the old birds a few days before. The time of ringing would probably not have mattered very much, but the nightingale, in country parlance, will desert her nest in the early days of incubation, if you look at it. Smooth rings were slipped on the old birds in each case, and

corrugated rings on the nestlings. With the robins we were scientific, for we took only two nests for the experiment, and having rings of two colours of rubber, we were able to mark them so that each family could be distinguished when full grown. We began by marking only two nests of nightingales in the same discriminating way, but one of our number, on a solitary idle day, ruined one portion of the experiment by discovering a fresh nest, liming the old birds and marking the whole lot. Thus, when summer ended, this was our position : —somewhere in the woods and fields of the world there were :—

A. Two full grown robins, carrying smooth white rings, and four nestling robins carrying corrugated white rings.

B. Two full grown robins, carrying smooth red rings, and five young ones carrying corrugated red rings.

C. Two old nightingales carrying smooth white rings, and six young ones carrying corrugated white wings.

D. Four " aged " nightingales carrying smooth red rings, and nine young ones carrying corrugated red rings.

It will be noted that this year in addition to a migratory species we had taken a resident species. The idea of this was to see how far the robin's wanderings in winter carry him :

whether he returns to his old nesting place ; and whether any survivors of his family accompany him.

By the next summer not even the sight of an oriole or a peregrine would have caused our frenzied search for robins' and nightingales' nests to hesitate. During the winter we had often seen five or six of the ringed robins about, as nests which were near the house had been selected for ringing, and we entertained every hope we should also find a few ringed nightingales nesting in the same glades where the ringed birds had nested the summer before. When the summer ended, we had the following results to chronicle.

A. One of the previous summer's young robins had a nest about eight yards from the spot where he himself had been hatched, but his mate was an unringed bird. None of the other white-ringed robins were traced at all.

B. The two red-ringed parent robins, after being frequently seen throughout the winter, nested in the same garden as before. This instance must not carry too much weight, as the birds had been regularly fed for several years on the lawn, and the old ones which we ringed had even been so tamed as to come in at an open French window for food at tea-time. Some of the red-ringed young ones were seen during the winter, but none of them were identified after summer came.

C. A very successful test ; the old birds returned to the same glade, and again reared a family there, while one of their young (a cock) brought an unringed hen with him, and nested about a quarter of a mile away in the same wood.

D. In this case we had serious cause to regret the indiscretion committed by one of our number the previous summer. Only one pair of birds carrying the red rings were discovered ; one of them had a smooth ring, the hen a corrugated one. Whether this hen was daughter to her present mate or no relation, the error of the previous summer made it impossible to determine. It will thus be seen that out of 34 birds ringed the previous summer, no more than eight were identified, and it must be added that this is a larger percentage than we ever obtained in continued experiments. But when the great winter mortality amongst all small birds is considered, and the possibility of failure to track and identify a bird so common as the robin is added to the probability that this "homing" instinct, however dominant, encounters many opposing considerations, the result is certainly to justify the belief which originated the test, that every bird has a sixth sense compounded of sight and memory, not to speculate at other factors, which may roughly be termed its " homing " instinct, though it may have diverse uses and manifestations. Since the tests described, others have been conducted on the same lines, with very similar results, no less successful, but not more so. The attempt requires an enormous amount of leisure and patience, and could best be made by the members of an ornithological society, who could devote their attention to some semi-common bird, of which they could count on tracking every single representative in the district in a given summer, and marking them by differentiated rings. Where an individual attempts it, or a handful of individuals, the most gratifying results are obtainable by choosing some rare but regular visitant, but the results so obtained are too limited and too partial to justify general deductions.

XLII

THE TROUT

"If wee consider of men and fishes in their natural stoliditie, wee shall find agreeable correspondence between them."—*A Booke of Angling*, by SAMUEL GARDINER, D.D., 1606.

AMONG all fresh-water fish, the trout is pre-eminent in the interest which it arouses. The salmon is revered as the monarch of the rivers ; but *salmo salar* passes some months of each year in the sea, and is not, strictly speaking, a fresh-water fish. In the waters of the United Kingdom, where trout are found, *salmo fario*, the commonest of the species, spends the whole of its life in rivers or lakes, and never descends to the open sea. The habitat of the brown trout is, therefore, in fresh water, though at the spawning season it will frequently travel a considerable distance, in search of a suitable place to deposit its spawn.

Many naturalists agree that there is evidence to support the view that the common brown trout is a descendant of the salmon trout, or sea trout (*salmo trutta*). It can be proved that sea trout, which remain for a lengthened period in the pools of rivers, lose their silvery hue, and assume the colour of brown trout. They may even develop the characteristic spots of the river species. There is no doubt that considerable mystery surrounds the evolution of the trout of fresh water, but it is established that the brown trout possesses a singular power of adapting itself to its environment.

We roughly designate as trout, the bull trout, a migratory fish found in some English rivers, the big lake trout, or ferox, of Scotland, and the gillaroo of the Irish loughs. There are, however, many salient points of dissimilarity in these varieties of the *salmo* family. Even the common trout of our rivers and brooks present very remarkable difference of form, weight, colour, and habits. Why is the flesh of one brown trout a pink colour when cooked, while the flesh of another is white? This distinction may be noted in specimens taken from one river, although in many waters the trout are either pink-fleshed or white-fleshed. Why are some common trout silvery, others golden-hued, and others again almost as darkly coloured as tench?

Let us first array the influences which determine the hue and the markings of river trout. The most important determinants of the colour of fish are the character of the stream bed and the nature of the water. In the translucent limestone rivers of Derbyshire, such as the Wye and the Lathkill, the trout are usually light in the colouring of the scales. On the other hand, the same species taken from a peaty brook among the Welsh hills will be almost black. In the Wye there are trout so light that they have become known to anglers as the "Wye ghosts."

Between these extremes, we find in trout varying degrees of shade and notable variation in the placing of spots. A "brandling trout," for instance, is barred with black stripes, commonly called "finger-marks." The trout from the gravel shallows of any particular river may be grey and dull, or sand-coloured; while their companions in an adjoining stretch of the stream, where the water is more sluggish and darker, may be bronzed, or reddish, and present a marked contrast in the colouring. These differences show how very susceptible trout are to the influences of their environment. Bright water, light fish; dark water, sober-coloured fish. This may be accepted as a fair generalization.

Just as the sand leopard, the ptarmigan, the hare, and, indeed, almost all animals are provided with fur or feathers which accord with the colour of their surroundings, so is the trout protected by this adaptation of colour to the water and the bed of the stream. A dark trout, poised just above the golden sand of a clear stream, is readily seen, whereas it needs the experienced eye of the fisherman to detect a sand-toned fish in such a haunt. This harmony between the trout and its surroundings is a partial protection against all the foes that prey upon it, such as the otter, heron, and predatory fish.

The weight of trout depends upon the food-yielding capacity of any given stream or lake. "As some pastures breed larger sheep," says Izaak Walton, "so do some rivers, by reason of the ground over which they run, breed larger trouts." The Thames produces trout of ten, twelve, and sometimes fifteen pounds in weight, while the Tay has yielded a trout of twenty-seven-and-a-half pounds to the rod of an angler. In the Scottish lochs trout grow to the weight of twenty pounds. Bala Lake in Wales contains fish of this species up to eight pounds.

A noteworthy instance of the growth capacity of trout is afforded by the quick increase in bulk of the fish of Blagdon Reservoir, near Bristol, where the rate of growth in weight has been more than a pound per year. As the water has been stocked with young fish, the increase in weight can be proved beyond all question. Yet there are llyns in Wales, and tarns in Cumberland, where, by reason of a scanty food supply, trout never attain to half-a-pound in weight. In Llyn Howel, near Harlech, the trout literally teem; but as the lake has a stony bottom, unfavourable to a plentiful production of insects, the fish are lean and ill-conditioned, and seldom grow to even half-a-pound. These mountain pools are also situated at such a height above the level of the sea that winged insects are scarce, and cannot thrive in the cold temperature. The trout are, therefore, debarred from surface food in the shape of flies and gnats, and can only gain meagre nutriment from the bed of the lake.

But if we descend about two hundred feet from Llyn Howel, we shall see a small mere of a different character, where there is an admixture of sand and mud in parts of the bed. A number of weeds and rushes will also be noted. Here, then, is a shallower pool, providing more generously for the trout that inhabit it, and although the fish do not grow to over a pound in weight, the average being about half-a-pound, they are not starved, and their bright handsome appearance contrasts strongly with that of the dull, attenuated trout in Llyn Howel.

The same conditions determine the weight of trout in rivers. Where water-snails, shrimps, the fry of small fish, and the larvæ of insects abound in the river, and the surface is often covered with flies and midges in spring and summer, the trout will be well-proportioned and healthy. Water-snails and fresh-water shrimps are a fattening diet for trout ; and the spring fare of flies, upon the surface of the water, soon restores the fish to condition after the strain of spawning.

The reproduction of trout from the ovum of the female and the milt of the male is termed spawning. Trout breed in the autumn, beginning in certain rivers during October, and in others as late as January. The spawning grounds, or " redds," are carefully chosen by the fish after pairing, and the male fish is assiduous in guarding his companion until the young are hatched from the egg. In February or March the water of a trout stream swarms with the alevins, or small fry of the fish. The young trout grow rapidly, but large numbers are destroyed by aquatic birds, and such coarse fish as may find their way into the stream, or are bred in it. Heavy floods, which bring down silt and mud, often cause havoc during the spawning season, the eggs being covered and destroyed by the matter. In a dry winter there is the danger that the tributary streams, which are often chosen as spawning places, may run low and leave the ova exposed. There are also risks from the attacks of fish upon the eggs, for all fish, even trout themselves, will eat spawn.

Guided by instinct, the alevin soon learns how to obtain nourishment. Its hunger is prodigious, and its dietary varied, for trout are almost omnivorous.

As we have seen, the rate of increase in bulk depends solely upon an ample food supply. Trout are both bottom and surface feeders. From March till October, whenever a genial atmosphere hatches insects in the water, or by the riverside, trout rise to the surface, and await a meal of the flies which float upon, or flutter just above, the water. It is then that the trout display remarkable avidity in feasting upon winged insects. During the " hatches " of blue duns and March browns, in the warm days of spring, the fish rise steadily to flies from eleven in the morning until four in the afternoon. A " rise " to these insects indicates that the trout are beginning to savour their diet of the warm months, and it is at this season that the fly-fisherman returns to his sport.

Later, in the summer months, trout are often sluggish during the day, especially if the weather is hot and thundery. But towards evening, when the surface of the river is frequently alive with several kinds of flies, the trout begin to feed eagerly. In July and August, trout sometimes quest actively for moths and flies during the whole of the night. Soon after sunrise the " rise " ceases, and the fish, gorged with food, seek their hiding-places under the banks and beneath sunken rocks.

The examination of the contents of a trout's stomach in the summer will show a varied and plentiful collection of dainties, such as shrimps, grubs, beetles, grasshoppers, flies of several kinds, and small fish. Trout may be described as gluttonous fish, though there are apparently periods when they are satiated with food. For example, after a fortnight's high living on the mayfly, trout are apt to refuse any bait which the angler may offer to them.

A flood in the river provides trout with a large and fresh supply of food. The turbid tributaries bring down innumerable insects, which are washed from the banks, and the rush of water stirs up provender from the bed of the river. At such times trout eat a large number of earth worms, and until the water clears they find their diet below the surface and in the sediment.

Trout eat the young of their own species as well as other small fish. They chase minnows and tiny fry in the shallows. In Bala Lake, they subsist largely upon young perch ; and the best lure for a big Thames trout is a bleak. A trout of a quarter-of-a-pound will seize and devour a trout of nearly an ounce in weight.

The streams most favourable to the liberal production of well-fed trout are those of our Southern Counties, especially the Hampshire Test, Itchen, and Avon. In the Itchen a trout of eight pounds in weight has been caught, and it is not unusual to take fish from this famous stream weighing over three pounds apiece. There are rivers in Hertfordshire and Buckinghamshire which almost rival the Hampshire streams in the quantity and quality of the trout bred in them.

As we travel westwards to the more rapid streams of Devon and Cornwall, we find productive waters but smaller fish. The Dart, the Teign and the Camel contain a good store of trout, but they rarely approach those of the Hampshire chalk streams in regard to weight. In Derbyshire also the average weight of the trout may be set down as a little less than half a pound, though there are many heavier fish in the pools of the Derwent at Matlock and Belper, and in parts of the Dove.

Wherever we turn there is great diversity in the weight of the trout frequenting the waters of a given area. Wales abounds with lakes and rivers which yield plenty of trout. Scotland has a much larger acreage of lochs, and many more and bigger rivers, all more or less supplied with *salmo fario*. The same conditions for the production of trout obtain in Ireland, especially in the north and west. Some of the Irish loughs contain large numbers of heavy trout, others swarm with small fish. In cold, rapid mountain streams, trout pass their lives in a severe struggle for existence. They have to contend with the force of the water at all times, and especially during spates after a heavy downpour of rain. As all fish swim, or " stand," with their heads to the current, it is obvious that in a heavy stream the mere exercise of the fins and tail, necessary to preserve a position in the feeding-places, is in itself fatiguing. No trout chooses to lurk in the full rush of a strong river ; but in boisterous streams it is difficult to avoid frequent battling against the flow. Eddies, slow pools, and the less troubled water behind a barrier of rock, afford the quieter feeding-places for the fish of impetuous rivers.

Mountain brooks are seldom stored with plentiful food for trout. There are long spells when no flies can be seen over the water, and at high altitudes insects are seldom abundant.

The life of a trout in the middle and lower reaches of the river is much less strenuous than that of the brook trout. In the main stream, there are large, quiet pools, more eddies, and better feeding-grounds. Those trout bred in the tributaries, which contrive to fight the hardest for sustenance, become the adventurous rovers that find their way to the big river. The affluents of a river may be called the nurseries of trout. It is in these brooks that the fish prefer to spawn.

Observation of the habits of trout proves that among fish they possess intelligence in a superior degree. A mature trout is very cautious in the choice of its feeding-place. It selects a position where it can " stand " without undue exertion, and command a view of the surface of the stream. With quick eyes it notes the slightest shadow across the water. It lurks, if possible, close to the broken waves of a rapid, in one of those glides between two currents, which claim the close attention of expert fishermen. Trout resort to the shade of boughs, to patches of weed on the river bottom, to dark-coloured eddies, and to harbours beneath shelving banks or submerged rocks.

Every trout stoutly maintains its right to the position which it takes up. If a wandering member of its species approaches, it turns and attacks the rival fiercely. With fins gently moving, and eyes wary, the feeding trout awaits the least tremor of the surface, and rises nimbly to seize a floating fly. When imprudent small fry venture near, it flashes after them, and endeavours to swallow one of their number. A big trout sucks down a fly gently, scarcely disturbing the water. Lesser trout seize their flies with more excitement and splash.

In a commercial sense, the trout ranks next to the salmon in value. Our markets are not plentifully supplied with this delicate fish on account of the stringency of the law against netting in fresh water. Trout are, nevertheless, obtainable in the fish markets during the season, but they fetch a somewhat high and always steady price per pound. The real value of the trout lies in the fact that enthusiastic anglers are willing to pay rents for lengths of trout streams, which appear fabulous in the estimation of those who have not the passion for fly-fishing.

Any water which is adapted for the rearing of trout is of greater value than land of the same acreage outside of a town. There are portions of streams which yield extremely high rentals to their owners, and there are miles of brooks and numbers of ponds, which are capable of being converted into trout preserves, that would prove remunerative property. The culture of trout for the purpose of replenishing rivers and lakes is now an important and increasing industry. Every year one notes the establishment of a fresh trout hatchery ; every year the rentals of fisheries rise higher.

The trout has won more praise from poets and prose-writers than even the much-flattered salmon. There is a large literature of the trout. Scientific, practical, poetic, and sporting writers have written with zeal concerning this highly-prized fish. It is the theme of a host of treatises, the subject of sundry monographs, and the inspiration to some admirable prose. From the days of Dame Juliana Berners to the age of

Walton, on to the time of Christopher North and Sir Walter Scott, and down to the present year, the pens of authors have never ceased to contribute fresh lore concerning trout and trout-fishing.

The trout is a " game fish " or " sporting fish," and has been held in the almost universal respect of fishermen for ages past. Ancient Greeks knew the art of fly-fishing, the Britons fished for trout in the Severn, Usk, and Dee. In the part of *Holinshed's Chronicles* written by William Harrison, we read of the trout in English rivers, and the various methods of rearing and preserving fish in ponds and stews. William Lauson, who wrote a book on angling in 1613, alludes to the esteem of his contemporaries for this fish. " The trout makes the angler the most gentlemanly and readiest sport of all other fishes."

XLIII

THE FOX

The fox jumps over the hedge so high
And the hounds all after him go.

Folk Song.

HOW difficult it seems to realise that a week-old fox cub—a chubby, snub-nosed ball of dark, slate-blue fur—will change into the sly, crafty, slinking, slaughter-loving plunderer, which it is the destiny of mature foxes to become. And, perhaps, it is still more difficult to think of a baby fox at the age of eight weeks—the embodiment of playfulness, smartness, energy, and grace of movement—as the disreputable, forlorn, uncared-for, mangy, and toothless object of a few years hence, driven by sheer starvation into a fowl-house.

It is given only to the most patient students of Nature and gamekeepers to become acquainted with the ways and wiles of the fox, so unapproachable, and so quick to scent danger is he. I speak of the true, wild fox, not the tame or semi-tame creature which runs risks that no decent, self-respecting fox, adorned with a luxuriant brush, clothed with a fine fur coat, and in his right mind, would ever dream of taking. The fact that foxes, as a rule, sleep by day and forage by night makes the study of their private lives doubly difficult.

When at Christmas the gamekeeper begins to reckon his remaining stock

FOXES.

From a photograph by
Charles Reid, Wishaw.

of scattered game, he also begins to hear the bark of amorous foxes ; and, once more, his thoughts turn resignedly to visions of havoc among his breeding game, sacrificed to the demands of strong litters of fox cubs, growing daily stronger.

Picture yourself standing in the depths of a great, silent wood on Christmas Night ; all things clothed with a mantle of virgin snow. Your eye may have caught the outline of a pheasant, you are wondering whether it is a cock or hen, and you pity the chilliness of its self-sought roost. While you still gaze at the pheasant form, the unnerving hoot of a brown owl makes you start, seeming to come from nowhere—from the realms of ghosts. You wait watching, and soon a shadowy form flits over the underwood with further unearthly greetings, to be echoed and answered by the salutations of its fellows.

And, as you muse upon this ghostly chorus, another sound which swells the voice of night catches your ear— the bark of a fox signalling to its mate. You become fascinated by these fox-calls—like the short, staccato yaps of a terrier, but with a weirdly guttural ending—at once full of utter sadness, loneliness, and appeal.

In spite of the various thoughts which occupy the fox's brain, thoughts of love, of food, and of traps and snares which beset his path, there is no lapse of vigilance by eye, ear, or nose—most useful of all. In spite of your motionless figure, and cautious breathing, that finest nose in the world of the woods has warned— one might almost say, automatically —its suspicious owner that a possible foe is abroad. You will be lucky to catch a glimpse of a sinuous form as it glides across the ride beyond the effective range of the hardest-shooting choke-bore.

Later on, when the lingering winter of February yields grudgingly to the importunities of spring, you may explore some thicket-skirted dell to gather the first, short-stalked primroses, enough, maybe, to call a bunch. In your search for each treasured bloom you notice signs of laborious toil at the mouth of what had always before been merely a rabbit burrow. This must be investigated, for your curiosity is roused by the way in which the soil is piled and pressed down outside the entrance. You know the rabbit method, which leaves the excavated soil drawn out in a long furrow, perhaps for three yards or more, the bulk being disposed at the sides of the furrow.

From the threshold of this new-made hole, a careful search will bring to light a few tawny hairs, which prove beyond doubt that the rabbits' burrow is being seriously thought of by a nursery-seeking vixen fox. If you push your stick far into the hole, a wrathful, pungent odour will tell you if her ladyship is at home to resent your intrusion. Generally, however, she is lying snugly in a cosy spot in some grassy hedgerow, or in a field of roots hard by, whose foliage " bolting " with spring's encouragement offers a luxuriant retreat.

You may fill up the hole in the dell, and again and again will the persevering vixen clean it out. So far as I know, this is the one instance in which a vixen forgives the intrusion, or even the taint, of man. It proves also the marvellous instinct, amounting almost, one would think, to reasoning power, of the mother fox. You may interfere repeatedly with the site she has chosen for her nursery, without causing her to forsake it for undiscovered quarters. But from the moment her litter has arrived, the slightest interference— often even your approach within a dozen yards—will be instantly resented, and during the following night she will remove her family to a new home. It is an interesting point in the preparations made by vixens that they invariably " draw out " an extra nursery earth, as a refuge in case of emergency.

About the middle of March fox cubs are cradled in a saucer-like depression far in the warm recesses of the nursery earth, which has taken the vixen's fancy. Gamekeepers call this fox-cradle the " oven " ; to which there is no lining—just the bare, dry soil—and, for the sake of dryness, it is always fashioned on a higher level than the tunnels leading to and from it.

The average fox family is half a dozen ; but, as in the case of dogs, litters of a dozen or more may be met with, which are occasionally found quartered above ground. I remember the discovery of no fewer than thirteen cubs, about a week old, nestled beneath the shelter of a dense holly bush. I am inclined to believe, however, that fox nurseries above ground are chosen, as a rule, because of the vixen's temporary inability to find or fashion to suit her requirements an under-ground retreat, owing to those she had prepared being discovered and intruded upon.

Moreover, foxes do not seem to have remained proof against the attractions of co-operative nurseries. I recall two vixens, who were nursing litters of six and seven respectively in the same earth. And even the wily old dog fox, evidently the proud father of the generous dozen, was interested in the arrangement, for he was seen carrying to the earth a shoulder of carrion mutton.

When in mid-April you seek again the primroses, now in the fullness of their simple glory, you will notice that the soil by the front door of the fox earth is smoothed down and polished. This is caused by the pattering of a couple of dozen or so of little feet, and shows that the cubs are about a month old, and eager to explore the great, wide, woodland world without.

A field-glass will tell you that the objects lying about the main entrance are tasty morsels, which the mother has brought as a first means of weaning her family and teaching them the diet which Nature decreed for their well-being. Beetles, mice, and rats are in great demand at this time, with little rabbits snatched from their warm furry nest in the " stop " which the doe had so carefully covered.

To spend an hour or two on some soft spring evening watching through a field-glass the play of little foxes is ample reward for a five-mile walk.

The more cubs play, the more they eat. Fully the hard-worked vixen realises the blessings of a growing family. Happy, indeed, is the mother of foxes in a district of many rabbits !

So long as there are foxes and game in the country, ceaseless will be the arguments as to whether or not foxes are injurious to game. When my opinion is asked, I reply that game is naturally the food of foxes, but the quality of damage they inflict depends much on circumstances, individual taste, and early teaching. Foxes, like human beings, live chiefly on that which is easiest to obtain, and costs least trouble or money—that is to say, when there are multitudes of juicy rabbits to be had for the trouble of snapping them up, foxes do comparatively little harm to more valuable game. Purely as a matter of taste and inclination, I believe that foxes, except in the nesting season of game birds, find in rabbits nine-tenths of their food. But, when Fate has decreed that a fox shall reside in a practically rabbitless locality, in which there is other nobler game, that fox must interfere with the prosperity of that game or—starve. For to resist temptation under such circumstances is neither human nor vulpine.

Unfortunately I have had sad experience of many foxes forced to live, so soon as they could eat, on game birds and hares. Is it not natural, when, in after life, such foxes see or smell a pheasant, partridge, or leveret, that they should say to themselves : " There is our breakfast, dinner, or supper ; come, let us take possession while we may."

Nature, in her arrangements for the adjustment of her idea of a perfect balance, has ordained that there shall be born into the world fewer female than male foxes ; this is also the case with stoats. I have often noticed among litters of foxes and stoats, numbering from six to eight, that there have been but one or two females.

You may be out for a country ramble, and rouse a full-grown fox, who was having a nap in the cosiness of a straw rick in the middle of a field ; and, if you have for a companion a countryman, he is almost certain promptly to announce its sex—a feat of woodcraft likely to arouse your curiosity. You are led to believe that to distinguish the sex of foxes, provided they are within sight, is as easy as to tell a cock from a hen pheasant. That a white "tag" at the end of a fox's brush denotes a dog fox, while its absence indicates a vixen, is one of the most popular countryside fallacies.

Again, an ancient legend would have one believe that a fox gazes at a pheasant or fowl safely perched on a tree until the power of its longing gaze causes the wretched bird to fall into the waiting jaws beneath.

The very fact that the sight of prowling foxes or foxy-looking dogs —such as are some Irish terriers —generally causes pheasants to fly to the handiest branch for refuge is sufficient to explode so pretty a fable.

For all that, foxes are not above resorting to ruses to gain their ends ; for instance, to allay the suspicions of feeding rabbits, a fox will roll as if in play, but contrive by each movement to bring himself nearer to the hoaxed rabbits, when an exquisitely calculated spring earns him a dainty supper. Besides, a fox is capable even of feigning death, as a final means of escape, when in sore straits. I remember a man who thought he had shot a fox, after digging within reach of its head, and, having pulled it out, threw it aside. But so soon as the man had put his gun down to examine the hole, in which there was a second fox (who was less fortunate), up sprang No. 1, and fled with the life he had won in spite of the superiority of man.